Penguin Education

Rules and Meanings

Edited by Mary Douglas

Penguin Modern Sociology Readings

Rules and Meanings

The Anthropology of Everyday Knowledge

Selected Readings

Edited by Mary Douglas

Penguin Education

Penguin Education,
A Division of Penguin Books Ltd,
Harmondsworth, Middlesex, England
Penguin Books Inc, 7110 Ambassador Road,
Baltimore, Md 21207, USA
Penguin Books Australia Ltd,
Ringwood, Victoria, Australia

First published 1973
This selection copyright © Mary Douglas, 1973
Introduction and notes copyright © Mary Douglas, 1973
Copyright acknowledgements in this volume
will be found on page 303

Made and printed in Great Britain by
Richard Clay (The Chaucer Press) Ltd, Bungay, Suffolk
Set in Monotype Times

Contents

Introduction

This collection of Readings does not conform precisely to any particular model. It claims philosophical forebears for a course of anthropology that I like to teach. A few selections come from books that I would regard as essential reading. Most of them are chosen to illustrate and to extend the relevance and increase the impact of a message which is, by my showing, elusive and hard to assimilate. The course is sometimes labelled Cognitive Anthropology; Cognition; Religion and Morals; or Symbolism. Whatever the name, I regard it as an essential perspective for anthropology – a sinking of artesian wells, as it were. Apart from this programme, the subject easily dries up and appears as a series of barren controversies cut off from the rest of human knowledge and vulnerable to the blowing of every fashionable wind. This is how I see the reader and it would be right to warn that the book expounds more of what this editor believes ought to be accepted in anthropology than what is actually accepted. There is a recognizable epistemological viewpoint, working through European literature, philosophy, linguistics and sociology, which strikes some students as novel when they meet it. It is not novel. It is old. It is not trivial, but important. Its recent foundations were in anthropology at the turn of the century. A conversation started in Europe then between philosophers and social scientists. The speakers started from a common concern with problems of commitment, solidarity and alienation. They knew only too well that there can be rules without meaning. They also assumed that there can be no meaning without rules. They drove the study of meaning straight to the study of social relations. Formal analysis would reveal the formal properties of a communication system, as a vehicle of meaning; the meanings conveyed would be uncovered only through social analysis. But once begun, this conversation, so hopeful of solving many epistemological problems, soon split up into the musings of diverse specialists. As a result, our knowledge of the social conventions which make understanding possible remains scarcely advanced from that beginning. If they had received each other's sayings, reflected and replied, our intellectual heritage would have been enriched. But the dialogue was broken off as the community of scholars was dispersed, either forcibly by the wars or voluntarily because they turned to speak more exclusively to their disciples. The selections offered here draw out of the sociological theory of knowledge a certain thread. The theme goes back to Hegel and Marx; that reality is socially constructed. Every thinking sociologist would now agree it in principle. But how far dare they follow it? And what can be known about the kinds of reality that are construable? Somewhere along the line the conversation that began with 'Primitive Classification' in 1901–2 got wafted out of general earshot, though it never stopped altogether. Marcel Mauss mentioned the work of the Cambridge psychologists at the end of his lecture on *Les Techniques du Corps* (1935). Evans-Pritchard used the notion of a social monitor of perception to make sense of the concept of collective conscience, and referred to the body of ideas developed in psychology through Head, Bartlett and Rivers (1934). But apart from Merleau Ponty's work, the theory of perception seemed to become thereafter mainly a concern of psychology, not of sociology. But what a pity that Merleau Ponty seems not to have read *The Nuer* and recognized there the parallel positive working out of his criticisms of contemporary philosophy. Other shared assumptions likewise became assigned to or appropriated by different disciplines. So when Malinowski pointed out that speech derives its meaning from the social context, the idea was hailed as profoundly original.

What Wittgenstein was saying about the logical scaffolding on which reality is constructed had already become the background assumption of social anthropologists and was consistently used for interpreting their work through the 1940s and onwards. It is curious now to hear Lévi-Strauss a quarter of a century later announce his discovery that all thought has a logical basis. It is curious to hear more recent phenomenologists declare afresh that knowledge is socially constructed. Ethno-methodologists bring great delicacy to analysing how the process of social interaction constructs the typifications and recipes which make social reality. They are aware of how the dimensions of time and space are socially constructed. But to take aboard the implication that the whole of physical nature must be endowed with its reality in the same way demands an imaginative effort which has been left to artists, novelists and poets. If only it were fully realized, urgent questions would be posed for the philosophy of science. But systematic inquiry into how many kinds of construction can be put upon physical nature is not treated as a serious enterprise. It is assumed that they may be infinite in number, and so they may in so far as the diversity of nature itself is susceptible of infinite interpretations. But we are less justified in assuming that the range of possible human societies varies so much. Since it is from here that the perspectives are controlled it will be worth asking what are the main varieties of society that produce the constructions of reality. At this point, when the possibility of cognition is at issue, the sociological programme is full circle back to philosophy. But by now the philosophers who started it have dropped out of the conversation. After narrowly bounding the reality they wish to investigate, so as better to control it, they have been exposed to criticisms of triviality. The refinement of their concepts makes it harder for them to come closer to us and comment critically upon the researches which they had originally inspired, but the task, however difficult, is still necessary. The same in reverse for linguists: de Saussure's programme was inspired by Durkheim; but his disciples travelled far away from sociology in the analysis of arbitrary sign systems. We shout, but only a faint and garbled version reaches across the gulf separating the disciplines. Similarly for ethno-scientists: they lost hold of the line that linked their progeny of problems to its sociological genesis.

This volume could well be reproached for what it has omitted of a large and topical subject matter. But it is not intended to represent all the current ideas about rules and the meanings carried along them. Such a fascinating project would fill ten volumes. Instead it has a single objective; to show an unbroken but submerged tradition, how it developed, how it relates to contemporary interests in apparently far removed fields. This tradition takes for granted that human thought serves human interests and therefore carries in itself at any given moment the social configurations of that time and place. Most of the deepest puzzles in philosophy and semantics arise from forgetting this and neglecting to find coherent ways of taking it into account. This train of thought is here best represented by two long articles, by Ralph Bulmer and S. J. Tambiah in Part Four, which analyse the classification of animals in New Guinea and Thailand respectively. They show the heavy social load that is carried by apparently innocent-looking taxonomic systems. In each case the classification of animal kinds is constitutive of social reality in that it assigns species to one category or another, shows them to be valued high or low and keeps them in their categories by rules of behaviour. Rules which forbid eating certain animals keep them in the set of inedible things. Rules which forbid domestication of a certain animal species keep it in the category of wild animals. Further, the very form of the rules applied to some animals is the same as the form of rules applied to some humans. For example, the incest rule in the Thai village requires that any person's great-grandchildren (that is, second cousins) should not intermarry. Another rule requires that buffaloes reared under the house should not be used for sacrifice on behalf of members of the house. Thus a homology between the two situations is conveyed by the formal identity of the rule; livestock and women are reared for exchange. Buffaloes are tethered under the sleeping quarters so that the analogy of sacrificial with sexual consummation is reinforced. Almost incredible complexity and richness of meaning is achieved in the rules which organize the space in and around the Berber house described by Pierre Bourdieu (Reading 18). If the author had limited himself to one system of signs, say furniture, or the house without the outside, or the whole material culture without the supporting rites and proverbs which he cites, he would have missed these meanings.

These three analyses, two of meanings carried in taxonomic systems, one of the structure of meaning in house design, are in direct line of descent from the early studies of totemism and of primitive classification. Australian totemism was always so obviously a local and peculiar manifestation that the studies of its various forms never forced the conclusion that we also, in modern society, construct a moral universe by the same processes. Primitive classification is presented by Durkheim and Mauss as carrying by definition a heavier affective load, as being more weighted and therefore distorted by social concerns, than modern scientific thought. Thus they fortified the already vigorous tendency to bracket away ourselves from the social phenomena we are observing. But these three studies, selected on account of their highly condensed presentation from a wide range of ethnographic work which tends in the same direction, are very suggestive the other way. Even in the laboratory, the researcher has options open to him. There are options for following this line of inquiry rather than that, of referring to these other works or omitting them. He must choose for the sake of structuring his own contribution. It is fitted into a conversation between scholars and so is pared down here and blown up there. The categories of valuable and useless areas of work are identified, ranked and bounded, elements assigned to the classes and sub-classes, rules made to hold the framework of knowledge steady. The alleged gap between what we know about the construction of everyday knowledge and the construction of scientific knowledge is not so big as is supposed.

The specialists have had half a century to confer with their inner circle of initiates and to evolve rules of discourse appropriate to the fields they have hedged off. The time is come for a renewal of the original community and of the free-ranging conversation about the social basis of knowledge that it once enjoyed. Philosophers will become conversant with totemic systems again as they used once to be. To their inquiries about the essence of redness they will have to add inquiries about the way that whole configurations of colour carve up the diversity of experience, or even learn to pose the question the other way round. A book that was a decade ahead of its time (though it should not have been) will have to be re-read and assimilated into the mainstream European tradition. I refer to the analysis of Dinka thought by Godfrey Lienhardt. After reading *Divinity and Experience* (1961) no one would be tempted to label some sensations as primary and others as secondary, or some experiences as concrete and others abstract. For it makes nonsense to try to say that a colour is a primary or concrete sense experience if it is known first through its name as the characteristic of a bird and as a member of a class to which all cattle exhibiting that colouring belong – and this is in a society in which children will know the cattle and the colour of their hides long before they encounter the bird and its plumage. If colour be not accorded status as a primary experience, how much less are physiological characteristics free of structuring by social requirements. It has long been accepted that there is in any culture just such a weighting, paring down here and liberating there of parts of the body according to the dominant interests of the culture. Yet this insight remains a realization in a vacuum. For example, its implications for sociology are obvious, but unexplored.

Ultimately led back to the limits of knowledge, the book reminds philosophers and linguists that speech is a social phenomenon, and that social decisions mark off the boundaries between different provinces of meaning. Total insulation between one field of experience and another is highly improbable as the passages on expression in Part Six show. In the media of dress, food, comportment, table-setting, the boundaries that are set up are kept in being by great effort and continual reminders. There is a tendency for meaning to overflow and for distinct provinces to inter-penetrate. Schutz has argued that there are separable, independent, finite provinces of meaning. But this becomes implausible when one observes the same formal rules being applied from one range of experience to another. The same form of rules will carry the same range of meanings with them. To achieve a small piece of behaviour which is not laden with significance overflowing from the rest of the self's concerns requires very contrived and specialized techniques of dissociation, as the lines quoted from John Cage demonstrate.

The collection as a whole points to the problems indicated in the last section. Sets of rules are metaphorically connected with one another, allow meaning to leak from one context to another along the formal similarities that they show. The barriers between finite provinces of meaning are always sapped either by the violent flooding through of social concerns or by the subtle economy which uses the same rule structure in each province. Since this is so, separate conversations will not go on for long without returning inevitably to their shared origins. In the end the puzzles that are insoluble within a particular discipline's means will be solved by downing the fences, recognizing the common pictorial form in which the problems are posed, and restating them in the wider sociological perspective. The time has come to treat everyday knowledge and scientific knowledge as a single field in sociology.

The editor gratefully acknowledges the help in research and organizing the material given by Mr Antony Wilson and the bibliographic assistance of Mr James Urry.

Part One
Tacit Conventions

How the moral order is known – how the inner experience of morality is
related to the moral order without – this depends on hidden processes.
Each person confronted with a system of ends and means (not necessarily
a tidy and coherent system) seems to face the order of nature, objective
and independent of human wishes. But the moral order and the knowledge
which sustains it are created by social conventions. If their man-made
origins were not hidden, they would be stripped of some of their authority.
Therefore the conventions are not merely tacit, but extremely inaccessible
to investigation. This book of readings is addressed to the question of how
reality is constructed, how it is given its moral bias and how the process of
construction is veiled. The dates of the selections are part of the theme and
deserve particular attention. Over and over the same questions are taken
up as if from scratch. The dates themselves show over fifty years how
repugnant and easy to forget is Plato's concept of the good lie, and how
difficult to contemplate steadily our responsibility for creating our own
environment.

read artistic for all investigation

Archaeolgicl excavation of the underpinnings of the art experience
Desire to see that art is a social convention rather than ontolgicl
reality

1 L. Wittgenstein

Understanding Depends on Tacit Conventions

Excerpt from L. Wittgenstein, *Tractatus Logico-Philosophicus*, Routledge & Kegan Paul, second edition of new translation, 1971, pp. 35–7. First published in 1921.

4.002 Man possesses the ability to construct languages capable of expressing every sense, without having any idea how each word has meaning or what its meaning is – just as people speak without knowing how the individual sounds are produced.

Everyday language is a part of the human organism and is no less complicated than it.

It is not humanly possible to gather immediately from it what the logic of language is.

Language disguises thought. So much so, that from the outward form of the clothing it is impossible to infer the form of the thought beneath it, because the outward form of the clothing is not designed to reveal the form of the body, but for entirely different purposes.

The tacit conventions on which the understanding of everyday language depends are enormously complicated.

2 A. Schutz

The Frame of Unquestioned Constructs

Excerpts from A. Schutz, *Collected Papers: I. The Problem of Social Reality*, Martinus Nijhoff, The Hague, 1967, pp. 13–14, 33, 61–2, first published in 1953 and 1954.

The social origin of knowledge

Only a very small part of my knowledge of the world originates within my personal experience. The greater part is socially derived, handed down to me by my friends, my parents, my teachers and the teachers of my teachers. I am taught not only how to define the environment (that is, the typical features of the relative natural aspect of the world prevailing in the in-group as the unquestioned but always questionable sum total of things taken for granted until further notice), but also how typical constructs have to be formed in accordance with the system of relevances accepted from the anonymous unified point of view of the in-group. This includes ways of life, methods of coming to terms with the environment, efficient recipes for the use of typical means for bringing about typical ends in typical situations. The typifying medium *par excellence* by which socially derived knowledge is transmitted is the vocabulary and the syntax of *everyday language*. The vernacular of everyday life is primarily a language of named things and events, and any name includes a typification and generalization referring to the relevance system prevailing in the linguistic in-group which found the named thing significant enough to provide a separate term for it. The pre-scientific vernacular can be interpreted as a treasure house of ready made pre-constituted types and characteristics, all socially derived and carrying along an open horizon of unexplored content. . .

We come, therefore, to the conclusion that 'rational action' on the common-sense level is always action within an unquestioned and undetermined frame of constructs of typicalities of the setting, the motives, the means and ends, the courses of action and personalities involved and taken for granted. They are, however, not merely taken for granted by the actor but also supposed as being taken for granted by the fellow-man. From this frame of constructs, forming their undetermined horizon, merely particular sets of elements stand out which are clearly and distinctly determinable. To these elements refers the common-sense concept of rationality. Thus we may say that on this level actions are at best partially rational and that rationality has many degrees. For instance, our assumption that our fellow-man who is involved with us in a pattern of interaction knows its rational elements will never reach 'empirical certainty' (certainty 'until further notice' or 'good until counter-evidence') but will always bear the character of plausibility, that is, of subjective likelihood (in contra-distinction to mathematical probability). We always have to 'take chances' and to 'run risks', and this situation is expressed by our hopes and fears which are merely the subjective corollaries of our basic uncertainty as to the outcome of our projected interaction.

To be sure, the more standardized the prevailing action pattern is, the more anonymous it is, the greater is the subjective chance of conformity and, therewith, of the success of intersubjective behavior. Yet – and this is the paradox of rationality on the common-sense level – the more standardized the pattern is, the less the underlying elements become analysable for common-sense thought in terms of rational insight . . .

Next we have to consider that the common-sense knowledge of everyday life is from the outset socialized in many respects.

It is, first, structurally socialized, since it is based on the fundamental idealization that if I were to change places with my fellow-man I would experience the same sector of the world in substantially the same perspectives as he does, our particular biographical circumstances becoming for all practical purposes at hand irrelevant. I propose to call this idealization that of the reciprocity of perspectives.

It is, second, genetically socialized, because the greater part of our knowledge, as to its content and the particular forms of typification under which it is organized, is socially derived, and this in socially approved terms.

It is, third, socialized in the sense of social distribution of knowledge, each individual knowing merely a sector of the world and common know-ledge of the same sector varying individually as to its degree of distinctness, clarity, acquaintanceship, or mere belief.

These principles of socialization of common-sense knowledge, and especially that of the social distribution of knowledge, explain at least par-tially what the social scientist has in mind in speaking of the functional structural approach to studies of human affairs. The concept of func-tionalism – at least in the modern social sciences – is not derived from the biological concept of the functioning of an organism, as Nagel holds. It refers to the socially distributed constructs of patterns of typical motives, goals, attitudes, personalities, which are supposed to be invariant and are then interpreted as the function or structure of the social system itself. The more these interlocked behavior patterns are standardized and institu-tionalized, that is, the more their typicality is socially approved by laws, folkways, mores, and habits, the greater is their usefulness in common-sense and scientific thinking as a scheme of interpretation of human behavior.

These are, very roughly, the outlines of a few major features of the constructs involved in common-sense experience of the intersubjective world in daily life, which is called *Verstehen*. As explained before, they are the first level constructs upon which the second level constructs of the social sciences have to be erected. But here a major problem emerges. On the one hand, it has been shown that the constructs on the first level, the common-sense constructs, refer to subjective elements, namely the *Verstehen* of the actor's action from his, the actor's, point of view. Consequently, if the social sciences aim indeed at explaining social reality, then the scientific constructs on the second level, too, must include a reference to the subjective meaning an action has for the actor. This is, I think, what Max Weber understood by his famous postulate of subjective interpretation, which has, indeed, been observed so far in the theory formation of all social sciences. The postulate of subjective interpretation has to be understood in the sense that all scientific explanations of the social world *can*, and for certain purposes *must*, refer to the subjective meaning of the actions of human beings from which social reality originates.

3 H. Garfinkel

Background Expectancies

Excerpt from H. Garfinkel, *Studies in Ethnomethodology*, Prentice-Hall, 1967, pp. 35–7.

The problem

For Kant, the moral order 'within' was an awesome mystery; for sociologists, the moral order 'without' is a technical mystery. From the point of view of sociological theory the moral order consists of the rule-governed activities of everyday life. A society's members encounter and know the moral order as perceivedly normal courses of action – familiar scenes of everyday affairs, the world of daily life known in common with others and with others taken for granted.

They refer to this world as the 'natural facts of life' which, for members, are through and through moral facts of life. For members, not only are matters so about familiar scenes, but they are so because it is morally right or wrong that they are so. Familiar scenes of everyday activities, treated by members as the 'natural facts of life', are massive facts of the members' daily existence both as a real world and as the product of activities in a real world. They furnish the 'fix', the 'this is it' to which the waking state returns one, and are the points of departure and return for every modification of the world of daily life that is achieved in play, dreaming, trance, theater, scientific theorizing, or high ceremony.

In every discipline, humanistic or scientific, the familiar common sense world of everyday life is a matter of abiding interest. In the social sciences, and in sociology particularly, it is a matter of essential preoccupation. It makes up sociology's problematic subject matter, enters the very constitution of the sociological attitude, and exercises an odd and obstinate sovereignty over sociologists' claims to adequate explanation.

Despite the topic's centrality, an immense literature contains little data and few methods with which the essential features of socially recognized 'familiar scenes' may be detected and related to dimensions of social organization. Although sociologists take socially structured scenes of everyday life as a point of departure they rarely see,[1] as a task of sociological inquiry in its own right, the general question of how any such common sense world is possible. Instead, the possibility of the everyday world is

1. The work of Alfred Schutz is a magnificent exception. Readers who are acquainted with his writings will recognize how heavily this paper is indebted to him.

either settled by theoretical representation or merely assumed. As a topic and methodological ground for sociological inquiries, the definition of the common sense world of everyday life, though it is appropriately a project of sociological inquiry, has been neglected. My purposes in this paper are to demonstrate the essential relevance, to sociological inquiries, of a concern for common sense activities as a topic of inquiry in its own right and, by reporting a series of studies, to urge its 'rediscovery'.

Making commonplace scenes visible

In accounting for the stable features of everyday activities sociologists commonly select familiar settings such as familial households or work places and ask for the variables that contribute to their stable features. Just as commonly, one set of considerations are unexamined: the socially standardized and standardizing, 'seen but unnoticed', expected, background features of everyday scenes. The member of the society uses background expectancies as a scheme of interpretation. With their use actual appearances are for him recognizable and intelligible as the appearances-of-familiar-events. Demonstrably he is responsive to this background, while at the same time he is at a loss to tell us specifically of what the expectancies consist. When we ask him about them he has little or nothing to say.

For these background expectancies to come into view one must either be a stranger to the 'life as usual' character of everyday scenes, or become estranged from them. As Alfred Schutz pointed out, a 'special motive' is required to make them problematic. In the sociologists' case this 'special motive' consists in the programmatic task of treating a societal member's practical circumstances, which include from the member's point of view the morally necessary character of many of its background features, as matters of theoretic interest. The seen but unnoticed backgrounds of everyday activities are made visible and are described from a perspective in which persons live out the lives they do, have the children they do, feel the feelings, think the thoughts, enter the relationships they do, all in order to permit the sociologist to solve his theoretical problems.

Almost alone among sociological theorists, the late Alfred Schutz, in a series of classical studies (1932, 1962, 1964, 1966) of the constitutive phenomenology of the world of everyday life, described many of these seen but unnoticed background expectancies. He called them the 'attitude of daily life'. He referred to their scenic attributions as the 'world known in common and taken for granted'. Schutz' fundamental work makes it possible to pursue further the tasks of clarifying their nature and operation, of relating them to the processes of concerted actions, and assigning them their place in an empirically imaginable society.

References

SCHUTZ, A. (1932), *Der Sinnhafte Aufbau der Sozialen Welt*, Springer.

SCHUTZ, A. (1962), *Collected Papers: I. The Problem of Social Reality*, ed. M. Natanson, Nijhoff.

SCHUTZ, A. (1964), *Collected Papers: II. Studies in Social Theory*, ed. A. Broderson, Nijhoff.

SCHUTZ, A. (1966), *Collected Papers: III. Studies in Phenomenological Philosophy* ed. I. Schutz, Nijhoff.

4 E. E. Evans-Pritchard

For Example, Witchcraft

Abridged from E. E. Evans-Pritchard, *Witchcraft, Oracles and Magic among the Azande*, Clarendon Press, 1937, pp. 64–7.

Unless the reader appreciates that witchcraft is quite a normal factor in the life of Azande, one to which almost any and every happening may be referred, he will entirely misunderstand their behaviour towards it. To us witchcraft is something which haunted and disgusted our credulous forefathers. But the Zande expects to come across witchcraft at any time of the day or night. He would be just as surprised if he were not brought into daily contact with it as we would be if confronted by its appearance. To him there is nothing miraculous about it. It is expected that a man's hunting will be injured by witches, and he has at his disposal means of dealing with them. When misfortunes occur he does not become awestruck at the play of supernatural forces. He is not terrified at the presence of an occult enemy. He is, on the other hand, extremely annoyed. Someone, out of spite, has ruined his ground-nuts or spoilt his hunting or given his wife a chill, and surely this is cause for anger! He has done no one harm, so what right has anyone to interfere in his affairs? It is an impertinence, an insult, a dirty, offensive trick! It is the aggressiveness and not the eeriness of these actions which Azande emphasize when speaking of them, and it is anger and not awe which we observe in their response to them.

Witchcraft is not less anticipated than adultery. It is so intertwined with everyday happenings that it is part of a Zande's ordinary world. There is nothing remarkable about a witch – you may be one yourself, and certainly many of your closest neighbours are witches. Nor is there anything awe-inspiring about witchcraft. We do not become psychologically transformed when we hear that some one is ill – we expect people to be ill – and it is the same with Azande. They expect people to be ill, i.e. to be bewitched, and it is not a matter for surprise or wonderment.

But is not Zande belief in witchcraft a belief in mystical causation of phenomena and events to the complete exclusion of all natural causes? The relations of mystical to common-sense thought are very complicated and raise problems that confront us on every page of this book. Here I wish to state the problem in a preliminary manner and in terms of actual situations.

I found it strange at first to live among Azande and listen to naïve explanations of misfortunes which, to our minds, have apparent causes, but after a while I learnt the idiom of their thought and applied notions of witchcraft as spontaneously as themselves in situations where the concept was relevant. A boy knocked his foot against a small stump of wood in the centre of a bush path, a frequent happening in Africa, and suffered pain and inconvenience in consequence. Owing to its position on his toe it was impossible to keep the cut free from dirt and it began to fester. He declared that witchcraft had made him knock his foot against the stump. I always argued with Azande and criticized their statements, and I did so on this occasion. I told the boy that he had knocked his foot against the stump of wood because he had been careless, and that witchcraft had not placed it in the path, for it had grown there naturally. He agreed that witchcraft had nothing to do with the stump of wood being in his path but added that he had kept his eyes open for stumps, as indeed every Zande does most carefully, and that if he had not been bewitched he would have seen the stump. As a conclusive argument for his view he remarked that all cuts do not take days to heal but, on the contrary, close quickly, for that is the nature of cuts. Why, then, had his sore festered and remained open if there were no witchcraft behind it? . . .

One of my chief informants, Kisanga, was a skilled woodcarver, one of the finest carvers in the whole kingdom of Gbudwe. Occasionally the bowls and stools which he carved split during the work, as one may well imagine in such a climate. Though the hardest woods be selected they sometimes split in process of carving or on completion of the utensil even if the craftsman is careful and well acquainted with the technical rules of his craft. When this happened to the bowls and stools of this particular craftsman he attributed the misfortune to witchcraft and used to harangue me about the spite and jealousy of his neighbours. When I used to reply that I thought he was mistaken and that people were well disposed towards him he used to hold the split bowl or stool towards me as concrete evidence of his assertions. If people were not bewitching his work, how would I account for that? Likewise a potter will attribute the cracking of his pots during firing to witchcraft. An experienced potter need have no fear that his pots will crack as a result of error. He selects the proper clay, kneads it thoroughly till he has extracted all grit and pebbles, and builds it up slowly and carefully. On the night before digging out his clay he abstains from sexual intercourse. So he should have nothing to fear. Yet pots sometimes break, even when they are the handiwork of expert potters, and this can only be accounted for by witchcraft. 'It is broken – there is witchcraft', says the potter simply.

Part Two
The Logical Basis of Constructed Reality

The logic of depiction requires that the whole of logical space be given as soon as one place in it is determined. A passage such as this one chosen from Wittgenstein's *Tractatus* is exactly illustrated by the analysis of Nuer society. For Nuer are supremely logical. 'Where the women are, the cattle are not.' Thus summed up is the series of matching propositions which constitute their rules of marriage and incest, their political allegiances and their distribution of property. Consanguinity and affinity are distinct and complementary relations which fill between them the whole social universe. Incest confuses the order of society and unleashes disease. So strong is the logical scaffolding that nature is invested with chains of causal necessity which uphold the distinction between different categories of relationship. An analysis which takes for granted the social genesis of logical operations is able to show how nature is found with its own *a priori* which seems independently to match that of the mind. In spite of this early work it is still possible for Faris to list a vast array of modern anthropological studies of the cognitive process which fail to give weight to the social boundaries within which cognition proceeds. There is more excuse for philosophers who make no claim to be conversant with anthropology. Yet it is a loss to us if everything Husserl's students say about cognition is said outside this tradition. For in fumbling about how the essence of redness involves an extremely complex cognitive act, he would have been surely helped by the discussion of how the Dinka experience of colour is mediated through cattle first and the rest of nature next, and of how the whole of their aesthetic and social experience is so profoundly embedded in a bovine idiom that it is even misleading to distinguish their knowledge of cattle from their knowledge of themselves as if each were not the medium of the other.

5 L. Wittgenstein

The World is Constructed on a Logical Scaffolding

Excerpts from L. Wittgenstein, *Tractatus Logico-Philosophicus*, Routledge & Kegan Paul, second edition of new translation, 1971, pp. 35–43. First published in 19–21.

3.42 A proposition can determine only one place in logical space: nevertheless the whole of logical space must already be given by it.

(Otherwise negation, logical sum, logical product, etc., would introduce more and more new elements – in coordination.)

(The logical scaffolding surrounding a picture determines logical space. The force of a proposition reaches through the whole of logical space.)

3.5 A propositional sign, applied and thought out, is a thought.

4 A thought is a proposition with a sense.

4.001 The totality of propositions is language.

4.003 Most of the propositions and questions to be found in philosophical works are not false but nonsensical. Consequently we cannot give any answer to questions of this kind, but can only point out that they are nonsensical. Most of the propositions and questions of philosophers arise from our failure to understand the logic of our language.

(They belong to the same class as the question whether the good is more or less identical than the beautiful.)

And it is not surprising that the deepest problems are in fact *not* problems at all.

4.0031 All philosophy is a 'critique of language' (though not in Mauthner's sense). It was Russell who performed the service of showing that the apparent logical form of a proposition need not be its real one.

4.01 A proposition is a picture of reality.

A proposition is a model of reality as we imagine it.

4.011 At first sight a proposition – one set out on the printed page, for example – does not seem to be a picture of the reality with which it is concerned. But neither do written notes seem at first sight to be a picture of a piece of music, nor our phonetic notation (the alphabet) to be a picture of our speech.

And yet these sign-languages prove to be pictures, even in the ordinary sense, of what they represent.

4.012 It is obvious that a proposition of the form 'aRb' strikes us as a picture. In this case the sign is obviously a likeness of what is signified.

4.013 And if we penetrate to the essence of this pictorial character, we see that it is *not* impaired by *apparent irregularities* (such as the use of ♯ and ♭ in musical notation).

For even these irregularities depict what they are intended to express; only they do it in a different way.

4.014 A gramophone record, the musical idea, the written notes, and the sound-waves, all stand to one another in the same internal relation of depicting that holds between language and the world.

They are all constructed according to a common logical pattern.

(Like the two youths in the fairy-tale, their two horses, and their lilies. They are all in a certain sense one.)

4.0141 There is a general rule by means of which the musician can obtain the symphony from the score, and which makes it possible to derive the symphony from the groove on the gramophone record, and, using the first rule, to derive the score again. That is what constitutes the inner similarity between these things which seem to be constructed in such entirely different ways. And that rule is the law of projection which projects the symphony into the language of musical notation. It is the rule for translating this language into the language of gramophone records.

4.015 The possibility of all imagery, of all our pictorial modes of expression, is contained in the logic of depiction.

4.016 In order to understand the essential nature of a proposition, we should consider hieroglyphic script, which depicts the facts that it describes.

And alphabetic script developed out of it without losing what was essential to depiction.

4.02 We can see this from the fact that we understand the sense of a propositional sign without its having been explained to us.

4.021 A proposition is a picture of reality: for if I understand a proposition, I know the situation that it represents. And I understand the proposition without having had its sense explained to me.

4.022 A proposition *shows* its sense.

A proposition *shows* how things stand *if* it is true. And it *says that* they do so stand.

4.023 A proposition must restrict reality to two alternatives: yes or no.

In order to do that, it must describe reality completely.

A proposition is a description of a state of affairs.

Just as a description of an object describes it by giving its external properties, so a proposition describes reality by its internal properties.

A proposition constructs a world with the help of a logical scaffolding, so that one can actually see from the proposition how everything stands logically *if* it is true. One can *draw inferences* from a false proposition.

4.024 To understand a proposition means to know what is the case if it is true.

(One can understand it, therefore, without knowing whether it is true.)

It is understood by anyone who understands its constituents.

4.025 When translating one language into another, we do not proceed by translating each *proposition* of the one into a *proposition* of the other, but merely by translating the constituents of propositions.

(And the dictionary translates not only substantives, but also verbs, adjectives, and conjunctions, etc.; and it treats them all in the same way.)

4.026 The meanings of simple signs (words) must be explained to us if we are to understand them.

With propositions, however, we make ourselves understood.

4.027 It belongs to the essence of a proposition that it should be able to communicate a *new* sense to us.

4.03 A proposition must use old expressions to communicate a new sense.

A proposition communicates a situation to us, and so it must be *essentially* connected with the situation.

And the connection is precisely that it is its logical picture.

A proposition states something only in so far as it is a picture.

4.031 In a proposition a situation is, as it were, constructed by way of experiment.

Instead of, 'This proposition has such and such a sense', we can simply say, 'This proposition represents such and such a situation.'

4.0311 One name stands for one thing, another for another thing, and they are combined with one another. In this way the whole group – like a *tableau vivant* – presents a state of affairs.

4.0312 The possibility of propositions is based on the principle that objects have signs as their representatives.

My fundamental idea is that the 'logical constants' are not representatives; that there can be no representatives of the *logic* of facts.

6 E. Durkheim and M. Mauss

The Social Genesis of Logical Operations

Excerpt from E. Durkheim and M. Mauss, *Primitive Classification*, Routledge & Kegan Paul, 1963, pp. 81–8. First published in 1903.

Primitive classifications are not singular or exceptional, having no analogy with those employed by more civilized peoples; on the contrary, they seem to be connected, with no break in continuity, to the first scientific classifications. In fact, however different they may be in certain respects from the latter, they nevertheless have all their essential characteristics. First of all, like all sophisticated classifications, they are systems of hierarchized notions. Things are not simply arranged by them in the form of isolated groups, but these groups stand in fixed relationships to each other and together form a single whole. Moreover, these systems, like those of science, have a purely speculative purpose. Their object is not to facilitate action, but to advance understanding, to make intelligible the relations which exist between things. Given certain concepts which are considered to be fundamental, the mind feels the need to connect to them the ideas which it forms about other things. Such classifications are thus intended, above all, to connect ideas, to unify knowledge; as such, they may be said without inexactitude to be scientific, and to constitute a first philosophy of nature.[1] The Australian does not divide the universe between the totems of his tribe with a view to regulating his conduct or even to justify his practice; it is because, the idea of the totem being cardinal for him, he is under a necessity to place everything else that he knows in relation to it. We may therefore think that the conditions on which these very ancient classifications depend may have played an important part in the genesis of the classificatory function in general.

1. As such they are very clearly distinguished from what might be called technological classifications. It is probable that man has always classified, more or less clearly, the things on which he lived, according to the means he used to get them: for example, animals living in the water, or in the air or on the ground. But at first such groups were not connected with each other or systematized. They were divisions, distinctions of ideas, not schemes of classification. Moreover, it is evident that these distinctions are closely linked to practical concerns, of which they merely express certain aspects. It is for this reason that we have not spoken of them in this work, in which we have tried above all to throw some light on the origins of the logical procedure which is the basis of scientific classifications.

Now it results from this study that the nature of these conditions is social. Far from it being the case, as Frazer seems to think, that the social relations of men are based on logical relations between things, in reality it is the former which have provided the prototype for the latter. According to him, men were divided into clans by a pre-existing classification of things; but, quite on the contrary, they classified things because they were divided by clans.

We have seen, indeed, how these classifications were modelled on the closest and most fundamental form of social organization. This, however, is not going far enough. Society was not simply a model which classificatory thought followed; it was its own divisions which served as divisions for the system of classification. The first logical categories were social categories; the first classes of things were classes of men, into which these things were integrated. It was because men were grouped, and thought of themselves in the form of groups, that in their ideas they grouped other things, and in the beginning the two modes of grouping were merged to the point of being indistinct. Moieties were the first genera; clans, the first species. Things were thought to be integral parts of society, and it was their place in society which determined their place in nature. We may even wonder whether the schematic manner in which genera are ordinarily conceived may not have depended in part on the same influences. It is a fact of current observation that the things which they comprise are generally imagined as situated in a sort of ideational milieu, with a more or less clearly delimited spatial circumscription. It is certainly not without cause that concepts and their interrelations have so often been represented by concentric and eccentric circles, interior and exterior to each other, etc. Might it not be that this tendency to imagine purely logical groupings in a form contrasting so much with their true nature originated in the fact that at first they were conceived in the form of social groups occupying, consequently, definite positions in space? And have we not in fact seen this spatial localization of genus and species in a fairly large number of very different societies?

Not only the external form of classes, but also the relations uniting them to each other, are of social origin. It is because human groups fit one into another – the sub-clan into the clan, the clan into the moiety, the moiety into the tribe – that groups of things are ordered in the same way. Their regular diminution in span, from genus to species, species to variety, and so on, comes from the equally diminishing extent presented by social groups as one leaves the largest and oldest and approaches the more recent and the more derivative. And if the totality of things is conceived as a single system, this is because society itself is seen in the same way. It is a whole, or rather it is *the* unique whole to which everything is related. Thus logical hierarchy is only another aspect of social hierarchy, and the unity of knowledge is nothing else than the very unity of the collectivity, extended to the universe.

Furthermore, the ties which unite things of the same group or different groups to each other are themselves conceived as social ties. We recalled in the beginning that the expressions by which we refer to these relations still have a moral significance; but whereas for us they are hardly more than metaphors, originally they meant what they said. Things of the same class were really considered as relatives of the individuals of the same social group, and consequently of each other. They are of 'the same flesh', the same family. Logical relations are thus, in a sense, domestic relations. Sometimes, too, as we have seen, they are comparable at all points with those which exist between a master and an object possessed, between a chief and his subjects. We may even wonder whether the idea of the pre-eminence of genus over species, which is so strange from a positivistic point of view, may not be seen here in its rudimentary form. Just as, for the realist, the general idea dominates the individual, so the clan totem dominates those of the sub-clans and, still more, the personal totems of individuals; and wherever the moiety has retained its original stability it has a sort of primacy over the divisions of which it is composed and the particular things which are included in them. Though he may be essentially Wartwut and partially Moiwiluk, the Wotjobaluk described by Howitt is above all a Krokitch or a Gamutch. Among the Zuñi, the animals symbolizing the six main clans are set in sovereign charge over their respective sub-clans and over creatures of all kinds which are grouped with them.

But if the foregoing has allowed us to understand how the notion of classes, linked to each other in a single system, could have been born, we still do not know what the forces were which induced men to divide things as they did between the classes. From the fact that the external form of the classification was furnished by society, it does not necessarily follow that the way in which the framework was used is due to reasons of the same origin. *A priori* it is very possible that motives of a quite different order should have determined the way in which things were connected and merged, or else, on the contrary, distinguished and opposed.

The particular conception of logical connections which we now have permits us to reject this hypothesis. We have just seen, in fact, that they are represented in the form of familial connections, or as relations of economic or political subordination; so that the same sentiments which are the basis of domestic, social, and other kinds of organization have been effective in this logical division of things also. The latter are attracted or opposed to each other in the same way as men are bound by kinship or opposed in the vendetta. They are merged as members of the same family are merged by common sentiment. That some are subordinate to others is analogous in every respect to the fact that an object possessed appears inferior to its owner, and likewise the subject to his master. It is thus states of the collective mind (*âme*) which gave birth to these groupings, and these states moreover are manifestly affective. There are sentimental affinities between things as between individuals, and they are classed according to these affinities.

We thus arrive at this conclusion: it is possible to classify other things than concepts, and otherwise than in accordance with the laws of pure understanding. For in order for it to be possible for ideas to be systematically arranged for reasons of sentiment, it is necessary that they should not be pure ideas, but that they should themselves be products of sentiment. And in fact, for those who are called primitives, a species of things is not a simple object of knowledge but corresponds above all to a certain sentimental attitude. All kinds of affective elements combine in the representation made of it. Religious emotions, notably, not only give it a special tinge, but attribute to it the most essential properties of which it is constituted. Things are above all sacred or profane, pure or impure, friends or enemies, favourable or unfavourable;[2] i.e. their most fundamental characteristics are only expressions of the way in which they affect social sensibility. The differences and resemblances which determine the fashion in which they are grouped are more affective than intellectual. This is how it happens that things change their nature, in a way, from society to society; it is because they affect the sentiments of groups differently. What is conceived in one as perfectly homogeneous is represented elsewhere as essentially heterogeneous. For us, space is formed of similar parts which are substitutable one for the other. We have seen, however, that for many peoples it is profoundly differentiated according to regions. This is because each region has its own affective value. Under the influence of diverse sentiments, it is connected with a special religious principle, and consequently it is endowed with virtues *sui generis* which distinguish it from all others. And it is this emotional value of notions which plays the preponderant part in the manner in which ideas are connected or separated. It is the dominant characteristic in classification.

It has quite often been said that man began to conceive things by relating them to himself. The above allows us to see more precisely what this anthropocentrism, which might better be called *sociocentrism*, consists of. The centre of the first schemes of nature is not the individual; it is society.[3]

2. For the adherent of many cults, even now, foodstuffs are classified first of all into two main classes, fat and lean, and we know to what extent this classification is subjective.

3. De la Grasserie has developed ideas fairly similar to our own, though rather obscurely and above all without evidence (1899, ch 3).

It is this that is objectified, not man. Nothing shows this more clearly than the way in which the Sioux retain the whole universe, in a way, within the limits of tribal space; and we have seen how universal space itself is nothing else than the site occupied by the tribe, only indefinitely extended beyond its real limits. It is by virtue of the same mental disposition that so many peoples have placed the centre of the world, 'the navel of the earth', in their own political or religious capital,[4] i.e. at the place which is the centre of their moral life. Similarly, but in another order of ideas, the creative force of the universe and everything in it was first conceived as a mythical ancestor, the generator of the society.

This is how it is that the idea of a logical classification was so hard to form, as we showed at the beginning of this work. It is because a logical classification is a classification of concepts. Now a concept is the notion of a clearly determined group of things; its limits may be marked precisely. Emotion, on the contrary, is something essentially fluid and inconsistent. Its contagious influence spreads far beyond its point of origin, extending to everything about it, so that it is not possible to say where its power of propagation ends. States of an emotional nature necessarily possess the same characteristic. It is not possible to say where they begin or where they end; they lose themselves in each other, and mingle their properties in such a way that they cannot be rigorously categorized. From another point of view, in order to be able to mark out the limits of a class, it is necessary to have analysed the characteristics by which the things assembled in this class are recognized and by which they are distinguished. Now emotion is naturally refractory to analysis, or at least lends itself uneasily to it, because it is too complex. Above all when it has a collective origin it defies critical and rational examination. The pressure exerted by the group on each of its members does not permit individuals to judge freely the notions which society itself has elaborated and in which it has placed something of its personality. Such constructs are sacred for individuals. Thus the history of scientific classification is, in the last analysis, the history of the stages by which this element of social affectivity has progressively weakened, leaving more and more room for the reflective thought of individuals. But it is not the case that these remote influences which we have just studied have ceased to be felt today. They have left behind them an effect which survives and which is always present; it is the very cadre of all classification, it is the ensemble of mental habits by virtue of which we conceive things and facts in the form of coordinated or hierarchized groups.

This example shows what light sociology throws on the genesis, and

4. Something understandable enough for the Romans and even the Zuñi, but less so for the inhabitants of Easter Island, called Te Pito-te Henua (navel of the earth); but the idea is perfectly natural everywhere.

consequently the functioning, of logical operations. What we have tried to do for classification might equally be attempted for the other functions or fundamental notions of the understanding. We have already had occasion to mention, in passing, how even ideas so abstract as those of time and space are, at each point in their history, closely connected with the corresponding social organization. The same method could help us likewise to understand the manner in which the ideas of cause, substance, and the different modes of reasoning, etc. were formed. As soon as they are posed in sociological terms, all these questions, so long debated by metaphysicians and psychologists, will at last be liberated from the tautologies in which they have languished. At least, this is a new way which deserves to be tried.

Reference

LA GRASSERIE, R. de (1899), *Des Religions comparées au point de vue sociologique*, Paris.

7 E. E. Evans-Pritchard

'Where the Women Are, the Cattle Are Not'

Abridged from E. E. Evans-Pritchard, 'Nuer rules of exogamy and incest', in M. Fortes, (ed.), *Social Structure*, Clarendon Press, 1949, pp. 85–101.[1]

The Nuer word *rual* means both incest and the misfortune which it causes. Syphilis and certain forms of yaws are believed to be especially a consequence of incest, though retribution may come in any form, from wild beasts, a spear, drowning, sickness, etc. These misfortunes can sometimes be avoided by sacrifice. On the other hand, they may fall not only on the partners to the sin (*dwer*) but also on their closest relatives, so that a man who commits incest may render himself responsible for homicide as well.

When it is forbidden to a man to have relations with a woman he may not, of course, marry her, and it will be simpler to begin this account by stating the rules of exogamy. Marriage is not permitted between clansfolk, close cognates, close natural kinsfolk, close kinsfolk by adoption, close affines, and persons who stand to one another as fathers and daughters in the age-set system.

A man may not marry a clanswoman and *a fortiori* a woman of his lineage. Agnatic kinship is recognized between some clans but it does not constitute a bar to intermarriage. The relationship is considered to be very distant and, in any case, the ancestor of the fraternal clans is believed to have cut an ox in twain to permit intermarriage between the descendants of his sons. Nuer accept the hypothesis that maximal lineages of the larger clans might one day split apart and marriage be allowed between them, but 'at present they are too close'. They say *Cike diel*; 'They have not yet reached ten generations (from their founder).' They perceive that the limits of clan exogamy have been arbitrarily fixed and are not unalterable.

A man may not marry any close cognate. Nuer consider that if relationship can be traced between a man and a woman through either father or mother, however many female links there may be, up to six generations (*kath*), though the number of generations is not absolutely fixed, marriage should not take place between them. . . . Stated in a slightly different way, a man or woman may marry into his, or her, mother's clan but not into

1. A preliminary account of this subject was given in a lecture delivered to the Royal Anthropological Institute on 20 November 1934 (summary in *Man*, xxxv, 1935).

her maximal lineage. Other clans do not allow a man to marry into his mother's clan in any circumstances.

When, as often happens among the Nuer, the physiological father, the *genitor*, is a different man from the sociological father, the *pater*, his sons will not marry into his minimal lineage because the physiological connection is socially recognized by the payment to the natural father of a cow of the bridewealth of his natural daughters. [. . .]

Generally a captured girl is brought up a member of her captor's household and is regarded as his daughter. He rubs ashes on the back of a sheep and tells his ancestral ghosts that the girl is 'our daughter and our sister'. Nuer say: 'Thus she is taken into the household (*gol*) and becomes a member of the household.' They also say: 'She will become our daughter and we will receive her bridewealth-cattle.' The cattle of her bridewealth give her kinship with the persons among whom it is distributed, as does also her right to receive in return the cows of the paternal aunt on the marriage of the daughters of the sons of her captor and foster-father. Marriage is therefore forbidden between her descendants and the descendants of these kinsmen in virtue of bridewealth, for several generations. She herself can be married to a clansman of her captor and foster-father so long as her husband does not belong to his minimal lineage, which is to say, so long as those who pay her bridewealth cannot also claim part of it, for those who can claim part of a girl's bridewealth are kin to her. Nuer state these rules in terms of cattle.

A man may not take his wife's sister or any near kinswoman of his wife as a second wife. A man may be on familiar terms with his wife's sister but sexual relations with her are incestuous and it is only permissible for him to marry her if his wife has died without having borne children.[2] It is said that were he to do so the children of the marriage would die. When I argued that there was no kinship between a man and his wife's sister, Nuer said that this was not true. 'What about the child?' they asked. They regard a man and his wife's sister as related through the child of the wife – for a woman is only fully married when she has a child and comes to live with her husband's people as their 'kinswoman', as they say, since her child is their child. Her sister is therefore also a kind of kinswoman since she is also the mother of their child. Your wife's sister, being your child's maternal aunt, is your sister (as we say, sister-in-law). Nuer also define this relationship in terms of cattle. When your daughter is married, her mother's sister receives a cow of her bridewealth, and Nuer hold that she cannot both receive this cow and be your wife at the same time, especially as the cow is regarded

2. A single case of marriage to two sisters at the same time was recorded. A well-known magician on the Sobat River defied the prohibition. When, however, one of his daughters fell sick with syphilis, or yaws, he gave up the second sister.

as part of the bridewealth still owing from your marriage to your wife. Also, when your wife's sister's daughter marries, your wife will receive a cow, and Nuer feel that there is something wrong about this cow coming to her if her sister is also her co-wife. In certain circumstances a woman may claim cattle on her sister's marriage, and in this case the man who pays the cattle would also be the receiver of them were a man to marry his wife's sister – a situation the Nuer regard as impossible. Hence Nuer say that a man may not marry his wife's sister either 'on account of her (the wife's) children' or 'on account of the cattle', which are different ways of saying that you cannot marry the child's maternal aunt. There is a further reason which would prevent a man from marrying his wife's sister while his wife is living, for, as will be explained later, a man may not have sexual relations with two closely related women at the same time. It follows that two brothers ought not to marry sisters or close cousins: 'That would be bad because if your brother died you could not take his wife.'

A man may not marry the daughter of an age-mate, a member of his age-set, 'because she is his daughter'. The blood age-mates have shed together into the ground at their initiation gives them a kind of kinship. In certain circumstances an age-mate may claim a cow, the *yang rica*, of the bridewealth of the daughter of one of his mates, and a man may not be in the position of paying bridewealth and being able to claim it. Nuer point out also that were a man to marry the daughter of an age-mate her parents would become his parents-in-law and the respect he would have to show them would be incompatible with the familiarity with which he should treat age-mates and their wives and the liberties he may take with them. He could not, for instance, eat and drink in their home, an abstention in glaring contradiction to the behaviour expected of age-mates. The prohibition on marriage with the daughter of an age-mate imposes no inconvenience on Nuer, for there would always be a great difference in age between the man and woman, and this is, in any case, an obstacle to marriage rarely surmounted in Nuerland. Strictly speaking, a breach of this prohibition is not *rual* but Nuer say that it is 'like *rual*'. The prohibition is said to have been ordained by God and it is believed that the guardian spirit of the age-set (*kwoth ricdien*) will avenge a breach of it.

It is said that in the past a man would not have been allowed to marry the daughters of his father's age-mates, for they are his sisters. It is still not permissible for such a marriage to take place if both the fathers are alive, since this would mean that the two age-mates would enter into a relationship characterized by mutual reserve and in conflict with the egalitarian status of age-mates towards one another. [. . .]

The exogamous rules I have recorded above can be generalized by saying, as the Nuer do, that a man may not marry a woman who is *mar* (kin) to him. In defining exogamy kinship is traced farther in some directions than in others and is of different kinds: the clan kinship of the *mut*, the common spear; the kinship of *buth*, of collateral lineage and of adoption; uterine kinship; kinship through the *genitor*; the kinship of cognation, *mar* in the usual sense of the word; kinship which the birth of a child creates between husband and wife; the kinship acknowledged by acceptance of bride-wealth; and the kinship by analogy of the *ric*, the age-set. . . .

It is not incestuous for a man to have relations with the daughters of men of his father's age-set and he would not hesitate to make love to them. In all other cases where it is forbidden for a man to marry a woman standing in a certain relationship to him it is also forbidden to him to be intimate with her, though the prohibition has not always the same force or extension. Before discussing the different degrees of seriousness with which Nuer view breaches of the various rules, I will mention the other relationships which carry the incest taboo besides those already recorded which exclude marriage either absolutely or contingently. [. . .]

The prohibition of a man having relations with a kinsman's wife is part of a more general regulation which forbids, as *rual*, two close kinsmen to have relations with the same woman, though, here again, 'bulls' do not come, altogether or to some extent, under the ban. Likewise, two closely related women must not have relations with the same man. Nuer youths, who make love to maidens very freely, are careful to inquire of a girl, if they are uncertain of her affairs, whether she has a sweetheart among their close kinsmen. A man may, however, start an affair with a girl as soon as a kinsman has broken off relations with her. The rule, which refers to court-ship and sweethearts rather than to casual intercourse, applies to father and son, uterine brothers, and to a lesser degree paternal half-brothers, and also in some degree to cousins, except to paternal parallel cousins, for they are 'bulls' and it does not matter if they share sweethearts. The pro-hibition is, however, only forcibly enunciated with regard to kinsfolk who form the same *dep*, dancing-line, which means kinsmen who are also members of the same village. Hence it is said that it is not very dangerous for a man and his mother's brother's son to make love to the same girl if they are not members of the same local community. The most dangerous incest of this kind, the consequences of which 'split a man in two' with pain, is when father and son have relations with the same woman, for the father goes from the woman to the mother, thus bringing her into a sexual relationship with her son. It is also highly dangerous for a mother and daughter to have relations with the same man.

There are, as we have seen, a very large number of relationships which carry the incest taboo and it is not surprising that there are frequent breaches of it. Indeed, Nuer discuss incest, except incest with the closest kin, without expressing horror or repugnance. It is a fact with which they are familiar and a subject on the surface of life, not a secret thing to be talked of with shame or embarrassment. Parents teach their sons at an early age the rules of sex: to avoid the wives of others and those who *teke mar*, have kinship. Not only must they refrain from making love to women who count as kin but they must avoid any licentious talk, to which the Nuer are much given, in their presence. The *nei ti gwa*, the unrelated people, they can joke with and make love to without fear of censure or retribution, so long as they are not wives to other men, for fornication with an unrelated girl, a *nya Nath*, as they say, is not regarded with disapprobation. The admonition of parents is enforced by the frequent discussions children hear about the exogamous permissibility of proposed marriages and by the sacrifices on account of incest they are bound to witness from time to time.

The incest taboo is not uniform in its force nor in the consequences its breach is believed to entail. Some incest is very bad and has very serious consequences. Other incest is not so bad, is even thought little of, and is not expected to bring about serious, or even any, consequences. The worst incest of all would be with the mother, and Nuer were astonished when I asked them if they had known of any cases of it: 'But that would be immediate death.' Incest with the uterine sister or the daughter is also terrible. [. . .] Generally speaking, the farther the man and woman are from one another genealogically the less seriously incest between them is regarded, especially if they live in different districts, and the taboo is less stringent and has a narrower range for natural kinsmen than for social kinsmen. [. . .] Relations with distant clanswomen and cognates are of frequent occurrence. They are with persons who are on the frontiers of exogamy and carry no moral stigma or much fear of consequences. Nuer, in the usual idiom of their culture, often condemn incest with kinsfolk by reference to bridewealth: 'Would you have relations with the daughter of your father's sister? Do you not receive cattle on her marriage?' 'What! Do you not want the cattle of your daughter's marriage and would you not die of *rual*?' And so forth. [. . .] To avoid the consequences of incest Nuer make sacrifices, and the weight they attach to the breach of the taboo may be estimated by the value of the thing they sacrifice. For slight incest, as with a distant clanswoman or the wife of a paternal cousin, they consider it sufficient to sacrifice one of the yellow fruits I have spoken of earlier or one of the pendulous fruits of the sausage tree. When a yellow fruit is sacrificed it is cut in two and the left half, 'the bad half', is thrown away, while the contents of the right half, 'the good half', are drunk by the partners to the sin as an infusion. They may get a magician to do this for them or they may do it for themselves. When incest has taken place with the wife of a kinsman who is not a 'bull' and is in Nuer reckoning a close kinsman, the wife's sleeping-skin is cut in two. This, of course, would only be done if one of the pair were sick enough to be more frightened of death than of the husband, for unlike the cutting of the fruits the rite cannot be performed secretly. In cases of incest with a close kinswoman and in all cases of what the Nuer regard as really bad incest, *wal ruali*, an antidote some people are said to possess and make use of when committing a slight incest, is no protection and a vicarious sacrifice no remedy. A goat or a sheep, or in the most serious cases an ox, must be cut vertically in twain and a leopard-skin chief must perform the sacrifice. The guilty persons drink incest medicines infused in the gall of the sacrificed animal. It is believed that retribution follows swiftly on the heels of the offence, so that if sacrifice is to be of any avail it must be performed at once. Nuer say that a sacrifice is unlikely to be efficacious when death is near and that it is little profit to make confession then.

The moral element in the retributive action which follows on a breach of the incest taboo is brought out by the fact that, except in cases of really bad incest, such as when a father and son have relations with the same woman, it is felt that no ill effects will follow an infraction if the incestuous pair were unaware that they were breaking it. It is common knowledge that children begin sexual play with kin and they are corrected if observed, but it is not thought that misfortune will follow, 'Because the children are ignorant of having done wrong'. [. . .]

I now make some general observations, within the scope of this essay, on Nuer exogamy and incest, or about the Nuer concept of *rual*. Nuer say that marriage to persons standing in certain relationships is forbidden because it would be *rual*, incestuous. Speaking sociologically, I think we may reverse this statement and say that sexual relations with persons standing in these relationships are considered incestuous because it would be a breach of exogamy to marry them. I would hold that the incest taboo can only be understood in the light of the rules of exogamy and that these rules are to be explained by their function in the Nuer kinship system and in their whole social structure.

It is evident that the incest prohibition is not derived from notions of consanguinity only, or even to any extent, but from a social definition of kinship. [. . .] The Nuer incest prohibition is a prohibition of sexual relations within relationships of certain kinds, and I contend that it is to be regarded primarily as a way of providing a moral norm, a reason, and a sanction for the exogamous regulations of their society and is therefore a product of their social structure. [. . .]

In view of the importance attached to children by Nuer in determining what is incest, or the degree of it, it may readily be understood why sexual relations with the wives of half-brothers, paternal uncles, and patrilineal cousins of every kind are regarded as being either incestuous peccadilloes or not incestuous at all. The wife of a 'bull' is, in a general social sense, the wife of all the 'bulls', of the joint family and of the lineage. She is 'our wife' and 'the wife of our cattle'. Likewise her children are the children of the lineage, of the agnatic group and of its cattle. Hence sexual relations with the wives of these agnates, if not approved, are condoned, for they are the wives of all. Hence also, whereas relations with, for example, the wife of the maternal uncle means relations with the *cek nara*, the maternal uncle's wife, and the mother of *gat nara*, the maternal uncle's child, relations with the wife of the father's brother's son are with *cekdan*, our wife, and the mother of *gatdan*, our child. The presence of a child does not alter the status of the persons concerned in the second case as it does in the first, for the wife is the wife of the lineage and the child is the child of the adulterer. When a man dies, therefore, there is no question of the widow being remarried to one of his brothers, for the brothers already count as her husbands. The dead man's lineage have a right to inherit his wife because she is their wife, the wife of their cattle. [. . .]

It is clear that the rules of exogamy, by differentiating between persons in Nuer society, indicate kinship status and are one of the most effective means of doing this and thereby of maintaining the kinship system, which is based on the distinctions between the various categories of relationships. The rules of exogamy prevent confusion between one relationship and another and the contradiction such confusion would cause between the patterns of behaviour in which the relationships are expressed. This conclusion is contained in the statements, some of them recorded in this essay, of Nuer themselves, who see that it is undesirable to obliterate or confuse the boundaries between kinship categories. Were marriage with the wife's sister permitted, to the child of it the mother's sister would also be the father's wife; were a man to marry the daughter of an age-mate, his age-mate would also be his father-in-law. But if the wife has died childless, marriage with her sister is permitted because the relationship of a man to his child's mother's sister is no longer at issue, and if one of two age-mates is dead the son of one may marry the daughter of the other because the fathers can no longer be brought into a relationship of affinity. This explanation of exogamous rules holds not only for the Nuer but, as Professor Radcliffe-Brown has taught for very many years, for all societies.

8 J. C. Faris

'Occasions' and 'Non-Occasions'

J. C. Faris, 'Validation in ethnographical description: the lexicon of "occasions" in Cat Harbour', *Man*, new series, vol. 3, no. 1, March 1968, pp. 112–24.[1]

In contemporary ethnographical studies one major focus of attention has been on the objective description of native taxonomies and folk classification.[2] Some ethnographers, however, have been concerned that rigorous description may not be sufficient for making cultural sense of indigenous classifications, and there have thus been a number of attempts to specify the cognitive processes or principles necessary to produce such empirical sets. Statements on principles vary from the gross speculations of Foster (1965) on the cognitive orientation of peasants to the genealogical determinism demanded by Lounsbury (1964, 1965) and co-workers for the generation of kinship terminologies.

A number of other workers in the field of ethnographical theory and method have discussed problems in the psychological and cultural reality of process demonstrations (notably Wallace 1965; Wallace and Atkins 1960; Romney and D'Andrade 1964; Schneider 1965), and the criticisms and comments surrounding the subject are legion (for the most relevant see the review by Colby (1966), its commentators and bibliography, and the notes by Coult (1966a, 1966b) and their associated replies).

But thus far most studies which have concentrated on the cognitive (or otherwise) principles which generate a native classification have tended to ignore certain other problems – such as the circumstances in which the processes become operative, and the cultural nature and formation of

1. A preliminary version of this article was read at a session of the Northeastern Anthropological Association Annual Meeting, Amherst, Massachusetts, on 27 March 1966.

Field research on which this article is based took place from January 1964 to March 1965, and was generously supported by the Institute of Social and Economic Research of the Memorial University of Newfoundland, Canada. Words and phrases in quotes are from published sources or indicate emphasis. Words and phrases in italics are Cat Harbour usage.

2. See Conklin (1955, 1962a); Frake (1961, 1964); Goodenough (1956); Lounsbury (1956); Metzger and Williams (1963a, 1963b, 1966), for some of the more discussed, significant and accessible examples.

the domain or concept itself.[3] A few ethnographers have commented on the lack of attention to certain of these considerations (compare Hymes, 1964, 1966; Keesing, 1966), and in the example which follows I hope to illustrate just how important such considerations may be. For a culturally valid description (by which I mean a description wherein the classificatory principles are derived from the culture itself) it is not enough to indicate in contrast sets, componential terms or other dimensions the discriminations between lexemes of a domain (components of a classification), or even to demonstrate the existence of a taxonomy or other logical structures (such a demonstration may be irrelevant to the elicitation of attribute definitions or markers (Kay, 1966)). Attention must also be given to the place of the domain in the wider corpus of local vocabulary, its formation, and to the relevance of symbolism and connotation from other spheres of the culture.

There appear to be two predominant and interrelated reasons for the lack of attention to these problems. First is the overwhelming concentration on the ordering of perceptual domains or concepts whose boundary definitions are *assumed*; and second is the aversion to systematic concern with diachronic problems in ethnography.

The determination of empirical sets

The most common contemporary ethnographical descriptions[4] are of perceptual orders – classifications of object-label phenomena. This is in many cases a function of their 'high codability' (Brown and Lenneberg, 1954) and the less optional, more 'obligatory' (Conklin, 1962a) nature of the component categories.

This emphasis has also arisen from the ease of domain boundary specification. The significant attributes of a colour classification, or a disease or plant taxonomy may often be specified in a precise sensory manner. Object-label categorisations eliminate or lessen the problem of reference to symbols derived from other spheres of experience, and perhaps lessen the strategies and decisions necessary for a native to classify.

Some anthropologists, convinced of the universality of their material, make assumptions of boundary definitions and pre-specify an 'etic grid'. These attempts include, for example, the *sui generis* assumptions for kinship and kinship terminology of Lounsbury and others (Henderson, 1967; Lounsbury, 1964, 1965; Murdock, 1949; Schneider, 1964).

3. 'Concept', 'empirical set', and 'domain' may be regarded as synonymous for the purposes of this article.
4. The exceptions include Frake (1964), and the work of Metzger and Williams (1963a, 1963b, 1966). See also the comments on 'perceptual emphasis' by Akhmanova (1966) and Keesing (1966).

It appears that unless we are prepared to accept *methodologically* the assumptions of 'etic grids' in some spheres of experience,[5] the most rigorous and sound techniques available at present for the specification of domains (either perceptual *or* conceptual domains) are along the lines of the eliciting procedures now being developed by Metzger and Williams (1963*a*, 1963*b*, 1966). This involves taking a fragment from a native text (a sure way to provide an authentic focus, even if an uneconomical way of proceeding toward a total ethnography) and asking a number of careful questions designed to (1) elicit the components of the domain (i.e. lexemes in most cases) and their denotata, and (2) force the informant to make minimal level discriminations between the components to enable the ethnographer to map a representation of the indigenous ordering of the set.

This, though one of the most fruitful approaches for the determination of a focus and for an approximation of the internal structure of a domain, still does not answer one of the most vexing problems facing ethnographers in the validation of description – just how the highest order lexeme in the lexicon (the most inclusive component, the 'fragment' taken from a text) actually 'fits' in broader considerations of the culture in question without prior assumptions not derived from the culture. What does this super-ordinate component 'mean', and what does this concept and its meaning reveal about the culture? What, in short, is the significatum of the domain? We must focus on the discovery of the *cultural* principles by which assignments are made to a domain as well as the structural order within the set.

It seems to me that the above queries bear directly on problems of ethnographical validity, and I suggest diachronic considerations may be one avenue of fruitful pursuit. This involves attention to the formation of concepts.

5. Foster's image of limited good (1965) might also be regarded as an 'etic grid'. It should be pointed out here that however useful and methodologically advantageous, I do not accept the proposition that adequate semantic theory necessarily demands an 'etic' reference base before 'emic' analysis is possible (cf. Henderson, 1967; Scheffler, 1967).

This is not necessarily to endorse the positions of Leach (1958) and Needham (1962) as reflections of 'adequate' general semantic theory; but neither can we necessarily assume genealogical bases (in kin terminological studies) nor ethological (i.e. libidinal, etc.) bases (in other spheres of behaviour) until we have much more data than are at present available. I would think much more attention should be paid to neuro-physiological researches if we are to progress toward general theory and less attention to universal assumptions on behavioural levels – which is squarely where Lounsbury's present theory rests (1965).

Concept formation

The distinction between concept formation and the categorizing of a set of 'attained concepts' (Bruner *et al.*, 1956), may be crudely expressed as the distinction between *inventing* and *identifying*. Undoubtedly similar cognition is involved in both, but it is the difference between the new, undefined, 'unthought-about' and unsorted material dealt with in inventing; and the previously defined, bounded, 'thought-about' and sorted material of identifying which is relevant for ethnography.

The classification of attained concepts has been discussed above. In the *formation* of a concept an inventor can only draw from the symbols and connotata of previously ordered domains, plus details from the ecological, social and psychological history of the spheres in which he is dealing to be able to decide on just what will serve to significate – or enable the native to attain – the new concept.

The inventor may have little latitude and he is in many ways a prisoner-victim of his experience and that of others before him – he could be said to be playing the 'original world game' solitaire (Brown 1958). One critical asset to the inventor is the frequent appeal to highly codable symbols to serve as perceptual cues (Bruner *et al.* 1956) in the formation of new concepts, however abstract they may be. Colby (1963) has called attention to the way certain symbols maintain a 'high symbolic load' or 'high meaning capacity', and by a careful study of such symbols and their acquisition as codable cues and their change in meaning through an individual's life cycle, ethnographers may be able to map and *explain* more objectively quite abstract conceptual domains in which these symbols are significant. Children may acquire the perceptual cues for an abstract concept long before they understand the concept (Jacobson and Halle 1956, Part 2), and it is of interest to the ethnographer to note just what differing connotata the perceptual cues evoke in the growth of a child's semantic associations (see Faris, 1969 for an example of the differential views of children about a specific domain). A child's sequential acquisition of the necessary and sufficient attributes of a concept may mirror in many respects the process of formation through time of a concept by an inventor.

It was only when I became aware that rigorously elicited Cat Harbour descriptions failed to make sense that I attempted to find out how such orders came to be – starting initially as do children with a semantic examination of the perceptual cues 'objectifying' the concept.

The background

Cat Harbour is a small (300 people) fishing community on the north-east coast of Newfoundland. The people are English speakers and the descendants of English West Countrymen. The settlement was established[6] in the eighteenth century on Newfoundland's roughest coast in an isolated and hostile setting to avoid apprehension by the authorities – for settlement was at this time (and until the second quarter of the nineteenth century) prohibited, both in the interests of British maritime supremacy and the economic interests of the West Country merchants who wanted to retain Newfoundland as a summer fishing station for their exclusive exploitation.

But although their inaccessible location discouraged apprehension by authorities, it made life difficult in the extreme for the early settlers, and they had to evolve techniques for coping with harsh and hostile surroundings, severe storms and ice, shallow and rough water, and the rocky and sandy coastline. There were also the raids of the native Indians of Newfoundland, the Beothucks (see Howley, 1915, for specific raids on Cat Harbour), and harassment from French fishermen frequenting their shores, English West Country merchant vessels and American privateers. Moreover, the lack of market access, the difficulty of procuring supplies and the lack of mercantile competition also meant that these illegal 'outports', as they are called, were (and continue to be) repeatedly subject to economic and political exploitation from the outside.

Though space prevents detail here, evidence is abundant that Cat Harbour's social and ecological history is quite important for understanding contemporary behaviour and conceptions (Faris, 1972), particularly in the indigenous cognition of the world outside the settlement (which is expressed as a generalised universe of danger and wickedness) and of its representative in the local community, the stranger (who is always suspect and regarded as potentially malevolent). Symbolism derived from these circumstances pervades a considerable portion of Cat Harbour's social life.

The Cat Harbour year centres very largely about the intense activity of the summer fishing voyage. Because of the Arctic ice flows and the North Atlantic storms, it may be that for only two or three months of the year are fishermen able to 'get on the water'. During this time men work from 5 or 6 a.m. to 12 or 1 a.m., and in the season everything else is secondary – there are few superfluous activities. There are no weddings and statistically, surprisingly few funerals. As one man said, *No one would think of dying, hands are too busy to bury them.* Most of the organised church services cease, and the circuit missionary is usually not seen again until autumn. People even joke about the cessation of sexual activities, expressing the

6. There is today a strong oral tradition on the north-east coast that the original settlers in the area were fugitives from justice and deserters from West Country vessels persecuting the Newfoundland fishery. These deserters settled in isolated and undesirable spots to be left alone (see Faris, 1972).

summer as the time of sleeping *back on* (i.e. back-to-back). But before this extremely busy season begins and as soon as the 'heavy' seas bring it to an end, and during the long, ice-locked winter, there are a number of what were to me 'special' events, some – but only some – of which were called by local people *occasions*.

Puzzled by the fact that some of my intuitive semantic assumptions did not adequately apply to the local domain or make sense of the utterances of informants, I asked a number of simple questions about the body of lexical items which I had determined were included by speakers under the gross label *occasions*.[7] I was then able to approximate some representation of the structure of this domain, but I found I could still not make sense of *occasions* until some time later – when I had learned a great deal more about the community and learned that this seemingly bizarre classification made perfectly good sense in terms of the community's history.

'Occasions' in Cat Harbour

People in Cat Harbour designate a number of collective social events *occasions*. Included in this category are *weddings*, *scoffs*, *funerals*, *birthdays*, *times*, and *mummers*. There are a number of events which are not regarded as *occasions*, and which do not have a category label. I will term these events 'non-*occasions*'. These include *union meetings* (Fishermen's Protective Union, historically – today the less active Federation of Fishermen), church services, christenings, *teas*, *banquets*, *socials*, *concerts*, *suppers*, and the evening shop gatherings of adult males. The common response when I asked about the definition of *occasions* was that *occasions* were simply *special*.

My series of rudimentary questions required people to contrast all the events which they had told me were *occasions*. By this means I hoped I might get some view of their structure of *occasions*. These questions did not ask *for* meanings, but forced informants to appeal to some referential meaning or some significant distinctions to make the decisions. I then arrived at a point where I could construct a type of model to represent the folk classification of *occasions*. One such model of the lexemes included in the lexicon of *occasions* is characterised by vertical inclusion and horizontal exclusion; it is both hierarchical and paradigmatic (Conklin, 1962b).

Scoffs are not *weddings*, yet both *scoffs* and *weddings* are *times*. *Funerals* are not *times*, yet both *times* and *funerals* are *occasions*. *Birthdays* are not *mummers* (or, more properly, events at which *mummers* are present, or *mummers*' *visits*), yet both *birthdays* and *mummers* can mean *scoffs*. This

7. I arrived at the lexicon by asking about what events were 'occasions' and what kinds of 'occasions' could there be. Mapping the internal structure simply involved contrasting each component with every other.

1·1 'non-*occasions*'	1·2 *occasions*			
	1·21 *funerals*	1·22 *times*		
		1·221 *weddings*	1·222a *birthdays*	1·222b *scoffs*	1·222c *mummers*

Figure 1 The lexicon of *occasions* in Cat Harbour

is not a very elegant model, it is simply a graphic representation.[8] But the levels of contrast and inclusion correspond to local distinctions, and it is one representation based on information about the way Cat Harbour folk classify '*occasions*'.

Even though helpful, this still did not tell me much about the semantic feature(s) they all had in common; that is, it did not tell me anything about *occasions* – what distinguished these events from those that were '*non-occasions*' (the lexical blank, cell 1.1., in figure 1). *Occasions* are 'special'. One can see that some of these look like 'fun' – but what about *funerals*? It is possible to consider that *funerals* may in fact be fun for some people, and certainly in Cat Harbour they are important social events – but people do not, however bizarre their behaviour, see 'funerals' as fun. Moreover, church *socials*, *concerts*, and *teas* were often fun – but were not *occasions*.

Of course several attributes strike one immediately which might be used to distinguish the components of the set from each other; the problem, however, was not what was different about *weddings* and *funerals* and *times*, but what was common about them all. I could approximate the internal structure of the indigenous domain, but I could not specify it culturally. I had no way of validating the description; I had no view of the significata of *occasions*. Further questions similar to those used to arrive at the internal order of the domain were unsuccessful, and I began to get answers like, *Everyone knows what a funeral is, sure, don't they have funerals where you come from?* So, in deference to rapport at this point, I put the puzzling model aside until later – for it was only after learning considerably more about the community that I began to see that the discriminating criteria between *occasions* and '*non-occasions*' (see Figure 1) reflected a crucial structural opposition pervading local cognition. This should become clear after a brief examination of some specific contextual data.

Let me take first, and most exhaustively, *scoffs*. *Scoffs* take place after

8. It is also not a precisely exhaustive presentation, for other events apart from *birthdays*, *scoffs* and *mummers*, may rarely be *times* depending on the behaviour and deviation involved. Figure 1 includes only those events *always* considered to be *occasions*.

harvest and into winter when game is available. A *birthday* may be the impetus and excuse for a *scoff*, but this is not necessary, and it may be decided upon spontaneously without the benefit of any other event. *Scoffs* are private affairs involving only a few couples – usually friends or a man's affines – couples of the same *race* (as the local generational levels are expressed) all of whom contribute something to the late supper, the *scoff*. People play cards, dance, and the men (rarely the women) drink. There is a considerable amount of sexual joking and licence, both men and women taking the initiative. The climax of the evening is the *scoff*, which invariably consists of potatoes, turnips, cabbage, salt beef, salt pork and the main fresh game – moose, rabbit, wild duck or goose.

Now the critical thing about the *scoff* is that all the ingredients are stolen – that is, taken from someone not invited. Vegetables are taken from someone's root cellar or from his garden, and the meat may be taken off a carcase hanging in someone's fish *store* (a shed in which fish are salted). But the term *stealing* is not used, for the ingredients taken for a *scoff* are *bucked*, a lexeme characterizing exactly the same action, that is, taking property without the consent of the owner, but being essentially legitimate. Cat Harbour folk say, *Oh no, bucking is not stealing*, and there are corresponding lexical differences for all aspects of a *scoff* versus a *meal* which has been 'stolen'. This can be represented in Table 1.

Table 1 **Lexical environment: scoff/meal**

	taking food termed:	*regarded as:*	*action taken:*
'Scoff'	*bucking*	a *time*	none, or *second plundering*
'Meal'	*stealing*	a *sin*	moral (gossip) or legal pressure

A *scoff*, then, is a *sanctioned deviation*; under other circumstances it would be considered improper behaviour. The legitimizing criteria are several. First, materials are not taken from those in dire need, and must be taken from persons not invited. Second, there must be more than one couple; it must be a social occasion, but not a public one. Third, the normal bounds of propriety are exceeded in several spheres as there is licence and behaviour normally frowned upon – behaviour regarded as uninhibited, exposed and characteristic (in local cognition) of the stranger and the outside world. Fourth, the actors must all be participants in the local moral community; that is, a local violator or a stranger is not accorded the privilege, and should he attempt it, his actions are regarded as illegitimate, as 'stealing'. And last, the participants must 'play the game' in that those not invited may try to take the *scoff* while it is cooking – that is, by *second plundering* – essentially stealing it from the initial thieves. People say, *second plunder is the sweetest*, and *plundering* goods initially *bucked* is regarded as legitimate. A *scoff* is, in summary, a private sanctioned deviation, an occasion of sanctioned licence, a legitimization of behaviour and action normally considered *sin*.

What of *weddings*? First, it should be pointed out that there is a difference between *marriages* and *weddings* in Cat Harbour. *Marriage* refers only to the formal ritual uniting the couple – a standardized, brief (and to the participants relatively unimportant) church service – and I here consider only *weddings*. Briefly, a *wedding* today occurs after the couple are married, but in former years it often took place before the couple were married, as missionaries visited Cat Harbour no more than once or twice a year. *Weddings* today are large public affairs. Attenders bring gifts, are admitted, and are reciprocally fed. There is dancing (favourites are jigs and reels with heavy sexual overtones), and while the women chat, gossip and serve meals, the men drink. Men who otherwise seldom drink are often intoxicated at *weddings*, but at this *occasion*, at this *time*, such behaviour is sanctioned. It is a role reversal, in essence, from the rigidly temperate and reserved façade normally maintained. After having heard from several persons of the evils of sexual licence and excessive drinking, I observed these same people participating with gusto in these activities at a *wedding* – only to be told again by them the following day of the evils of sexual licence and excessive drinking. Children are told that drunks are dangerous, and it is significant that some of the rare fights which have occurred in the outport have taken place at *weddings*. It was expressed to me, *At weddings men are likely to get black if they get too much to drink – a little rum and some fellows get full sail* (i.e. uninhibited). The term *black* here – referring to serious quarrels leading to physical aggression – is part of the same symbolism used to characterise the stranger and the behaviour regarded as typical of the outside world. Let me explain more of this symbolism, for these highly-codable perceptual cues carry a broad semantic load, and the connotata of several abstract concepts are objectified by such symbols.

The crow, or anything black by nature, has sinister associations, and a general black/white symbolism pervades the entire community. The Devil is often the *Blackman*, and *hard* looks – that is, evil faces and frowns – are called *black looks*. Roman Catholics, with whom the earliest settlers fought, are referred to as *pretty dark*, and *mummers*, the disguised individuals who come from house to house during Christmastide, are sometimes called *the Dark Ones*. *Mummers* are in essence symbolic strangers. (See Faris, 1969.) And, other things being equal, men regard a white sled dog or horse as more dependable, trustworthy, stronger and worth more than a black one. When two men get too far into a heated argument, they are said to be *getting black*, and the logic behind this symbolism can be seen most succinctly in a conversation between two men who had not seen each other for some time: *I hadn't seen you for days, you're a proper stranger. Yep, I'm just as black as the Devil.* In fact, if a person wishes to refer to a stranger with whom others may not be familiar (such as myself, someone directly from the outside) as opposed to a stranger having been in the community for many years (such as women marrying in – who remain strangers), he will speak of a *black stranger* or *blackest kind of stranger*.

Moreover, people are extremely frightened of the dark,[9] and adults will not go out alone at night. This fear and these conceptual associations are kept alive by the threats made by parents, for they constantly use these symbols to correct misbehaving children: *Do you want us to let the stranger get you?* and, *If you don't straighten up we'll put you in the dark.* Local people never knock before entering a house, but strangers and *mummers* do; so parents sometimes knock on a wall or a table to distract children, saying quickly, *Here come the mummers*, or *Here's strangers.* Children know well the portent of a knock and learn the perceptual indicators long before they fully understand the concepts which they symbolize.[10] Children are taught to avoid close personal relationships with their peers, that emotional expression is to be avoided, and that any exposure can lead to exploitation. At an early age they begin to learn the values placed on predictable behaviour and perfected response, and experience early the caution, reserve, inhibition and formality characteristic of adult Cat Harbour behaviour. Even the universal physical familiarity prior to marriage is accompanied by a remarkable lack of emotional expression.[11]

Returning to the lexical domain, *weddings*, *scoffs*, *birthdays*, and *mummers*, then, are *times*. I should now like briefly to consider *funerals* – the most puzzling component of the lexicon, and in local perspective, neither *fun* nor *sin*. In fact, the major problem in my assumptions about

9. This was documented over 100 years ago by Jukes (1842):
'... and to my great astonishment, I found that, though an active daring boatman, he was absolutely afraid to venture fifty yards in the dark and that his fear did not seem unnatural to the rest'.

10. Part of the adoption of object cues prior to understanding the abstract concept (and thus increasing the semantic load a symbol evokes) may be related to the degree to which verbal learning (as opposed to observation) is minimised in Cat Harbour (Faris, 1966b).

11. Szwed (1966) documents a similar situation on the south coast of Newfoundland, where children are warned against the dangers of over-emotional expression and over-zealous friendships and interaction.

the domain was just why it was that *funerals*, which contrast so much to the essentially gay events described above, were also called *occasions*. I could see all manner of ways in which they contrasted, but not what critical attributes they shared with *special* events of the lexicon *occasions*.

The short, formal service held in the church is, as is the marriage ceremony, simply a standardised ritual prescribed by the outside institutional structure. But other activities surrounding a death and the categorisations of the participants involved are not so defined, and are a product of local cognition.

There are three categories of persons: *mourners*, *helpers* and the rest. The latter are those who attend the service, come to the home of the deceased to console the survivors, bring plastic flowers (rather as a token of admission) and view the body, but who are neither *mourners* nor *helpers* – in other words, everyone else. *Funerals*, like *weddings*, are community-wide social occasions, even cross-cutting a strong religious cleavage in Cat Harbour, so that everyone falls into one or the other of these categories. *Mourners* are defined exclusively by kinship – that is, the local kin categories dictate those who are to be regarded as *mourners*. It is important to keep this in mind, for everyone in Cat Harbour is related by blood or marriage to everyone else.

Helpers are pall bearers, those who dress the corpse, dig the grave and those (people or things) involved in the logistics of burial. *Mourners* have no contact at all with the deceased (with whom they were in closest contact in normal life), and the *helper* category takes care of all the physical arrangements. They are never *close* kinsmen, at least not of the category of relatives which serves to define *mourners*,[12] though usually of the same *race* (generation) as the deceased and usually his or her closest non-kin friends and associates in life. *Helpers* are, in a real way, necessary *close outsiders*. *Close* kinsmen – those who are *mourning* – are engaged in an activity which places them in a special category characterized by special behaviour and symbolism, and excluded from participation in any other activities in which they might normally engage. They wear small black ribbons on their lapels, are required to keep down the shades in their houses (or at least those facing the house of the deceased)[13] for a specified period,

12. Biology is not very relevant in these discriminations; genealogically-distant relatives may be 'mourners', while certain 'helpers' may be closer (biologically) kinsmen (cf. Faris, 1972).

13. Children, in learning the rules of mourning behaviour, first believe shades are drawn to *keep out the dead*, and that *if you see the box* [coffin] *you'll die sure*. Adults articulate the shade drawing as *respect*. Children also fear visiting persons whose shades are drawn (i.e. *mourners*), but I documented no fear to associate with *helpers* – those having actually handled the corpse. Children are never, prior to adolescence, *mourners* or *helpers*, even if the deceased is a sibling or a close friend.

and sit in a special reserved section of the church, demarcated for the event by black ribbon.

The *helpers*, on the other hand, wear small white ribbons, and in this category are included the minister or lay reader handling the service, the pall bearers, and the horse and sleigh (or pick-up truck in good weather) used to pull the bier. I have seen both horses and trucks with small white ribbons tied to them when used for this purpose. And *helpers* sit in a special section of the church marked off by white ribbons.

'Mourners', then, are in a real sense removed from normal social intercourse (especially with the deceased), and their behaviour, symbolically and actually, is distinguished from that expected in the usual course of events. They are placed in an 'outsider' position, so to speak, from the mundane and prosaic aspects of daily life. Their role is considered potentially a very emotional expression, and any overt emotional exposure is regarded as potentially dangerous and avoided in Cat Harbour. This is symbolized in the small black ribbon and is cognitively similar, I suggest, to the other conceptual spheres labelled *black* in Cat Harbour (or potentially *black*) – those spheres surrounded by an aura of danger, exposure and licence. In marked contrast, the *helpers*, those who *belong to the place* and who are *closest*, yet not *kinsmen* of the deceased, wear white, and are needed in a particular way.

This brings me to the position of suggesting a more culturally appropriate definition of the highest order lexical element in our set, *occasions*. *Special* events, *occasions*, are conceptually *social events of sanctioned deviation*. All of the subordinate lexemes in the set are situations of essentially deviant behaviour, sanctioned by the *occasion*. If this significatum is necessary and sufficient for this lexical category, then we can suggest that the lexical blank (cell 1.1, figure 1) labelled tentatively *non-'occasions'* would be something like *ordinary events*, or social events of no conceptual deviation. Based on this significatum, the semantic discriminations between lexemes within the domain might be that suggested in table 2. This latter, however, is somewhat speculative. But let me summarize what can be learned from this seemingly bizarre classification about Cat Harbour society, past and present, and about concept formation in general.

If one is to adopt (voluntarily or non-voluntarily) a reversed or deviant role (i.e. a *special* role), even briefly and ritually (i.e. in a sanctioned circumstance – an *occasion*), such a role or such behaviour must be defined as deviant or reverse in some way by the experience and tradition of the individual adopting it. This seems to me fundamental – deviations from the limited role alternatives available locally must be within the conceptual scope of the 'outport' individual. The sanctioned deviation, then, which I suggest as the significatum of the domain *occasions*, is culturally-defined; we need to look at the local criteria of deviation. I have tried to show that Cat Harbour folk draw their cognition of cultural deviance from the beliefs and expectations, the symbols and the behaviour they regard as characterising the stranger – the most stereotypically deviant and abnormal category with which they are familiar. Only an examination of the history of the settlement and the way children learn abstract concepts could reveal this, conveniently coded in the colour (or rather, black/white) symbolism. It is significant that *occasions* are largely devoid of children – they participate neither in the saturnalia of the *times* nor in the *mourning* at funerals. But they participate with gusto in the 'non-*occasion*' fun events such as *socials*, *concerts*, and *suppers*.

Table 2 Lexicon of 'occasions': suggested semantic discriminations

		semantic discrimination
dimension	.x	——— /sanctioned deviance
	.ox	non-voluntary/voluntary
	.oox	public/private

Now this is not a very elegant presentation, and it may also not be a convincing presentation (much more detailed data are available in Faris, 1966*a* and 1966*b*; 1968). But I think it clearly shows that simply a rigorous description of the ordering of an indigenous domain may not be wholly adequate for understanding the principles by which it is ordered – for explaining how it is culturally significant.

My analysis appeals to what Leach (1965) has called 'worn-out residues of history', and the simple fears and associations of children, to attempt to show that meaningful descriptions and validation of a taxonomy cannot always be divorced from considerations of its formation. A plea for consideration of concept formation is a plea for diachronic considerations. We are creatures not only of our own experience but also of the experience of others – of tradition. Children do not learn all the discriminating attributes of a concept or domain at once, and an examination of the sequential acquisitions and changes in semantic associations of children may reveal much about the formation of cultural concepts. The Cat Harbour example would suggest that a systematic concern with antecedents of an order and the development of techniques for their elicitation are necessary in ethnographical validation, particularly of less perceptual, more abstract conceptual orders of experience.

References

AKHMANOVA, O. (1966), 'Comments: on ethnographic semantics', B. N. Colby, *Curr. Anthrop.*, vol. 7, pp. 3–32.

BROWN, R. (1958), *Words and Things*, Free Press.

BRUNER, R. (1954), 'A study in language and cognition', *J. Abnorm. soc. Psychol.*, vol. 49, pp. 454–62.

COLBY, B. (1963), 'Comments: on the sociopsychological analysis of folk-tales', *Curr. Anthrop.*, vol. 4, pp. 235–95.

CONKLIN, H. (1955), 'Hanunoo color categories', *S. West. J. Anthrop.*, vol. 11, pp. 339–44.

COULT, A. (1966a), 'On the justification of untested componential analyses', *Amer. Anthrop.*, vol. 68, pp. 1014–5.

COULT, A. (1966b), 'A simplified method for the transformational analysis of kinship terms', *Am. Anthrop.*, vol. 68, pp. 1476–83.

FARIS, J. (1966), 'The dynamics of verbal exchange: a Newfoundland example', *Anthropologica*, vol. 8, pp. 235–48.

FARIS, J. (1969), 'Mummers in an outport fishing settlement: a description and suggestions on a cognitive complex', in H. Harpert and G. Story (eds.), *Christmas Mummers in Newfoundland*, University of Toronto Press.

FARIS, J. (1972), *Cat Harbour: a Newfoundland Fishing Settlement*, St John's Institute of Social and Economic Research.

FOSTER, G. (1965), 'Peasant society and the image of limited good', *Amer. Anthrop.*, no. 67, pp. 293–315.

FRAKE, C. (1961), 'The diagnosis of disease among the Subanun of Mindanao', *Amer. Anthrop.*, no. 63, pp. 11–32.

FRAKE, C. (1964), 'A structural description of Subanun "religious behaviour"', in W. Goodenough (ed.), *Explorations in Cultural Anthropology*, McGraw-Hill.

GOODENOUGH, W. (1956), 'Componential analysis and the study of meaning', *Language*, no. 32, pp. 195–216.

HENDERSON, R. (1967), 'Onitsha Ibo kinship terminology: a formal analysis and its functional applications', *S. West. J. Anthrop.*, no. 23, pp. 15–51.

HOWLEY, J. (1915), *A History of the Beothucks or Red Indians*, Cambridge University Press.

HYMES, D. (1966), 'Comments: on ethnographic semantics', B. N. Colby, *Curr. Anthrop.*, vol. 7, pp. 3, 32.

JAKOBSON, R., and HALLE, M. (1956), *Fundamentals of Language*, Mouton.

JUKES, J. B. (1942), *Excursions In and About Newfoundland in the Years 1839 and 1840*, London.

KAY, P. (1966), 'Comments: on ethnographic semantics', B. N. Colby, *Curr. Anthrop.* no. 7, pp. 3–32.

KEESING, R. (1966), 'Comments: on ethnographic semantics', B. N. Colby, *Curr. Anthrop.*, vol. 7, pp. 3–32.

LEACH, E. (1958), 'Concerning the Trobriand Clans and the kinship category *tabu*', in J. Goody (ed.), *The Development Cycle in Domestic Groups*, Cambridge University Press.

LEACH, E. (1965), Review of C. Levi-Strauss, *Mythologiques le cru et le cuit*, *Amer. Anthrop.*, no. 67, pp. 776–80.

LOUNSBURY, F. (1956), 'A semantic analysis of the Pawnee kinship usage', *Language*, no. 32, pp. 158–94.

LOUNSBURY, F. (1965), 'Another view of the Trobriand kinship categories', in E. Hammel (ed.), *Formal Semantic Analysis*, AMA.

METZGER, D., and WILLIAMS, G. (1963*a*), 'Tenejapa medicine: 1. The curer', *S. West. J. Anthrop.*, no. 19, pp. 216–34.

METZGER, D., and WILLIAMS, G. (1963*b*), 'A formal ethnographic analysis of Tenejapa ladino weddings', *Amer. Anthrop.*, no. 65, pp. 1076–101.

METZGER, D., and WILLIAMS, G. (1966), 'Some procedures and results in the study of native categories: Tzoltal "firewood"', *Amer. Anthrop.*, no. 68, pp. 389–407.

MURDOCK, G. (1949), *Social Structure*, Macmillan.

NEEDHAM, R. (1962), *Structure and Sentiment*, Chicago University Press.

ROMNEY, A. K., and D'ANDRADE, R. G. (eds.) (1964), 'Cognitive aspects of English kin terms', in *Transcultural Studies in Cognition*, AMA.

SCHEFFLER, H. (1967), 'On scaling kinship terminologies', *S. West. J. Anthrop.*, no. 23, pp. 159–75.

SCHNEIDER, D. (1964), 'The nature of kinship', *Man*, no. 64, pp. 180–81.

SCHNEIDER, D. (1965), 'American kin terms and terms for kinsmen: a critique of Goodenough's componential analysis of Yankee kinship terminology', in E. Hammel (ed.), *Formal Semantic Analysis*, AMA.

SZWED, J. (1966), 'Gossip, drinking and social control: consensus and communication in a Newfoundland parish', *Ethnology*, no. 5, pp. 434–41.

WALLACE, A. (1965), 'The problem of psychological validity of componential analysis', in E. Hammel (ed.), *Formal Semantic Analysis*, AMA.

WALLACE, A., and ATKINS, J. (1960), 'The meaning of kinship terms', *Amer. Anthrop.*, no. 62, pp. 58–80.

9 E. Husserl

The Essence of Redness

Excerpts from E. Husserl, *The Paris Lecture* (given in 1929), Martinus Nijhoff, The Hague, 1970, pp. 8–10 and 14–15; and E. Husserl, *The Idea of Phenomenology* (Lectures given in 1907), Martinus Nijhoff, The Hague, 1964, pp. 44–6. First published 1950.

This ubiquitous detachment from any point of view regarding the objective world we term the *phenomenological epoché*. It is the methodology through which I come to understand myself as that ego and life of consciousness in which and through which the entire objective world exists for me, and is for me precisely as it is. Everything in the world, all spatio-temporal being, exists for me because I experience it, because I perceive it, remember it, think of it in any way, judge it, value it, desire it, etc. It is well known that Descartes designates all this by the term *cogito*. For me the world is nothing other than what I am aware of and what appears valid in such *cogitationes*. *The whole meaning and reality of the world rests exclusively on such cogitationes.* My entire worldly life takes its course within these. I cannot live, experience, think, value, and act in any world which is not in some sense in me, and derives its meaning and truth from me. If I place myself above that entire life and if I abstain from any commitment about reality, specifically one which accepts the world as existing, and if I view that life exclusively as consciousness *of* the world, then I reveal myself as the pure ego with its pure stream of *cogitationes*.

I certainly do not discover myself as one item among others in the world, since I have altogether suspended judgement about the world. I am not the ego of an individual man. I am the ego in whose stream of consciousness the world itself – including myself as an object in it, a man who exists in the world – first acquires meaning and reality.

We have reached a dangerous point. It seems simple indeed to understand the pure ego with its *cogitationes* by following Descartes. And yet it is as if we were on the brink of a precipice, where the ability to step calmly and surely decides between philosophic life and philosophic death. Descartes was thoroughly sincere in his desire to be radical and presuppositionless. However, we know through recent researches – particularly the fine and penetrating work of Messrs Gilson and Koyré – that a great deal of Scholasticism is hidden in Descartes' meditations as unarticulated prejudice. But this is not all. We must above all avoid the prejudices, hardly noticed by us, which derive from our emphasis on the mathematically oriented natural sciences. These prejudices make it appear as if the phrase *ego cogito* refers to an apodictic and primitive axiom, one which, in conjunction with others to be derived from it, provides the foundation for a deductive and universal science, a science *ordine geometrico*. In relation to this we must under no circumstances take for granted that, with our apodictic and pure ego, we have salvaged a small corner of the world as the single indubitable fact about the world which can be utilized by the philosophizing ego. It is not true that all that now remains to be done is to infer the rest of the world through correct deductive procedures according to principles that are innate to the ego.

Unfortunately, Descartes commits this error, in the apparently insignificant yet fateful transformation of the ego to a *substantia cogitans*, to an independent human *animus*, which then becomes the point of departure for conclusions by means of the principle of causality. In short, this is the transformation which made Descartes the father of the rather absurd transcendental realism. We will keep aloof from all this if we remain true to radicalism in our self-examination and with it to the principle of pure intuition. We must regard nothing as veridical except the pure immediacy and givenness in the field of the *ego cogito* which the *epoché* has opened up to us. In other words, we must not make assertions about that which we do not ourselves *see*. In these matters Descartes was deficient. It so happens that he stands before the greatest of all discoveries – in a sense he has already made it – yet fails to see its true significance, that of transcendental subjectivity. He does not pass through the gateway that leads into genuine transcendental philosophy.

The independent *epoché* with regard to the nature of the world as it appears and is real to me – that is, 'real' to the previous and natural point of view – discloses the greatest and most magnificent of all facts: I and my life remain – in my sense of reality – untouched by whichever way we decide the issue of whether the world is or is not. To say, in my natural existence, 'I am, I think, I live', means that I am one human being among others in the world, that I am related to nature through my physical body, and that in this body my *cogitationes*, perceptions, memories, judgements, etc. are incorporated as psycho-physical facts. Conceived in this way, I, we, humans, and animals are subject-matter for the objective sciences, that is, for biology, anthropology, and zoology, and also for psychology. The life of the psyche, which is the subject-matter of all psychology, is understood only as the psychic life in the world. The methodology of a purified Cartesianism demands of me, the one who philosophizes, the phenomenological *epoché*. This *epoché* eliminates as worldly facts from my field of judgement both the reality of the objective world in general and the sciences of the world. *Consequently, for me there exists no 'I' and there are no psychic actions, that is, psychic phenomena in the psychological sense.* To myself I do not exist as a human being, [nor] do my *cogitationes* exist as components of a psycho-physical world. But through all this I have discovered my true self. I have discovered that I alone am the pure ego, with pure existence and pure capacities (for example, the obvious capacity to abstain from judging). Through this ego alone does *the being of the world.* and, for that matter, any being whatsoever, make sense *to me* and has possible validity. [. . .]

In relation to the preceding we must thus call attention to the fact that the transcendental *epoché* performed with respect to the existing world, containing all those objects which we actually experience, perceive, remember, think, judge, and believe, does not change the fact that the world – i.e. the objects as pure phenomena of experience, as pure *cogitata* of the momentary *cogitationes* – must become a central concern of phenomenological description. In that case, what is the nature of the abysmal difference between phenomenological judgements about the world of experience and natural-objective judgements? The answer can be given in these terms: as a phenomenological ego I have become a pure observer of myself. I treat as veridical only that which I encounter as inseparable from me, as pertaining purely to my life and being inseparable from it, exactly in the manner that genuine and intuitive reflection discloses my own self to me. Before the *epoché*, I was a man with the natural attitude and I lived immersed naively in the world. I accepted the experience as such, and on the basis of it developed my subsequent positions. All this, however, took place in me without my being aware of it. I was indeed interested in my experiences, that is, in objects, values, goals, but I did not focus on the experiencing of my life, on the act of being interested, on the act of taking a position, on my subjectivity. I was a transcendental ego even while in the living natural attitude, but I knew nothing about it. In order to become aware of my true being I needed to execute the phenomenological *epoché*. Through it I do not achieve – as Descartes attempted – a critique of validity, or, in other words, the resolution of the problem of the apodictic trustworthiness of my experience and consequently of the reality of the world. Quite to the contrary, I will learn that the world and how the world is for me the *cogitatum* of my *cogitationes*. I will not only discover that the *ego cogito* precedes apodictically the fact that the world exists for me, but also familiarize myself thoroughly with the concrete being of my ego and thereby *see* it. The being that I am when, immersed, I live and experience the world from the natural attitude consists of a particular transcendental life, namely, one in which I naively trust my experiences, one in which I continue to occupy myself with a naively acquired world view, etc. Therefore, the phenomenological attitude, with its *epoché*, consists in that *I reach the ultimate experiential and cognitive perspective thinkable. In it I become the disinterested spectator of my natural and worldly ego and its life.* In this manner, my natural life becomes merely one part or one particular level of what now has been disclosed as my transcendental life. I am detached inasmuch as I 'suspend' all worldly interests (which I nonetheless possess); and to the degree that I – the philosophizing one – place myself above them and observe them, and take these as themes for description, as being my transcendental ego. . . .

The particular cognitive phenomenon, coming and going in the stream of consciousness, is not the sort of thing about which phenomenology establishes its conclusions. Phenomenology is directed to the 'sources of cognition', to general origins which can be 'seen', to general absolute data which present the universal basic criteria in terms of which all meaning, and also the correctness, of confused thinking is to be evaluated, and by which all the riddles which have to do with the objectivity of cognition are to be solved.

Still, are real *universality*, universal essences, and the universal states of affairs attaching to them capable of self-givenness in the same sense as a *cogitatio*? *Does not the universal as such transcend knowledge?* Knowledge of universals is certainly given as an absolute phenomenon; but in this we shall seek in vain for the universal which is to be identical, in the strictest sense, in the equally immanent contents of innumerable possible cases of cognition.

Of course, we answer, as we have already answered: to be sure, the universal has this kind of transcendence. Every genuine (*reell*) constituent of the cognitive phenomenon, this phenomenological particular, is also a particular; and so the universal, which certainly is no particular, cannot be really contained in the consciousness of the universal. But the objection to *this* kind of transcendence is nothing more than a prejudice, which stems from an inappropriate interpretation of cognition, one which is not based on the source of cognition. Thus one has to get especially clear about the fact that we accord the status of absolute self-givenness to the absolute phenomenon, the *cogitatio* which has undergone reduction, not because it is a particular, but because it displays itself in pure 'seeing' after phenomenological reduction, *precisely as absolute self-givenness*. But in pure 'seeing' we find that universality no less displays *just* such an absolute givenness.

Is this actually the case? Let us now consider some cases in which a universal is given, i.e., cases where a purely immanent consciousness of the universal is built up on the basis of some 'seen' and self-given particular. I have a particular intuition of redness, or rather several such intuitions. I stick strictly to the pure immanence; I am careful to perform the phenomenological reduction. I snip off any further significance of redness, any way in which it may be viewed as something transcendent, e.g., as the redness of a piece of blotting paper on my table, etc. And now I fully grasp in pure 'seeing' the *meaning* of the concept of redness in general, redness *in specie*, the *universal* 'seen' as *identical* in this and that. No longer is it the particular as such which is referred to, not this or that red thing, but redness in general. If we really did this in pure 'seeing', could we then still intelligibly doubt what redness is in general, what is meant by this expression, what it may be in its very essence? We truly 'see' it; there it is, the very object of our intent, this species of redness. Could a deity, an infinite intellect, do more to lay hold of the essence of redness than to 'see' it as a universal?

And if now perhaps two species of redness are given to us, two shades of red, can we not judge that this and that are similar to each other, not this particular, individual phenomenon of redness, but the type, the shade as such? Is not the relation of similarity here a general absolute datum?

Again, this givenness is also something purely immanent, not immanent in the spurious sense, i.e. existing in the sphere of an individual consciousness. We are not speaking at all of the act of abstraction in the psychological subject, and of the psychological conditions under which this takes place. We are speaking of the general essence of meaning of redness and its givenness in general 'seeing'.

Thus it is now senseless still to raise questions and doubts as to what the essence of redness is, or what the meaning of redness is, provided that while one 'sees' redness and grasps it in its specific character, one means by the word 'red' just exactly that which is being grasped and 'seen' there. And in the same way it is senseless, with respect to the essence of cognition and the fundamental structure of cognition, to wonder what its meaning is, provided one is immediately given the paradigmatic phenomena and the type in question in a purely 'seeing' and eidetic (*ideierender*) reflection within the sphere of phenomenological reduction. However, cognition is certainly not so simple a thing as redness; a great many forms and types of it are to be distinguished. And not only that; their essential relations to one another need to be investigated. For to understand cognition we must generally clarify the *teleological interconnections* within cognition, which amount to certain essential relations of different essential types of intellectual forms.

10 G. Lienhardt

Configurations of Colour Structure the Diverse Field of Experience

Excerpt from G. Lienhardt, *Divinity and Experience: the Religion of the Dinka*, Oxford University Press, 1961, pp. 10–15.

Animal sacrifice is the central religious act of the Dinka, whose cattle are in their eyes perfect victims; and therefore the chapters which follow must take for granted a full understanding of the nature of the Dinkas' interest in their herds. The economic importance of cattle to a predominantly pastoral people is readily appreciated, and has here, therefore, been touched upon only briefly; but it is their wider social importance which particularly fits cattle for the part of victim in the blood sacrifices later described.

There is a vast Dinka vocabulary referring to cattle, and particularly to the varieties of their colouring and shading in their almost innumerable blends and configurations. The interest and, one might almost say, obsession which produces and develops this vocabulary is not primarily practical in nature; for the colour-configuration of a beast is not related to its usefulness as a source of food or other material necessities and, moreover, the rich metaphorical cattle-vocabulary of the Dinka relates primarily to oxen, which are of least utilitarian importance.

Information about this vocabulary has been published by Professor and Mrs Seligman (1932), writing about the Bor Dinka, and by Professor Evans-Pritchard, who collected a list of terms from a Ngok Dinka and published them with their Nuer equivalents (1934). Father P. A. Nebel has also published a list of some of the cattle-colour names of the Western Dinka (1948). The first two of these authorities give examples of complex metaphorical associations between configurations of colour in cattle and features of the natural and social environment which these colours call to mind. These metaphors show to what extent and in what detail Dinka thought is orientated towards their herds, and how each configuration of colour can form the centre of a whole field of diverse experience, linking one apperception with another.[1]

1. Professor Evans-Pritchard first indicated something of the wider sociological interest of these colour-names and metaphors in writing: '. . . little is known at present about Nilotic cattle-names, which are of great interest sociologically, illustrating language as a technique of economic relations, and showing the ways in which symbols referring to colours and their distribution are formed' (Evans-Pritchard, 1934, p. 628).

Cattle are described by many composite terms, each indicating by a prefix or suffix the sex and stage of maturity of a beast, combined with a term for its particular kind of colour-configuration. Bulls and oxen have the prefix *ma*, and if it is necessary to distinguish between the whole and the castrated beast the former takes as a suffix the term *thon*, meaning 'whole male', and the latter the term *bwoc*, castrated. A short-horn bull is further distinguished by the term *acoot*. Heifers have the prefix *nya*, 'young female', and cows the prefix *a*. Bull-calves may have the prefix *manh*, from *meth*, child, added to their other names.

There is a general parallelism between the prefix for 'bull' and 'ox', and for men's personal names, and between that for 'cow', and women's personal names, so that on the whole personal names with the prefix *ma*, for 'bull', are likely to be the names of men, and those with the prefix *a*, for 'cow', are likely to be the names of women. Though some personal names have no connection with cattle-names, many of the personal names, and all the cattle-names, which occur later in texts and descriptions may be understood to be formed in this way.

The following is an example of the terms for beasts of the configuration *ma kuei*, which are black with white on the head. The basic term for this configuration is *kuei*, the word for the fish-eagle, a striking bird of similar black and white marking. A bull of this configuration is *ma kuei(n) thon*; an ox, *ma kuei(n) bwoc* or merely *ma kuei*; a bull-calf, *manh ma kuei*; and a cow-calf or heifer, *nya(n) kuei*. A cow is *a kuei*. A short-horn bull would be *ma kuei(n) acoot*, and there are other terms which might be added to indicate different shapes of horns and stages of growth.

In most cases the term which denotes the colour-configuration has also another meaning, as the name of something of similar configuration in nature or Dinka culture, and the Dinka explicitly connect the basic colour-terms for their beasts with the source from which they derive. So, in the example above, the connection between the *kuei* colouring in cattle and the *kuei*, the fish-eagle, is consciously made.

Almost the whole extensive colour vocabulary of the Dinka is one of cattle-colours. A particular pattern or colour in newly imported cloth or beads is thus necessarily referred to by the name of the configuration of colour in cattle which it is thought most to resemble. A black and white spotted cloth, for example, would be *alath (-nh) ma kuac*, *ma kuac* being the term for a spotted bull or ox, which is itself connected explicitly with the spots of the leopard, *kuac*. A striped cloth would be *alath (-nh) ma nyang*, *ma nyang* being the term for a brindled bull, which is connected with the brindling of the crocodile, *nyang*. I think that the only Western Dinka words for colours, other than terms connected also with colour-configurations in cattle, are *toc*, green, which also means rawness and freshness in vegetables, and *thith*, red, which means also the redness of raw meat. These colours are not in any case found in cattle.[2] *Agher*, white, which refers to bright white light, may be connected with the term *yor* or *yar* in the names for white cattle, and *col*, black and also 'soot', though absent from the term for a black bull, *ma car*, is included in the names for black cows and heifers, *a col* and *nyan col*.

The basic vocabulary of names for configurations of colour in cattle is fixed and traditional, consisting of words for colours and combinations of light and shade which a Dinka learns to use from childhood, perhaps without initially having seen what it is, in wild nature, to which they refer. Thus any spotted pattern in which the spots generally resemble in size and distribution those of the leopard will be called *ma kuac*, and in this and many other cases the child may well have seen the *ma kuac* configuration in cattle before he has seen the leopard, *kuac*, to the configuration of which the name refers. A Dinka may thus recognize the configuration in nature by reference to what he first knows of it in the cattle on which his attention, from childhood, is concentrated.

The Dinkas' very perception of colour, light, and shade in the world around them is in these ways inextricably connected with their recognition of colour-configurations in their cattle. If their cattle-colour vocabulary were taken away, they would have scarcely any way of describing visual experience in terms of colour, light, and darkness. Other Nilotic peoples, who have lost many of their cattle and much of their material dependence upon them, have yet retained a colour vocabulary based upon cattle-colours, and develop poetic images on the basis of these cattle-colour names, as I now describe for the Dinka.[3]

When boys reach manhood they take the colour-names of oxen in addition to the personal names they have been previously known by, and are called by intimate friends and age-mates by the ox-names they have then taken at initiation. A young man then becomes in a manner identified with an ox of some particular colour, which he proudly displays before the girls. He will praise his ox in songs, delighting in inventing new ways of referring to its appearance, and in introducing into song imagery fitting to an ox of that colour. The ability to create new imagery based upon the traditional colour-names of cattle is considered a mark of intelligence in a man; and though some men are acknowledged to be more gifted than others in this respect, every Dinka can attempt a measure of poetic ingenuity and originality.

2. Though *thith* may be added to the term for a brown beast to indicate a strong reddish tone – *malual thith*, 'a very red-brown ox'.

3. The Anuak, for example, now have few cattle, but still use metaphorical praise-names based upon cattle-colour names.

The type of imagery developed may be illustrated by the following names for a man with a black display-ox. In song, or when addressed by his age-mates, he will not be content with the basic name for a black ox (*ma car*), but will be known by one or more other names, all explained ultimately as deriving from the blackness of his ox seen in relation to darkness in other things. He may therefore be known as *tim atiep*, 'the shade of a tree'; or *kor acom*, 'seeks for snails', after the black ibis which seeks for snails; or *bun anyeer*, 'thicket of the buffalo', which suggests the darkness of the forest in which the dark buffalo rests; or *akiu yak thok*, 'cries out in the spring drought', after a small black bird (*adhjiec*), which gives its characteristic cry at this time of the year; or *arec luk*, 'spoils the meeting', after the dark clouds which accompany a downpour of rain and send the Dinka who are having a meeting (*luk*) running for shelter. The following list indicates but a few of these metaphorical cattle-names, from which the extent and direction of imaginative interest may be judged:

For a white ox (*mabior*): 'bull of the women' (*muor diar*), because the women are anxious to get white European salt; *matoordit*, after the bright scales of the *atoor* fish; 'the moon brightens the cattle camp' (*dhol pei wut*); 'the cows await the moon' (*atit ghok pei*), the white bull in the camp thus being likened to the moon, and indeed a white beast is discerned clearly in a cattle-camp on a darkish night; 'elephant tusk' (*tung akoon*).

For a red-brown ox (*malual*): 'the game rest at midday' (*col lai piny*), after the antelope of this colour; 'it shakes the clump of bushes' (around an ant-hill) (*ayek but*), after the behaviour of a lion which is here seen to be of this colour, though it figures also in the metaphorical names developed around the basic term for tawny yellow beasts; 'it loves the pool' (*anhiar kol*), after the hippopotamus which is of this colour; 'it lies in the pool' (*atoc kol*), also after the hippopotamus; 'what makes women's elbows creak' (*ke dhiau tik kok*), when they grind, that is, to make beer which is reddish.

For a grey ox (*malou*) (*lou* is the bustard): 'big game' (*landit*), after the elephant which is of this colour; 'breaks up trees' (*abeng tim*), after the elephant; 'respecter of the cattle-byre' (*athek luak*), after the elephant which does not pursue people into a cattle-byre; 'game killed by the foreigners' (*lan a jur nok*), again after the elephant, as is 'spoor of the grey one' (*duopelou*).

For a black and white ox of the *majok* configuration: 'marking of the creator' (*bung aciek*), based upon an association between Divinity, and white and black, later described; *wel jok*, 'exchange *jok*', after a custom of the Dinka by which an elder brother has first claim on bulls of this configuration in exchange for some other; '*jok* ivory armlet' (*jok apyok*), emphasizing the whiteness of the white parts in contrast to the black; 'sacred ibis' (*arumjok*), after the black and white markings of this bird; 'spoiler of the marriage' (*are cruai*), because this is one of the most valued configurations and people want it among marriage cattle, but the owners do not wish to part with it; 'flour' (*abik*), the reference being to the whiteness of flour spread out to dry against the dark earth.

For a black and white ox of the *maker* configuration: 'soldier ant' (*ajing* or *majing*), after the columns of these black ants carrying white particles, grain, ants' eggs, or termites; 'of the thicket', in reference to the leopard; 'totem of the Nuer' (*yanh Nuer*), after the monitor lizard (*agany*), in which the light and shade are seen in this pattern, and which most Nuer will not eat; 'star-ox' (*makuel*), after the brightness of the stars in a dark sky; '*ker*-fish-eagle' (*kerkuei*), referring to a bull of this configuration with a white head, like the fish-eagle and like the *makuei* configuration, which is much admired; 'brought by drizzle' (*a bei nyir*), referring to the spots of a light shower on a man's body.

For a brindled ox of the *manyang* (crocodile) configuration: 'mongoose' (*agor*), after the stripes of this creature; 'spoiler of the fish-battue' (*arec mai*), referring to the crocodile which frightens the Dinka from the river; 'striker of the canoe' (*ayup riai*), again after the crocodile, as is 'wild-dog crocodile' (*magol-nyang*), referring to the brindling of the dog and also perhaps to the story of the dog which slit open the crocodile's mouth.

For a grey ox of the *malith* (*lith* – the chanting goshawk) colour: 'it finishes the cultivations' (*athol dom*), referring to the baboon which raids the gardens and is said to be of this colour; 'wants chickens' (*kor ajith*), after the habits of the chanting goshawk; 'master of the birds' (*beny diet*), again after the goshawk; 'tree of the birds' (*matiem diet*), referring to the way in which the chanting goshawk is attacked in a tree by tiny birds on which it has been preying.

Such names are almost inexhaustible, and are clearly not all necessary for practical convenience in referring to and distinguishing different beasts. They show the interdependence of the Dinkas' perception of colour and shading in nature and in cattle, and represent a deliberate effort to link cattle with features of the natural and social environment through perceived similarities of colour and shading. In such metaphors a wide range of Dinka experience is referred to the central theme of cattle; and such metaphorical associations are also the basis of a colour symbology important for an understanding of Dinka religious thought and practice.

Sometimes practical and aesthetic values may be in conflict. Some cattle-colours are preferred to others, and particularly desirable are those bold pied markings, called in Dinka *majok* and *marial*. It is said that when a bull-calf of one of these colours is born, the friends of its owner may tear off his beads and scatter them, for his happiness is such that he must show indifference to these more trivial forms of display. He is made sufficiently handsome by the beauty of his beast.

References

EVANS-PRITCHARD, E. E. (1934), *Imagery in Ngok Dinka Cattle Names*, Bulletin of the School of Oriental Studies, London Institution, vol. 7, part 3.
NEBEL, P. A. (1948), *Dinka Dictionary*, Verona.
SELIGMAN, C. G., and SELIGMAN, B. (1932), *Pagan Tribes of the Nilotic Sudan*, Clarendon Press.

Part Three
Orientations in Time and Space

Phenomenology seeks the lived experience in order to transcend it. To transcend the experience of time we would need a tenseless language such as Quine's standard grammar. Any object would be seen to be extended in four dimensions, up and down, north and south, east and west and also extended between the hence and the ago. In these terms Evans-Pritchard's perception of the Nuer lineage structure shows it as tenseless; tapered towards the ago, yes, open and eternally about to expand towards the hence; in reality poised and static, all changes being concealed and lost in the middle. It would be misleading to philosophers to suggest that anthropologists have made a comparable series of time studies over the last thirty years and that a mass of comparative material lies to hand. With Edmund Leach's discussion of the time dimension in *The Political Systems of Highland Burma* and John Barnes's discussion of the structuring of time among the Ngoni we have the best of the list and the main work is still to be done. The selections in this part show how time and space are constructed as dimensions of social relations.

11 E. Husserl

Lived Experiences of Time

Excerpt from E. Husserl, *The Phenomenology of Internal Time Consciousness* (lectures given from 1904 to 1910), Martinus Nijhoff, The Hague, 1964, pp. 27–9. First published in 1928.

In conformity with these reflections, we also understand the difference between the phenomenological question (i.e. from the standpoint of theory of knowledge) and the psychological with regard to the origin of all concepts constitutive of experience, and so also with regard to the question of the origin of time. *From the point of view of theory of knowledge, the question of the possibility of experience* (which, at the same time, is *the question of the essence of experience*) necessitates a return to the phenomenological data of which all that is experienced consists phenomenologically. Since what is experienced is split owing to the antithesis of 'authentic' and 'unauthentic' (*'eigentlich' und 'uneigentlich'*), and since authentic experience, i.e. the intuitive and ultimately adequate, provides the standard for the evaluation of experience, the phenomenology of 'authentic' experience is especially required.

Accordingly, the question of the essence of time leads back to the question of the 'origin' of time. The *question of the origin* is oriented toward the *primitive* forms of the consciousness of time in which the primitive differences of the temporal are constituted intuitively and authentically as the originary (*originären*) sources of all certainties relative to time. The question of the origin of time should not be confused with the *question of its psychological origin* – the controversial question between *empiricism and nativism*. With this last question we are asking about the *primordial material of sensation out of which arises objective intuition of space and time* in the human individual and even in the species. We are indifferent to the question of the empirical genesis. What interest us are lived experiences as regards their objective sense and their descriptive content. Psychological apperception, which views lived experiences as psychical states of empirical persons, i.e. *psycho-physical subjects*, and uncovers relationships, be they purely psychical or psycho-physical, between them, and follows their development, formation, and transformation according to *natural laws* – this psychological apperception is something wholly other than the *phenomenological*. We do not classify lived experiences according to any particular form of reality. We are concerned with reality only in so far as it is intended, represented, intuited, or conceptually thought. With reference to the problem of time, this implies that we are interested in *lived experiences* of time. That these lived experiences themselves are temporally determined in an objective sense, *that they belong in the world of things and psychical subjects* and have their place therein, their *efficacy*, their empirical origin and their being – that does not concern us, of that we know nothing. On the other hand, it does interest us that 'objective-temporal' data are *intended* in these lived experiences. Acts which belong to the domain of phenomenology can be described as follows: the acts in question intend this or that 'objective' moment; more precisely, these acts are concerned with the exhibition of *a priori* truths which belong to the moments constitutive of objectivity. We try to clarify the *a priori* of *time* by investigating *time-consciousness*, by bringing its essential constitution to light and, possibly, by setting forth the content of apprehension and act-characters pertaining specifically to time, to which content and characters the *a priori* characters of time are essentially due. Naturally, I am referring here to self-evident laws such as the following:

1. That the fixed temporal order is that of an infinite, two-dimensional series;
2. That two different times can never be conjoint;
3. That their relation is a non-simultaneous one;
4. That there is transitivity, that to every time belongs an earlier and a later, and so on.

So much for the general introduction.

12 E. E. Evans-Pritchard

Time is not a Continuum

Excerpt from E. E. Evans-Pritchard, *The Nuer*, Clarendon Press, 1940, pp. 100–108.

In my experience Nuer do not to any great extent use the names of the months to indicate the time of an event, but generally refer instead to some outstanding activity in process at the time of its occurrence, e.g. at the time of early camps, at the time of weeding, at the time of harvesting, etc., and it is easily understandable that they do so, since time is to them a relation between activities. During the rains the stages in the growth of millet and the steps taken in its culture are often used as points of reference. Pastoral activities, being largely undifferentiated throughout the months and seasons, do not provide suitable points.

There are no units of time between the month and day and night. People indicate the occurrence of an event more than a day or two ago by reference to some other event which took place at the same time or by counting the number of intervening 'sleeps' or, less commonly, 'suns'. There are terms for today, tomorrow, yesterday, etc., but there is no precision about them. When Nuer wish to define the occurrence of an event several days in advance, such as a dance or wedding, they do so by reference to the phases of the moon: new moon, its waxing, full moon, its waning, and the brightness of its second quarter. When they wish to be precise they state on which night of the waxing or waning an event will take place, reckoning fifteen nights to each and thirty to the month. They say that only cattle and the Anuak can see the moon in its invisible period. The only terms applied to the nightly succession of lunar phases are those that describe its appearance just before, and in, fullness.

The course of the sun determines many points of reference, and a common way of indicating the time of events is by pointing to that part of the heavens the sun will then have reached in its course. There are also a number of expressions, varying in the degree of their precision, which describe positions of the sun in the heavens, though, in my experience, the only ones commonly employed are those that refer to its more conspicuously differentiated movements: the first stroke of dawn, sunrise, noon, and sunset. It is, perhaps, significant that there are almost as many points of reference between 4 and 6 a.m. as there are for the rest of the day. This may be chiefly due to striking contrasts caused by changes in relations of earth to sun during these two hours, but it may be noted, also, that the points of reference between them are more used in directing activities, such as starting on journeys, rising from sleep, tethering cattle in kraals, gazelle hunting, etc., than points of reference during most of the rest of the day, especially in the slack time between 1 and 3 p.m. There are also a number of terms to describe the time of night. They are to a very limited extent determined by the course of the stars. Here again, there is a richer terminology for the transition period between day and night than during the rest of the night and the same reasons may be suggested to explain this fact. There are also expressions for distinguishing night from day, forenoon from afternoon, and that part of the day which is spent from that part which lies ahead.

Except for the commonest of the terms for divisions of the day they are little used in comparison with expressions which describe routine diurnal activities. The daily timepiece is the cattle clock, the round of pastoral tasks, and the time of day and the passage of time through a day are to a Nuer primarily the succession of these tasks and their relations to one another. The better demarcated points are taking of the cattle from byre to kraal, milking, driving of the adult herd to pasture, milking of the goats and sheep, driving of the flocks and calves to pasture, cleaning of byre and kraal, bringing home of the flocks and calves, the return of the adult herd, the evening milking, and the enclosure of the beasts in byres. Nuer generally use such points of activity, rather than concrete points in the movement of the sun across the heavens, to coordinate events. Thus a man says, 'I shall return at milking', 'I shall start off when the calves come home', and so forth.

Ecological time-reckoning is ultimately, of course, entirely determined by the movement of the heavenly bodies, but only some of its units and notations are directly based on these movements, e.g. month, day, night, and some parts of the day and night, and such points of reference are paid attention to and selected as points only because they are significant for social activities. It is the activities themselves, chiefly of an economic kind, which are basic to the system and furnish most of its units and notations, and the passage of time is perceived in the relation of activities to one another. Since activities are dependent on the movement of the heavenly bodies and since the movement of the heavenly bodies is significant only in relation to the activities one may often refer to either in indication of the time of an event. Thus one may say, 'In the *jiom* season' or 'At early camps', 'The month of *Dwat*' or 'The return to villages', 'When the sun is warming up' or 'At milking'. The movements of the heavenly bodies permit Nuer to select natural points that are significant in relation to activities. Hence in linguistic usage nights, or rather 'sleeps', are more clearly defined units of time than days, or 'suns', because they are undifferentiated units of social activity, and months, or rather 'moons', though they are clearly differentiated units of natural time, are little employed as points of reference because they are not clearly differentiated units of activity, whereas the day, the year, and its main seasons are complete occupational units.

Certain conclusions may be drawn from this quality of time among the Nuer. Time has not the same value throughout the year. Thus in dry season camps, although daily pastoral tasks follow one another in the same order as in the rains, they do not take place at the same time, are more a precise routine owing to the severity of seasonal conditions, especially with regard to water and pasturage, and require greater coordination and cooperative action. On the other hand, life in the dry season is generally uneventful, outside routine tasks, and ecological and social relations are more monotonous from month to month than in the rains when there are frequent feasts, dances and ceremonies. When time is considered as relations between activities it will be understood that it has a different connotation in rains and drought. In the drought the daily time-reckoning is more uniform and precise while lunar reckoning receives less attention, as appears from the lesser use of names of months, less confidence in stating their order, and the common East African trait of two dry-season months with the same name (*tiop in dit* and *tiop in tot*), the order of which is often interchanged. The pace of time may vary accordingly, since perception of time is a function of systems of time-reckoning, but we can make no definite statement on this question.

Though I have spoken of time and units of time the Nuer have no expression equivalent to 'time' in our language, and they cannot, therefore, as we can, speak of time as though it were something actual, which passes, can be wasted, can be saved, and so forth. I do not think that they ever experience the same feeling of fighting against time or of having to coordinate activities with an abstract passage of time, because their points of reference are mainly the activities themselves, which are generally of a leisurely character. Events follow a logical order, but they are not controlled by an abstract system, there being no autonomous points of reference to which activities have to conform with precision. Nuer are fortunate.

Also they have very limited means of reckoning the relative duration of periods of time intervening between events, since they have few, and not well-defined or systematized, units of time. Having no hours or other small units of time they cannot measure the periods which intervene between positions of the sun or daily activities. It is true that the year is divided into twelve lunar units, but Nuer do not reckon in them as fractions of a unit. They may be able to state in what month an event occurred, but it is with great difficulty that they reckon the relation between events in abstract numerical symbols. They think much more easily in terms of activities and of successions of activities and in terms of social structure and of structural differences than in pure units of time.

We may conclude that the Nuer system of time-reckoning within the annual cycle and parts of the cycle is a series of conceptualizations of natural changes, and that the selection of points of reference is determined by the significance which these natural changes have for human activities. In a sense all time is structural since it is a conceptualization of collateral, coordinated, or cooperative activities: the movements of a group. Otherwise time concepts of this kind could not exist, for they must have a like meaning for every one within a group. Milking-time and meal-times are approximately the same for all people who normally come into contact with one another, and the movement from villages to camps has approximately the same connotation everywhere in Nuerland, though it may have a special connotation for a particular group of persons. There is, however, a point at which we can say that time concepts cease to be determined by ecological factors and become more determined by structural interrelations, being no longer a reflection of man's dependence on nature, but a reflection of the interaction of social groups.

The year is the largest unit of ecological time. Nuer have words for the year before last, last year, this year, next year, and the year after next. Events which took place in the last few years are then the points of reference in time-reckoning, and these are different according to the group of persons who make use of them: joint family, village, tribal section, tribe, etc. One of the commonest ways of stating the year of an event is to mention where the people of the village made their dry season camps, or to refer to some evil that befell their cattle. A joint family may reckon time in the birth of calves of their herds. Weddings and other ceremonies, fights, and raids, may likewise give points of time, though in the absence of numerical dating no one can say without lengthy calculations how many years ago an event took place. Moreover, since time is to Nuer an order of events of outstanding significance to a group, each group has its own points of reference and time is consequently relative to structural space, locally considered. This is obvious when we examine the names given to years by different tribes, or sometimes by adjacent tribes, for these are floods, pestilences, famines, wars, etc., experienced by the tribe. In course of time the names of years are forgotten and all events beyond the limits of this crude historical reckoning fade into the dim vista of long long ago. Historical time, in this sense of a sequence of outstanding events of significance to a tribe, goes back much farther than the historical time of smaller groups, but fifty years is probably its limit, and the farther back from the present day the sparser and vaguer become its points of reference.

However, Nuer have another way of stating roughly when events took place; not in numbers of years, but by reference to the age-set system. Distance between events ceases to be reckoned in time concepts as we understand them and is reckoned in terms of structural distance, being the relation between groups of persons. It is therefore entirely relative to the social structure. Thus a Nuer may say that an event took place after the *Thut* age-set was born or in the initiation period of the *Boiloc* age-set, but no one can say how many years ago it happened. Time is here reckoned in sets. If a man of the *Dangunga* set tells one that an event occurred in the initiation period of the *Thut* set he is saying that it happened three sets before his set, or six sets ago. Here it need only be said that we cannot accurately translate a reckoning in sets into a reckoning in years, but that we can roughly estimate a ten-year interval between the commencement of successive sets. There are six sets in existence, the names of the sets are not cyclic, and the order of extinct sets, all but the last, are soon forgotten, so that an age-set reckoning has seven units covering a period of rather under a century.

The structural system of time-reckoning is partly the selection of points of reference of significance to local groups which give these groups a common and distinctive history; partly the distance between specific sets in the age-set system; and partly distances of a kinship and lineage order. Four generation-steps (*kath*) in the kinship system are linguistically differentiated relations, grandfather, father, son, and grandson, and within a small kinship group these relationships give a time-depth to members of the group and points of reference in a line of ascent by which their relationships are determined and explained. Any kinship relationship must have a point of reference on a line of ascent, namely a common

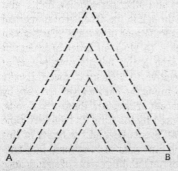

Figure 1

ancestor, so that such a relationship always has a time connotation couched in structural terms. Beyond the range of the kinship system in this narrow sense the connotation is expressed in terms of the lineage system. We will limit further discussion of this subject to an explanatory comment on Figure 1. The base line of the triangle represents a given group of agnates and the dotted lines represent their ghostly agnatic forebears, running from this base to a point in lineage structure, the common ancestor of every member of the group. The farther we extend the range of the group (the longer becomes the base line) the farther back in lineage structure is the common ancestor (the farther from the base line is the apex of the triangle). The four triangles are thus the time depths of four extensions of agnatic relationship on an existential plane and represent minimal, minor, major, and maximal lineages of a clan. Lineage time is thus the structural distance between groups of persons on the line AB. Structural time therefore cannot be understood until structural distance is known, since it is a reflection of it, and we must, therefore, ask the reader to forgive a certain obscurity at this point and to reserve criticism till we have had an opportunity of explaining more clearly what is meant by structural distance.

We have restricted our discussion to Nuer systems of time-reckoning and have not considered the way in which an individual perceives time. The subject bristles with difficulties. Thus an individual may reckon the passage of time by reference to the physical appearance and status of other individuals and to changes in his own life-history, but such a method of reckoning time has no wide collective validity. We confess, however, that our observations on the matter have been slight and that a fuller analysis is beyond our powers. We have merely indicated those aspects of the problem which are directly related to the description of modes of livelihood which has gone before and to the description of political institutions which follows.

We have remarked that the movement of structural time is, in a sense, an illusion, for the structure remains fairly constant and the perception of time is no more than the movement of persons, often as groups, through the structure. Thus age-sets succeed one another for ever, but there are never more than six in existence and the relative positions occupied by these six sets at any time are fixed structural points through which actual sets of persons pass in endless succession. Similarly, for reasons which we explain later, the Nuer system of lineages may be considered a fixed system, there being a constant number of steps between living persons and the founder of their clan and the lineages having a constant position relative to one another. However many generations succeed one another, the depth and range of lineages does not increase unless there has been structural change.

Beyond the limits of historical time we enter a plane of tradition in which a certain element of historical fact may be supposed to be incorporated in a complex of myth. Here the points of reference are the structural ones we have indicated. At one end this plane merges into history; at the other end into myth. Time perspective is here not a true impression of actual distances like that created by our dating technique, but a reflection of relations between lineages, so that the traditional events recorded have to be placed at the points where the lineages concerned in them converge in their lines of ascent. The events have therefore a position in structure, but no exact position in historical time as we understand it. Beyond tradition lies the horizon of pure myth which is always seen in the same time perspective. One mythological event did not precede another, for myths explain customs of general social significance rather than the interrelations of particular segments and are, therefore, not structurally stratified. Explanations of any qualities of nature or of culture are drawn from this intellectual ambient which imposes limits on the Nuer world and makes it self-contained and entirely intelligible to Nuer in the relation of its parts. The world, peoples, and cultures all existed together from the same remote past.

It will have been noted that the Nuer time dimension is narrow. Valid history ends a century ago, and tradition, generously measured, takes us back only ten to twelve generations in lineage structure, and if we are right in supposing that lineage structure never grows, it follows that the distance between the beginning of the world and the present day remains unalterable. Time is thus not a continuum, but is a constant structural relationship between two points, the first and last persons in a line of agnatic descent. How shallow is Nuer time may be judged from the fact that the tree under which mankind came into being was still standing in Western Nuerland a few years ago!

Beyond the annual cycle, time-reckoning is a conceptualization of the social structure, and the points of reference are a projection into the past of actual relations between groups of persons. It is less a means of co-ordinating events than of coordinating relationships, and is therefore mainly a looking-backwards, since relationships must be explained in terms of the past.

13 J. A. Roth

Benchmarks

Excerpts from J. A. Roth, *Timetables*, Bobbs-Merrill, 1963, pp. 3–7 and 10–14.

Although the focus of the patient's timetable is on discharge from the hospital, an effort is made to time other events along the way. Some parts of the timetable may be defined by arbitrary hospital regulations. Thus, Hamilton does not give a pass until three months after admission and three months after surgery and then allows each patient a set number of hours each month thereafter. At Makawer, patients are held six months after promotion to the exercise classes and nine months after surgery (if there are no complications or relapses). It would seem that, in areas where the time schedule is not established administratively, far more flexibility and variability would be possible. The patients, however, find such variability disturbing and press for norms.

Thus Sunny Sanitarium, a private hospital, does not have regulations covering passes. However, the patients observe the doctor's decisions to see how soon after admission he is willing to give a pass and how frequent and how long are the passes he subsequently gives. These observations are then translated by the patients into obligations. The patient is *entitled to* a pass two months after admission. He is *entitled to* at least one weekend each month thereafter. And if he does not get it, he feels cheated.

In hospitals with a rigid classification system the steps of promotion become important items in the timetable. At Makawer, if a patient starts out in Class 2, he *should* get a promotion within four months. If he starts out in Class 3, he *should* be promoted within a year if he does not get surgery. If he is not promoted within the expected time, he is either 'real sick' or is being neglected by the staff. Here again, the details of the timetable vary from hospital to hospital, but in each case norms of some sort exist.

A classification system contains within it a series of restrictions and privileges. Where no rigid classification system exists, these privileges themselves become part of the timetable. How soon after admission (or after surgery or after some other reference point) is the patient allowed to go to the bathroom, to the dayroom, to see movies, to the occupational therapy shop? How long is it before he is allowed two hours a day 'up time' (that is, the amount of time permitted out of bed)? Four hours a day? Six hours a day? When is he allowed to go outside for walks? When can he get a pass every month? *These privileges are desired not only in themselves, but for their symbolic value.* They are signs that the treatment is progressing, that the patient is getting closer to discharge. In fact, many privileges are taken surreptitiously by patients long before they are officially granted, but the patient still looks forward to getting them officially because they show that he is moving ahead. A patient with two hours' 'up time' may actually be spending eight hours a day out of bed and at the same time be pressuring the doctor to give him four hours' 'up time'.

Betty MacDonald tells us how the privileges granted a patient served as benchmarks of progress in the pre-chemotherapy days (before tuberculosis was treated with drugs):[1]

The only way we could tell whether we were getting well or dying was by the privileges we were granted. If we were progressing satisfactorily at the end of one month we were given the bathroom privilege and fifteen minutes a day reading-and-writing time. At the end of two months, if we continued to progress our reading-and-writing time was increased to half an hour, we were allowed to read books and were given ten minutes a day occupational therapy time. At the end of three months we were given a chest examination, along with the other tests, and if all was still well we were given three hours' time up, one hour occupational therapy time and could go to the movies. [. . .] (MacDonald, 1948).

Some aspects of diagnosis and treatment may also be used as reference points in the timetable if they occur with some regularity (or the patients believe they occur with regularity). The regularly repeated conferences on each patient's case in themselves serve to break up the long stretch of time from admission to discharge. Patients use the possible conference decisions as a means of guessing when they will be discharged. Thus, Dover patients often calculate the minimum possible stay for an active case as six months. Your first checkup comes six weeks after the admission examination, the second checkup three months after that. Your X-ray could be stable (a usual criterion for discharge) at the earliest between the first and second checkups. Then you have to wait at least six weeks while your final gastric cultures are run. This adds up to six months. Recognizing that X-rays are seldom regarded as stable by the staff as early as the second checkup, patients more commonly think of the minimum as nine months unless you can talk the doctor into giving you an earlier conference or giving you a leave of absence while awaiting the results of the cultures. A patient who is past the chance of getting out in the minimum time still makes estimates on the basis of conference periods.

1. This form of therapy became common only in the early 1950s. Before then therapy was less specific, less effective, and longer, and depended largely on bed rest.

It was November 1956 when she came in, and at the rate she is going now she can't see any chance of getting out before 1958. Her next conference won't be until the early part of October. Even then, if her X-rays are stationary, he (the doctor) will probably want her to have cultures run and keep her for at least one more conference and this would take her into 1958.[2]

The time of surgery is important in the timetable because patients always have a definite conception of how long one has to remain in the hospital after surgery. The expected time following pulmonary resection (excision of part or all of a lung) varies from four months at Hamilton to nine months at Makawer, but in each hospital, the patient kept much longer than the expected time thinks of himself as being kept overtime.

A final series of three gastric cultures is commonly used in many hospitals as an assurance that the patient is 'negative' before being discharged. These cultures are incubated for six weeks (eight weeks in some hospitals) before being regarded as negative. A patient who gets his 'gastrics' therefore assumes that he will get out in six weeks.

Patients with the more serious disease are usually started on INH (iso-nicotinic acid hydrazide, the most commonly used medicine in the treatment of TB) and streptomycin (an injection medicine) at Dover Sanatorium. Since semi-weekly injections are a great inconvenience for an outpatient clinic to administer, patients are usually switched to INH and PAS (paraminosalicylic acid, one of the three most commonly used TB drugs – an oral medicine) some time before discharge. As a result, patients have come to regard being changed from streptomycin to PAS as a sign of approaching discharge and observe the cases of other patients whose medication has been changed in this way in an effort to find out how many more conference periods are likely to pass before they are considered for discharge. [. . .] As an ex-schoolteacher at Dover put it:

You never seem to get anywhere because people here don't pay too much attention to the classifications. I've been here now since November and I'm still in Group 1. My husband comes to visit me and looks at this tag and thinks I'm never going to get promoted. He wonders what's going on. Then when you *do* get promoted to Group 2, you don't know what it means, anyway. You have no idea what additional privileges you have. You have no idea what you can do that you couldn't do before or what restrictions you had to observe before that you no longer have to observe. It's like an ungraded school room.

In such a situation the patients do not simply throw up their hands and say that there is no way of finding out when you can expect anything to happen or how long you have to stay in the hospital. They keep searching for clues – the poorer and fewer the clues, the more desperate the search. They grasp at anything that looks as if it might be a benchmark in the

2. Illustrations and quotations are taken from my field notes, unless otherwise stated.

progress of time. A visit from the rehabilitation worker makes them wonder whether this may be a regular thing and whether one may now count on a certain length of time before discharge. Only the repeated failure of the rehabilitation worker to visit other patients who are later discharged causes this clue to be abandoned. The change from streptomycin to PAS is not made consistently at a given stage of treatment, but still some patients hold to this as an important clue and try to guess their remaining period of hospitalization from this reference point.

The patients at Hamilton Hospital who do not require surgery have much the same difficulty determining timetable norms as the Dover patients, especially in the latter part of their stay. Almost all have bathroom privileges from the very beginning; occupational therapy and movie privileges are usually given early in the treatment; 'up time' privileges are not used; and the classification scale is ignored by the doctors and cannot be depended on. In an effort to establish a more precise timetable, the patients here too grasp at anything that looks like a move toward discharge. Thus, when many patients began to be moved to Ward 4W before they were discharged, this ward came to be regarded as an exercise or 'going out' ward, and patients talked about how long it took to get to this ward and how long it took to be discharged once you got there. However, the hospital was quite new and in a constant process of reorganization. Some patients were still discharged from other wards and, at the same time, some patients who were far from discharge – for example, some being readied for surgery – were placed on the 'exercise ward'. Therefore, the shift to this ward could not be counted on. Likewise, there was some feeling among patients that one could expect discharge two months after a final series of three gastric tests, but it became increasingly clear that the doctors did not consider these tests as 'final' as the patients at first thought.

Benchmarks for a timetable can never be done away with entirely because some degree of regularity is inherent in the treatment of TB and in the operation of a hospital. It is these regularities that the patients make use of in constructing timetable norms. If the clues become poorer, the patients are more likely to be wrong in making estimates about discharge time, about what stages they have reached on the way to discharge, and about how their cases compare to those of other patients. In desperation, they are more likely to grasp at inappropriate clues. However, whether the clues are relatively clear-cut and consistent as at Makawer and Valentine, or relatively confusing and inconsistent as at Dover and, for non-surgery patients, at Hamilton, the constant effort to develop and revise a timetable never ceases. [. . .]

When norms for the various privileges and diagnostic and treatment procedures have been more or less established, each patient can look forward to these intermediate steps on the way to discharge. If he fails to get a privilege, test, promotion in class, or discharge within the expected time, he is faced with the question: 'Am I *that sick*, or is the doctor giving me the runaround?' In cases where the patient is quite weak or has a fever, cough, or other obvious symptoms, the decision to hold him back may seem reasonable, both to him and to other patients. However, when the patient is feeling quite well and the doctors base their decision to delay promotion or privileges on subtle details of the chest X-rays or other diagnostic procedures that are not readily understandable by patients, the patient may well consider the doctors' action unjustified. It is in such cases that conflict over the timetable is most likely to occur. Thus, the 'normal' timetable can be used by the patients as a measuring stick of their own progress ('Am I doing better or worse than most?') or of the attention they are getting from the medical staff ('Are they moving me along as fast as possible or holding me back for no good reason?').

When I speak of patients constructing the norms of their timetable, I do not mean that they keep records of the times at which they and other patients get certain privileges or diagnostic or treatment procedures or get discharged. The norms arise through the pooling of limited and unsystematic observations from which there develops a group consensus – a consensus subject to modification with time and circumstances. According to my observations, however, the norms are quite close to the averages of actual practice. If anything, the points on the timetable tend to be a trifle premature in comparison with the actual averages. Thus, there is always a good proportion of the patients who are slightly behind the timetable; and few, if any, are very far ahead of it. As a result, many patients are constantly 'pulling at the bit', fearing that they may fall behind in the race to get well just as fast as the next man.

Reference

MACDONALD, B. (1948), *The Plague and I*, Hammond, Hammond.

14 H. Garfinkel

Time Structures the Biography and Prospects of a Situation

Excerpts from H. Garfinkel, *Studies in Ethnomethodology*, Prentice-Hall, 1967, pp. 164–7 and 148.

In contrast to homosexuals and transvestites, it was Agnes' conviction that she was naturally, originally, really, after all female. No mockery or masquerading accompanied this claim that we were able to observe. In this respect Agnes shared, point for point, the outlook of 'normals'.

But important differences nevertheless existed between Agnes and 'normals' in that 'normals' are able to advance such claims without a second thought whereas for her such claims involved her in uncertainties of responses from others. Her claims had to be bolstered and managed by shrewdness, deliberateness, skill, learning, rehearsal, reflectiveness, test, review, feedback, and the like. Her achieved rights to treat others and be treated herself as a natural female were achieved as the result of the successful management of situations of risk and uncertainty. Let me review some of the measures whereby she was able to secure and guarantee her claims.

Her devices were carried out within the conditions of, and were motivated by, a knowledge of herself that was, for almost every occasion of contact with others, none of somebody's business who was nevertheless important to her. As I have noted, the concealed knowledge of herself was regarded by her as a potentially degrading and damaging disclosure. She was realistically convinced that there would be little by way of an available remedy by which other persons might be 'set right' if the disclosure occurred. In this respect, the phenomena of Agnes' passing are amenable to Goffman's descriptions of the work of managing impressions in social establishments (1956). This amenability however is only superficial for reasons that will be apparent over the course of the discussion.

When I say that Agnes achieved her claims to the ascribed status of a natural female by the successful management of situations of risk and uncertainty, I do not mean thereby that Agnes was involved in a game, or that it was for her an intellectual matter, or that ego control for her extended to the point where she was able to switch with any success, let alone with any ease, from one sex role to the other. I have already mentioned several evidences of this. Other evidences can be cited. Even in imagination Agnes found it not only difficult to contemplate herself performing in the 'male' way but found it repugnant. Some memories were so exceptionally painful to her as to be lost as grounds of deliberate action. When she learned that the decision had been made to operate, the knowledge that she was committed to the operation as a decision was accompanied by a fear that when she was on the table, because the decision would then be entirely out of her hands, the doctors without consulting her would decide to amputate her breasts rather than her penis. The thought provoked a mild depression until she was assured that nothing of the sort was the case. The natural female was a condition that her various strategies had to satisfy. Agnes was not a game player. The 'natural female' was one among many institutional constraints, 'irrational givens', a *thing* that she *insisted upon* in the face of all contrary indications and the seductions of alternative advantages and goals. It attenuated the deliberateness of her efforts, the actual availability, let alone exercise of choices, and the consistency of her compliance with norms of strict utility and effectiveness in her choices of means. It furnished 'constraints' upon the exercise of certain rational properties of conduct, particularly of those rational properties that are provided for when certain games are used as procedural models to formulate formal properties of practical activities.

Not only is it necessary to stress the shortcomings of strategy analysis in discussing her 'management devices', but the very phrase 'management device' is only temporarily helpful. It is useful because it permits an enumerated account of these devices. For the same reason that it facilitates the enumeration it also clouds the phenomena that it is necessary to come to terms with. *These phenomena consist of Agnes in on-going courses of action directed to the mastery of her practical circumstances by the manipulation of these circumstances as a texture of relevances.* The troublesome feature encountered over and over again is the cloudy and little-known role that time plays in structuring the biography and prospects of present situations over the course of action as a function of the action itself. It is not sufficient to say that Agnes' situations are played out over time, nor is it at all sufficient to regard this time as clock time. There is as well the 'inner time' of recollection, remembrance, anticipation, expectancy. Every attempt to handle Agnes' 'management devices' while disregarding this time, does well enough as long as the occasions are episodic in their formal structure; and all of Goffman's analyses either take episodes for illustration, or turn the situations that his scheme analyses into episodic ones. But strategic analyses fail whenever these events are not episodic. Then to keep the analysis in good repair, there is required the exercise of theoretical ingenuity, and a succession of theoretical elections, one compounded on the other, with the frantic use of metaphor in the hope of bringing these events to faithful representation. This caveat can be summarized, although poorly, by pointing out that it would be incorrect to say of Agnes that she has passed. The active mode is needed; she is passing. Inadequate though this phrasing is, it summarizes Agnes' troubles. It stands as well for *our* troubles in describing accurately and adequately what her troubles were. [. . .]

Another common set of occasions arose when she engaged in friendly conversation without having biographical and group affiliation data to swap off with her conversational partner. As Agnes said:

Can you imagine all the blank years I have to fill in? Sixteen or seventeen years of my life that I have to make up for. I have to be careful of the things that I say, just natural things that could slip out . . . I just never say anything at all about my past that in any way would make a person ask what my past life was like. I say general things. I don't say anything that could be misconstrued.

Agnes said that with men she was able to pass as an interesting conversationalist by encouraging her male partners to talk about themselves. Women partners, she said, explained the general and indefinite character of her biographical remarks, which she delivered with a friendly manner, by a combination of her niceness and modesty. 'They probably figure that I just don't like to talk about myself.'

Reference

GOFFMAN, E. (1956), *The Presentation of Self in Everyday Life*, University of Edinburgh Social Sciences Research Centre.

15 J. Cage

Musical Time and Other Time

Excerpts from J. Cage, *Silence*, Calder & Boyars, 1968, pp. 9 and 40.

Musical habits include scales, modes, theories of counterpoint and harmony, and the study of the timbres, singly and in combination of a limited number of sound-producing mechanisms. In mathematical terms these all concern discrete steps. They resemble walking – in the case of pitches, on steppingstones twelve in number. This cautious stepping is not characteristic of the possibilities of magnetic tape, which is revealing to us that musical action or existence can occur at any point or along any line or curve or what have you in total sound-space; that we are, in fact, technically equipped to transform our contemporary awareness of nature's manner of operation into art. [. . .]

There are certain practical matters to discuss that concern the performance of music the composition of which is indeterminate with respect to its performance. These matters concern the physical space of the performance. These matters also concern the physical time of the performance. In connection with the physical time of the performance, where that performance involves several players (two or more), it is advisable for several reasons to give the conductor another function than that of beating time. The situation of sounds arising from actions which arise from their own centers will not be produced when a conductor beats time in order to unify the performance. Nor will the situation of sounds arising from actions which arise from their own centers be produced when several conductors beat different times in order to bring about a complex unity to the performance. Beating time is not necessary. All that is necessary is a slight suggestion of time, obtained either from glancing at a watch or at a conductor who, by his actions, represents a watch. Where an actual watch is used, it becomes possible to foresee the time, by reason of the steady progress from second to second of the second hand. Where, however, a conductor is present, who by his actions represents a watch which moves not mechanically but variably, it is not possible to foresee the time, by reason of the changing progress from second to second of the conductor's indications. Where this conductor, who by his actions represents a watch, does so in relation to a part rather than a score – to, in fact, his own part, not that of another –

his actions will interpenetrate with those of the players of the ensemble in a way which will not obstruct their actions. The musical recognition of the necessity of time is tardy with respect to the recognition of time on the part of broadcast communications, radio, television, not to mention magnetic tape, not to mention travel by air, departures and arrivals from no matter what point at no matter what time, to no matter what point at no matter what time, not to mention telephony. It is indeed astonishing that music as an art has kept performing musicians so consistently beating time together like so many horseback riders huddled together on one horse. It is high time to let sounds issue in time independent of a beat in order to show a musical recognition of the necessity of time which has already been recognized on the part of broadcast communications, radio, television, not to mention magnetic tape, not to mention travel by air, departures and arrivals from no matter what point at no matter what time, to no matter what point at no matter what time, not to mention telephony.

16 M. L. J. Abercrombie

Face to Face

Excerpts from M. L. J. Abercrombie, 'Face to face – proximity and distance',
Journal of Psychosomatic Research, vol. 15, no. 4, December 1971, pp. 399–401.

The spatial relationships of objects convey information about the roles of the people who use them. In some institutions, the size of rooms allocated to members of staff goes up with status, as though the more important person needs more cubic feet of air to breathe. The furnishings of a lecture theatre or classroom show the relationship of the teacher and the taught. The teacher sits at a desk or stands on a platform and is the only person who can see everybody and whom everyone can see. The arrangements of furniture in courtrooms, which are places for conversation, reflect national variations in the accepted relationships of the accused, the jury, the counsels and the judge. Almost invariably the judge's seat is raised, and when the bench is collegial, the presiding judge has a chair whose back protrudes several inches above the rest. In a British or American courtroom the jury sits in a box, but in Geneva it is not separated from the judge, for the judge retires with the jurymen, and shares with them the decision of guilt and punishment. Conventions of this kind not only demonstrate the roles to be played by people, but support the people in their roles and make it difficult for them to adopt alternative ones.

The effect of seating arrangements was known to King Arthur and his Knights of the Round Table. It is in order to encourage similar flexibility of roles that, in group analytic psychotherapy, therapists and patients sit in similar chairs about a round table, as different a situation as can be from the psychoanalytic one in which the patient lies recumbent and the therapist sits, all powerful, out of sight behind him.

Even well-practised chairmen may prefer to sit at the head of a rectangular table: others sit in the middle of a long side of it, and may be quite disconcerted at being placed elsewhere. The arguments that went on about the shape of the table for the Vietnam Peace Talks illustrate how seriously such an apparently simple thing may affect communication: was it to emphasize that there were two participants in the debate, or two pairs, or four? A round table with a hint of a division into two sides was chosen, but square and rectangular shapes had been considered.

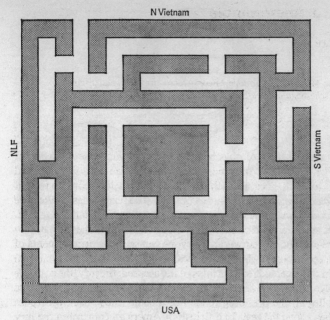

Figure 1　The Vietnam peace table：
Adapted from a cartoon in *The Times*, 17 December 1968

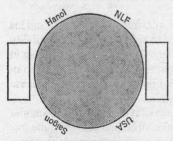

Figure 2　The accepted table

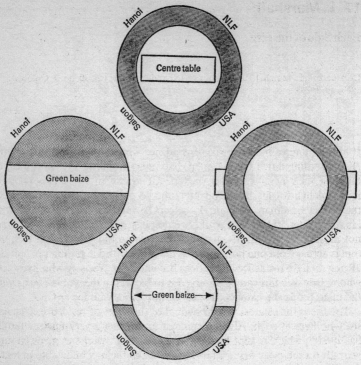

Figure 3 Some of the rejected suggestions:
from *The Times*, 17 January 1969.

17 L. Marshall

Each Side of the Fire

Excerpt from L. Marshall, '!Kung bushman bands', *Africa*, vol. 30, no. 4, October 1960, pp. 342–3.

It always amuses me to speak of residence when I visualize the nomadic !Kung settling down for the night, like migrating birds in the bushes, or building their nest-like grass shelters for a stay of a few weeks. And it is a delightful insistence on precision to say that Lame ≠Gao (23), the young headman of Band 1, before he married in 1959, lived with his elder sister, !U 22, not with his eldest sister, Di!ai 3, when they were not more than two arms' lengths apart because the sisters liked to hand things across from one household to the other without getting up. Yet the !Kung do have residence and it does become clear precisely who lives with whom. One way this can be observed is to see whom the woman feeds with the plant foods she gathers. It was !U, not Di!ai, who fed ≠Gao.

The fire is the clearest visible symbol of the place of residence. One can see who lives at each. Always, summer and winter, every nuclear family has its fire, which is kept burning all night. The desert sun gives enough warmth on the clear dry winter days to make them comfortable unless a fierce wind is blowing from the Antarctic. The fires are customarily covered with ashes during the day, and the coals are fanned up only when they are wanted for cooking. In the later afternoon men and women go from the camp to gather dead wood for the night fires. There is plenty of wood for them. Their use is conservative. Even the night fires are not large. You can draw closer together around a small fire and have less smoke in your eyes.

The fire is the nuclear family's home, its place to be. In a way a fire is a more unchanging home than a house on a spot on the ground from which a family might depart. A fire-home is always where the family is.

The family hangs its possessions in the bushes near by, sits around the fire, cooks at it, sleeps beside it – with two exceptions. The unmarried boys from about the age of puberty eat and sit and, in general, live by their family's fire in the day-time but at night they all sleep at a boys' fire. The unmarried girls of that age, likewise, sleep away from their parents' fire, at the fire of a grandmother or some other woman who can chaperon them.

The pattern of settlement of the !Kung has only a few constant elements. The !Kung settle at some distance from a water-hole, half a mile or so away in any direction. This is not to enable them to hunt at night from a blind at the water-hole, which is an extremely rare type of hunting for the !Kung to adopt because their big game antelopes do not need to drink regularly and seldom come to the water-holes. The predators do, however. The Bushmen and our expedition shared a water-hole for three months with a family of lions. The adult lions minded their own business, the rambunctious cubs were merely playful when they destroyed our water pump, but we all slept the better for keeping our distance.

The !Kung do not settle twice in exactly the same spot and never return to old shelters once abandoned. They return to the same water-holes and to the same gathering areas season after season, year after year, but there is plenty of space and they choose a fresh, clean spot each time.

The families in a band always settle close together, and the brown and clustered encampment makes me think of a swarm of bees. Band 1 with 32 persons living at 8 family fires usually occupies, on an average, a space of about 40 feet by 20 feet. In a small space the warmth and light of the many little night fires combine to wall the band in from darkness and space and predators.

Within the encampment, the families demarcate themselves consistently. Each nuclear family has its own fire. The fires of the nuclear families which compose an extended family are always near each other, not scattered about in the encampment. Adult dependants have their own fires near the families they live with. In other ways the pattern is variable. The encampment can take almost any shape: roughly circular, oddly angular or serpentine, but I never saw one look much like a square.

Fires are not placed in a fixed pattern with reference to the headman or father of an extended family, nor with reference to the points of the compass or anything I know of except nearness together. A convenient nearby bush to hang things on, a bit of shade, a relatively smooth and thorn-free place on the ground or sand determine the particular choice of spot. I have been referring to the settlement pattern in terms of family fires rather than shelters because the fires are constant, the shelters are whims.

The building of the shelters is the work of women. It is an aspect of the gathering of growing things. From 12 to 20 light, flexible branches about 5 to 6 feet long are gathered from bushes to make the frame. With their digging sticks the women dig a line of little holes in the shape of a crescent and tamp the branches into them. They weave the tops of the branches together. This makes a frame a half-hemisphere in shape, usually about 4 to 5 feet wide on its open side, 3 or 4 feet deep, 4 to 5 feet high at the peak. The women then gather armloads of grass and lay these over the frame in unbound bundles, grass heads downward like a thatch. In the summer during the rains, when the thunderstorms are awesome, and in winter when the dry, cold winds are strong, women sometimes bind the grass to the frame by drawing strands of fibre or bark from one side of the entrance around the shelter to the other, with perhaps a turn or two over the top, but the women are haphazard about the tying and often they do not bind the grass at all and the winds take it.

They face the shelters in any direction of the compass: into or back to the winds, rains, and sun, inwardly toward each other or outwardly back to back, face to face, side by side, touching each other or not – all by pure whim.

It takes the women only three-quarters of an hour to an hour to build their shelters, but half the time at least the women's whim is not to build shelters at all. In this case they sometimes put up two sticks to symbolize the entrance of the shelter so that the family may orient itself as to which side is the man's side and which the woman's side of the fire (see Marshall, 1959). Sometimes they do not bother with the sticks.

Reference

MARSHALL, L. (1959), 'Marriage among /Kung Bushmen', *Africa*, vol. 29, no. 4, p. 354.

18 P. Bourdieu

The Berber House

Excerpts from P. Bourdieu, 'The Berber house or the world reversed', *Echanges et communications: Mélanges offerts à Claude Lévi-Strauss à l'occasion de son 60*^e *anniversaire*, Mouton, 1971, pp. 151–61 and 165–9.

The interior of the Kabyle house is rectangular in shape and is divided into two parts at a point one third of the way along its length by a small lattice-work wall half as high as the house. Of these two parts, the larger is approximately 50 centimeters higher than the other and is covered over by a layer of black clay and cow dung which the women polish with a stone; this part is reserved for human use. The smaller part is paved with flagstones and is occupied by the animals. A door with two wings provides entrance to both rooms. Upon the dividing wall are kept, at one end, the small clay jars or esparto-grass baskets in which provisions awaiting immediate consumption, such as figs, flour and leguminous plants, are conserved; at the other end, near the door, the water-jars. Above the stable there is a loft where, next to all kinds of tools and implements, quantities of straw and hay to be used as animal-fodder are piled up; it is here that the women and children usually sleep, particularly in winter. Against the gable wall, known as the wall (or, more exactly, the 'side') of the upper part or of the *kanun*, there is set a brick-work construction in the recesses and holes of which are kept the kitchen utensils (ladle, cooking-pot, dish used to cook the bannock, and other earthenware objects blackened by the fire) and at each end of which are placed large jars filled with grain. In front of this construction is to be found the fireplace; this consists of a circular hollow, two or three centimeters deep at its centre, around which are arranged in a triangle three large stones upon which the cooking is done.[1]

1. All the descriptions of the Berber house, even the most exact and methodical ones (such as R. Maunier, 1930a and b), or those that are most rich in detail concerning the interior organization of space (such as those made by E. Laoust, 1912, 1920, or by H. Genevois, 1955) contain, in their extreme meticulousness, regular omissions, particularly when it is a question of precisely situating things and activities. The reason for this is that these descriptions never consider objects and actions as part of a symbolic system. The postulate that each of the observed phenomena derives its necessity and its meaning from its relation with all the others was the only way of proceeding to a systematic observation and examination capable of bringing out facts which escape any unsystematic observation and which the observers are incapable of yielding since they appear self-evident to them. This postulate is rendered valid by the very results of the

In front of the wall opposite the door stands the weaving-loom. This wall is usually called by the same name as the outside front wall giving onto the courtyard (*tasga*), or else wall of the weaving-loom or opposite wall, since one is opposite it when one enters. The wall opposite to this, where the door is, is called wall of darkness, or of sleep, or of the maiden, or of the tomb; a bench wide enough for a mat to be spread out over it is set against this wall; the bench is used to shelter the young calf or the sheep for feast-days and sometimes the wood or the water-pitcher. Clothes, mats and blankets are hung, during the day, on a peg or on a wooden cross-bar against the wall of darkness or else they are put under the dividing bench. Clearly, therefore, the wall of the *kanun* is opposed to the stable as the top is to the bottom (*adaynin*, stable, comes from the root *ada*, meaning the bottom) and the wall of the weaving-loom is opposed to the wall of the door as the light is to the darkness. One might be tempted to give a strictly technical explanation to these oppositions since the wall of the weaving-loom, placed opposite the door, which is itself turned towards the east, receives the most light and the stable is, in fact, situated at a lower level than the rest; the reason for this latter is that the house is most often built perpendicularly with contour lines in order to facilitate the flow of liquid manure and dirty water. A number of signs suggest, however, that these oppositions are the centre of a whole cluster of parallel oppositions, the necessity of which is never completely due to technical imperatives or functional requirements.

The dark and nocturnal, lower part of the house, place of objects that are moist, green or raw – jars of water placed on benches in various parts of the entrance to the stable or against the wall of darkness, wood and green fodder – natural place also of beings – oxen and cows, donkeys and mules – and place of natural activities – sleep, the sexual act, giving birth – and the place also of death, is opposed, as nature is to culture, to the light-filled, noble, upper part of the house: this is the place of human beings and, in particular, of the guest; it is the place of fire and of objects created by fire – lamp, kitchen utensils, rifle – the symbol of the male point of honour (*ennif*) and the protector of female honour (*ḥorma*) – and it is the place of the weaving-loom – the symbol of all protection; and it is also the place of the two specifically cultural activities that are carried out in the space of the house: cooking and weaving. These relationships of opposition are expressed through a whole set of convergent signs which establish the relationships

research-programme which it establishes: the particular position of the house within the system of magical representations and ritual practices justifies the initial abstraction by means of which the house is taken out of the context of this larger system in order to treat it as a system itself.

at the same time as receiving their meaning from them. Whenever there is a guest to be honoured (the verb, *qabel*, 'to honour' also means to face and to face the east), he is made to sit in front of the weaving-loom. When a person has been badly received, it is customary for him to say: 'He made me sit before his wall of darkness as in a grave', or: 'His wall of darkness is as dark as a grave.' The wall of darkness is also called wall of the invalid and the expression 'to keep to the wall' means to be ill and, by extension, to be idle: the bed of the sick person is, in fact, placed next to this wall, particularly in winter. The link between the dark part of the house and death is also shown in the fact that the washing of the dead takes place at the entrance to the stable. It is customary to say that the loft, which is entirely made of wood, is carried by the stable as the corpse is by the bearers, and the word *tha'richth* refers to both the loft and to the stretcher which is used to transport the dead. It is therefore obvious that one cannot, without causing offence, invite a guest to sleep in the loft which is opposed to the wall of the weaving-loom like the wall of the tomb.

In front of the wall of the weaving-loom, opposite the door, in the light, is also seated or rather, shown off, like the decorated plates which are hung there, the young bride on her wedding-day. When one knows that the umbilical cord of the girl is buried behind the weaving-loom and that, in order to protect the virginity of the maiden, she is made to pass through the warp, going from the door towards the weaving-loom, then the magic protection attributed to the weaving-loom becomes evident. In fact, from the point of view of the male members of her family, all of the girl's life is, as it were, summed up in the successive positions that she symbolically occupies in relation to the weaving-loom which is the symbol of male protection: before marriage she is placed behind the weaving-loom, in its shadow, under its protection, as she is placed under the protection of her father and her brothers; on her wedding-day she is seated in front of the weaving-loom with her back to it, with the light upon her, and finally she will sit weaving with her back to the wall of light, behind the loom. 'Shame,' it is said, 'is the maiden', and the son-in-law is called 'the veil of shames' since man's point of honour is the protective 'barrier' of female honour.

The low and dark part of the house is also opposed to the high part as the feminine is to the masculine: besides the fact that the division of work between the sexes, which is based upon the same principle of division as the organization of space, entrusts to the woman the responsibility of most objects which belong to the dark part of the house – water-transport, and the carrying of wood and manure, for instance – the opposition between the upper part and the lower part reproduces within the space of the house the opposition set up between the inside and the outside. This is the opposition between female space and male space, between the house and its garden, the place *par excellence* of the *ḥaram*, i.e. of all which is sacred and forbidden, and a closed and secret space, well-protected and sheltered from intrusions and the gaze of others, and the place of assembly (*thajma'th*), the mosque, the café, the fields or the market: on the one hand, the privacy of all that is intimate, on the other, the open space of social relations; on the one hand, the life of the senses and of the feelings, on the other, the life of relations between man and man, the life of dialogue and exchange. The lower part of the house is the place of the most intimate privacy within the very world of intimacy, that is to say, it is the place of all that pertains to sexuality and procreation. More or less empty during the day, when all activity – which is, of course, exclusively feminine – is based around the fireplace, the dark part is full at night, full of human beings but also full of animals since, unlike the mules and the donkeys, the oxen and the cows never spend the night out of doors; and it is never quite so full as it is during the damp season when the men sleep inside and the oxen and the cows are fed in the stable. It is possible here to establish more directly the relationship which links the fertility of men and of the field to the dark part of the house and which is a particular instance of the relationship of equivalence between fertility and that which is dark, full (or swollen) or damp, vouched for by the whole mythico-ritual system: whilst the grain meant for consumption is, as we have seen, stored in large earthenware jars next to the wall of the upper part, on either side of the fireplace, the grain which is intended for sowing is placed in the dark part of the house, either in sheep-skins or in chests placed at the foot of the wall of darkness; or sometimes under the conjugal bed, or in wooden chests placed under the bench which is set against the dividing wall where the wife, who normally sleeps at a lower level, beside the entrance to the stable, rejoins her husband. Once we are aware that birth is always rebirth of the ancestor, since the life circle (which should be called the *cycle of generation*) turns upon itself every third generation (a proposition which cannot be demonstrated here), it becomes obvious that the dark part of the house may be at the same time and without any contradiction the place of death and of procreation, or of birth as resurrection.

In addition to all this, at the centre of the dividing wall, between 'the house of the human beings' and 'the house of the animals' stands the main pillar, supporting the governing beam and all the framework of the house. Now this governing beam which connects the gables and spreads the protection of the male part of the house to the female part (*asalas alemmas*, a masculine term) is identified explicitly with the master of the house, whilst the main pillar upon which it rests, which is the trunk of a forked tree (*thigejdith*, a feminine term), is identified with the wife (the Beni Khellili call it 'Mas'uda', a feminine first name which means 'the happy woman'), and their interlocking represents the act of physical union (shown in mural paintings in the form of the union of the beam and the pillar by two superimposed forked trees). The main beam, which supports the roof, is identified with the protector of family honour; sacrifices are often made to it, and it is around this beam that, on a level with the fireplace, is coiled the snake who is the 'guardian' of the house. As the symbol of the fertilizing power of man and the symbol also of death followed by resurrection, the snake is sometimes shown (in the Collo region for example) upon earthen jars made by the women and which contain the seed for sowing. The snake is also said to descend sometimes into the house, into the lap of the sterile woman, calling her mother, or to coil itself around the central pillar, growing longer by the length of one coil of its body after each time that it takes suck. In Darna, according to René Maunier, the sterile woman ties her belt to the central beam which is where the foreskin is hung and the reed which has been used for circumcision; when the beam is heard to crack the Berbers hastily say 'may it turn out well', because this presages the death of the chief of the family. At the birth of a boy, the wish is made that 'he be the governing beam of the house', and when he carries out his ritual fast for the first time, he takes his first meal on the roof, that is to say, on the central beam (in order, so it is said, that he may be able to transport beams).

A number of riddles and sayings explicitly identify the woman with the central pillar: 'My father's father's wife carries my father's father who carries his daughters'; 'The slave strangles his master'; 'The woman supports the man'; 'The woman is the central pillar'. To the young bride one says: 'May God make of you the pillar firmly planted in the middle of the house.' Another riddle says: 'She stands but she has no feet'; a forked tree open at the top and not set upon her feet, she is female nature and, as such, she is fertile or, rather, able to be fertilized. Against the central pillar are piled the leather bottles full of *hij* seeds, and it is here that the marriage is consummated. Thus, as a symbolic summing up of the house, the union of *asalas* and *thigejdith*, which spreads its fertilizing protection over all human marriage, is in a certain way primordial marriage, the marriage of the ancestors which is also, like tillage, the marriage of heaven and earth. 'Woman is the foundations, man is the governing beam,' says another proverb. *Asalas*, which a riddle defines as 'born in the earth and buried in the sky', fertilizes *thigejdith*, which is planted in the earth, the place of the ancestors who are the masters of all fecundity, and open towards the sky.

Thus, the house is organized according to a set of homologous oppositions: fire: water; cooked: raw; high: low; light: shadow; day: night; male: female; *nif*: *horma*; fertilizing: able to be fertilized; culture: nature. But in fact the same oppositions exist between the house as a whole and the rest of the universe. Considered in its relationship with the external world, which is a specifically masculine world of public life and agricultural work, the house, which is the universe of women and the world of intimacy and privacy, is *haram*, that is to say, at once sacred and illicit for every man who does not form part of it (hence the expression used when taking an oath: 'May my wife – or my house – become illicit – *haram* – to me if . . .'). As the place of the sacred or the left-hand side, appertaining to the *horma* to which are linked all those properties which are associated with the dark part of the house, the house is placed under the safeguard of the masculine point of honour (*nif*) as the dark part of the house is placed under the protection of the main beam. Any violation of the sacred space takes on therefore the social significance of a sacrilege: thus, theft in an inhabited house is treated in everyday usage as a very serious fault inasmuch as it is offence to the *nif* of the head of the family and an outrage upon the *horma* of the house and consequently of all the community. Moreover, when a guest who is not a member of the family is introduced to the women, he gives the mistress of the house a sum of money which is called 'the view'.

One is not justified in saying that the woman is locked up in the house unless one also observes that the man is kept out of it, at least during the day.[2] As soon as the sun has risen he must, during the summer, be in the fields or at the assembly house; in the winter, if he is not in the field, he has to be at the place of assembly or upon the benches set in the shelter of the pent-roof over the entrance door to the courtyard. Even at night, at least during the dry season, the men and the boys, as soon as they have been circumcised, sleep outside the house, either near the haystacks upon the threshing-floor, beside the donkey and the shackled mule, or upon the fig-dryer, or in the open field, or else, more rarely, in the *thajma'th*. The man who stays too long in the house during the day is either suspect or ridiculous: he is 'the man of the home', as one says of the importunate man who stays amongst the women and who 'broods at home like a hen in the henhouse'. A man who has respect for himself should let himself be seen, should continuously place himself under the gaze of others and face them (*qabel*). He is a man amongst men (*argaz yer irgazen*). Hence the importance accorded to the games of honour which are a kind of dramatic action, performed in front of others who are knowing spectators, familiar with the text and all the stage business and capable of appreciating the slightest variations. It is not difficult to understand why all biological activities such as eating, sleeping and procreating are excluded from the specifically cultural universe and relegated to the sanctuary of intimacy and the refuge for the secrets of nature which is the house, the woman's world. In opposition to man's work which is performed outside, it is the nature of

2. In order to hint at how much the men are ignorant of what happens in the house, the women say: 'O man, poor unfortunate, all day in the field like a mule at pasture.'

woman's work to remain hidden ('God conceals it'): 'Inside the house, woman is always on the move, she flounders like a fly in whey; outside the house, nothing of her work is seen.' Two very similar sayings define woman's condition as being that of one who cannot know of any other sojourn than that tomb above the earth which is the house and that subterranean house which is the tomb: 'Your house is your tomb'; 'Woman has only two dwellings, the house and the tomb.'

Thus, the opposition between the house and the assembly of men, between the fields and the market, between private life and public life, or, if one prefers, between the full light of the day and the secrecy of the night, overlaps very exactly with the opposition between the dark and nocturnal, lower part of the house and the noble and brightly-lit, upper part. The opposition which is set up between the external world and the house only takes on its full meaning therefore if one of the terms of this relation, that is to say, the house, is itself seen as being divided according to the same principles which oppose it to the other term. It is therefore both true and false to say that the external world is opposed to the house as male is to female, or day to night, or fire to water, etc., since the second term of these oppositions divides up each time into itself and its opposite.[3]

In short, the most apparent opposition: male (or day, fire, etc.)/female (or night, water, etc.) may well mask the opposition: male/female–male/female–female, and in the same way, the homology male/female; female–male/female–female. It is obvious from this that the first opposition is but a transformation of the second, which presupposes a change in the field of reference at the end of which the female–female is no longer opposed to the female–male and instead, the group which they form is opposed to a third term: female–male/female–female $\rightarrow$ female ($=$ female–male $+$ female–female)/male.

As a microcosm organized according to the same oppositions which govern all the universe, the house maintains a relation with the rest of the universe which is that of a homology: but from another point of view, the world of the house taken as a whole is in a relation with the rest of the world which is one of opposition, and the principles of which are none other than those which govern the organization of the internal space of the house as much as they do the rest of the world and, more generally, all

3. This structure is also to be found in other areas of the mythico–ritual system: thus, the day is divided into night and day, but the day itself is divided into a diurnal–diurnal part (the morning) and a diurnal–nocturnal part (the evening); the year is divided into a dry season and a wet season, and the dry season is comprised of a dry–dry part and a dry-wet part. There should also be an examination of the relation between this structure and the structure which governs the political order and which is expressed in the saying: 'My brother is my enemy, my brother's enemy is my enemy.'

the areas of existence. Thus, the opposition between the world of female life and the world of the city of men is based upon the same principles as the two systems of oppositions that it opposes. It follows from this that the application to opposed areas of the same *principium divisionis*, which in fact forms their very opposition, provides, at the least cost, a surplus of consistency and does not, in return, result in any confusion between these areas. The structure of the type $a : b; b_1 : b_2$ is doubtless one of the simplest and most powerful that may be employed by a mythico-ritual system since it cannot oppose without simultaneously uniting (and inversely), while all the time being capable of integrating in a set order an infinite number of data, by the simple application of the same principle of division indefinitely repeated.

It also follows from this that each of the two parts of the house (and, by the same token, all of the objects which are put there and all of the activities which take place there) is in a certain way qualified to two degrees, namely, firstly as female (nocturnal, dark, etc.) inasmuch as it participates in the universe of the house, and secondly as male or female inasmuch as it participates in one or the other of the divisions of this universe. Thus, for example, when the proverb says: 'Man is the lamp of the outside and woman the lamp of the inside,' it is to be understood that man is the true light, that of the day, and woman the light of the darkness, the dark light; moreover, she is, of course, to the moon what man is to the sun. In the same way, when she works with wool, woman produces the beneficent protection of weaving, the whiteness of which symbolizes happiness; the weaving-loom, which is the instrument *par excellence* of female activity and which faces the east like the plough, its homologue, is at the same time the east of the internal space of the house with the result that, within the system of the house, it has a male value as a symbol of protection. Likewise, the fireplace, which is the navel of the house (itself identified with the womb of the mother), where smoulder the embers, which is a secret, hidden and female fire, is the domain of woman who is invested with total authority in all matters concerning the kitchen and the management of the food-stores; she takes her meals at the fireside whilst man, turned towards the outside, eats in the middle of the room or in the courtyard. Nevertheless, in all the rites where they play a part, the fireplace and the stones which surround it derive their potent magic from their participation in the order of fire, of that which is dry and of the solar heat, whether it is a question of providing protection against the evil eye or against illness or to summon up fine weather. The house is also endowed with a double significance: if it is true that it is opposed to the public world as nature is to culture, it is also, in another respect, culture; is it not said of the jackal, the incarnation of all that is savage in nature, that it does not have a home?

But one or the other of the two systems of oppositions which define the house, either in its internal organization or in its relationship with the outside world, will take prime importance according to whether the house is considered from the male point of view or the female point of view: whereas, for the man, the house is less a place one goes into than a place from which one goes out, the woman can only confer upon these two movements and the different definitions of the house which form an integral part with them, an inverse importance and meaning, since movement towards the outside consists above all for her of acts of expulsion and it is her specific role to be responsible for all movement towards the inside, that is to say, from the threshold towards the fireplace. The significance of the movement towards the outside is never quite so apparent as in the rite performed by the mother, on the seventh day after a birth, 'in order that her son be courageous': striding across the threshold, she sets her right foot upon the carding comb and simulates a fight with the first boy she meets. The sallying forth is a specifically male movement which leads towards other men and also towards dangers and trials which it is important to *confront* like a man, a man as spiky, when it is a question of honour, as the points of the comb. Going out, or more exactly, opening (*fataḥ*), is the equivalent of 'being in the morning' (*sebaḥ*). A man who has respect for himself should leave the house at daybreak, morning being the day of the daytime, and the sallying forth from the house, in the morning, being a birth: whence the importance of things encountered which are a portent for the whole day, with the result that, in the case of bad encounters (blacksmith, woman carrying an empty leather bottle, shouts or a quarrel, a deformed being), it is best to 'remake one's morning' or 'one's going out'.

Bearing this in mind, it is not difficult to understand the importance accorded to the direction which the house faces: the front of the main house, the one which shelters the head of the family and which contains a stable, is almost always turned towards the east, and the main door – in opposition to the low and narrow door, reserved for the women, which opens in the direction of the garden, at the back of the house – is commonly called the door of the east (*thabburth thacherqith*) or else the door of the sheet, the door of the upper part or the great door. Considering the way in which the villages present themselves and the lower position of the stable, the upper part of the house, with the fireplace, is situated in the north, the stable is in the south and the wall of the weaving-loom is in the west. It follows from this that the movement one makes when going towards the house in order to enter it is directed from the east to the west, in opposition to the movement made to come out which, in accordance with the supreme direction, is towards the east, that is to say, towards the height, the light and the good: the ploughman turns his oxen towards the east when he

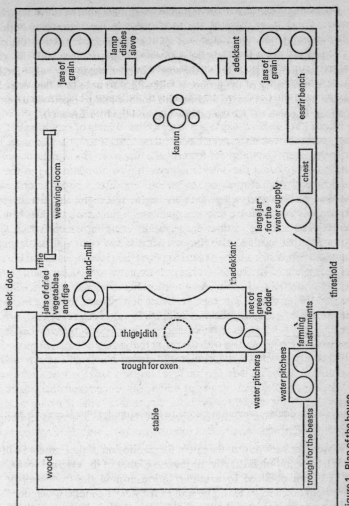

Figure 1 Plan of the house

harnesses them and also when he unharnesses them, and he starts ploughing from west to east; likewise, the harvesters arrange themselves opposite the *qibla* and they cut the throat of the sacrificial ox facing the east. Limitless are the acts which are performed in accordance with this principal direction, for these are all the acts of importance involving the fertility and the prosperity of the group. It will suffice to note that the verb *qabel* means not only to face, to affront with honour and to receive in a worthy manner, but also to face the east (*lqibla*) and the future (*qabel*).

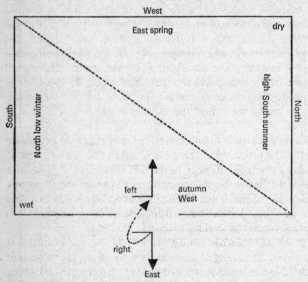

Figure 2 The double space orientation of the house (the right-angle arrows indicate the person's position)

If we refer back now to the internal organization of the house we will see that its orientation is exactly the inverse of that of the external space, as if it had been obtained by a semi-rotation around the front wall or the threshold taken as an axis. The wall of the weaving-loom, which one faces as soon as one crosses the threshold, and which is lit up directly by the morning sun, is the light of the inside (as woman is the lamp of the inside), that is to say, the east of the inside, symmetrical to the external east, whence it derives its borrowed light. The interior and dark side of the front wall represents the west of the house and is the place of sleep which is left behind when one goes from the door towards the *kanun*; the door corresponds symbolically to the 'door of the year', which is the beginning of the wet season and the agrarian year. Likewise, the two gable walls, the wall of the stable and the wall of the fireplace, take on two opposed meanings depending on which of their sides is being considered: to the external north corresponds the south (and the summer) of the inside, that is to say, the side of the house which is in front of one and on one's right when one goes in facing the weaving-loom; to the external south corresponds the inside north (and the winter), that is to say, the stable, which is situated behind and on the left when one goes from the door towards the fireplace. The division of the house into a dark part (the west and north sides) and a light part (the east and south sides) corresponds to the division of the year into a wet season and a dry season. In short, to each exterior side of the wall (*essur*) there corresponds a region of interior space (which the Kabyles refer to as *tharkunt*, which means, roughly, the side) which has a symmetrical and inverse sense signification in the system of internal oppositions; each of the two spaces can therefore be defined as the set of movements made to effect the same change of position, that is to say a semi-rotation, in relation to the other, the threshold acting as the axis of rotation.

It is not possible completely to understand the importance and symbolic value attached to the threshold in the system, unless one is aware that it owes its function as a magic frontier to the fact that it is the place of a logical inversion and that, as the obligatory place of passage and of meeting between the two spaces, which are defined in relation to socially qualified movements of the body and crossings from one place to another, it is logically the place where the world is reversed.

Thus, each of the universes has its own east and the two movements that are most pregnant with meaning and magical consequences, the movement from the threshold to the fireplace, which should bring plenitude and whose performance or ritual control is the responsibility of woman, and the movement from the threshold towards the exterior world which, by its inaugural value, contains all that the future holds and especially the future of agrarian work, may be carried out in accordance with the beneficent direction, that is to say from west to east. The twofold orientation in the space of the house means that it is possible both to go in and to go out starting from the right foot, both in the literal and the figurative sense, with all the magical benefit attached to this observance, without there ever being a break in the relation which unites the right to the upper part, to the light and to the good. The semi-rotation of the space around the threshold ensures then, if one may use the expression, the maximization of the magical benefit since both centripetal and centrifugal movement are performed in a space which is organized in such a way that one comes into it facing the light and one goes out of it facing the light.

The two symmetrical and inverse spaces are not interchangeable but hierarchized, the internal space being nothing but the inverted image or the mirror-reflection of the male space. It is not by chance that only the direction which the door faces is explicitly prescribed whereas the interior organization of space is never consciously perceived and is even less desired to be so organized by the inhabitants. The orientation of the house is fundamentally defined from the outside, from the point of view of men and, if one may say so, by men and for men, as the place from which men come out. The house is an empire within an empire, but one which always remains subordinate because, even though it presents all the properties and all the relations which define the archetypal world, it remains a reversed world, an inverted reflection. 'Man is the lamp of the outside and woman the lamp of the inside.'

References

GENEVOIS, H. (1955), *L'Habitation Kabyle*, Fort-National.

LAOUST, E. (1912), *Etude sur la Dialecte Berbère du Cherona*, Levoux.

LAOUST, E. (1920), *Mots et Choses Berbères*, Maisonneuve Larose.

MAUNIER, R. (1930a), 'Le culte domestique en Kabylie', in *Mélanges de sociologie Nord-Africaine*, Alcan.

MAUNIER, R. (1930b), 'Les rites de la construction en Kabylie', in *Mélanges de sociologie Nord-Africaine*, Alcan.

19 P. Gidal

Eight Hours or Three Minutes

Excerpt from P. Gidal, 'Warhol', *Films and Filming*, vol. 17, no. 7, April 1971, p. 28.

A film such as *Empirés* (eight hours) emphasis is on the nature of film reality, the gradation of shades from black to white *on film*, the nature of time's (forward-) movement past a nonentity (which the Empire State Building certainly is; so 'nothing' that it attains neutrality), and the emotive connotations thereof through the description of nothingness (a traditional art-concern, by now). When one alters one's critical apparatus sufficiently, one can begin to look at film life in a totally different way, and that openness to change affects one's (viewing of) art and life. One can argue that Warhol's 'time' is relatively short: eternity is felt in three minutes in a Warhol film. Viewing the 'same' image for eight hours heightens (through use of such an extreme) the capacity of viewing for three minutes. Also, the physical and retinal reaction to eight hours is so different from the reaction to three minutes that in that difference one learns, hypnotically, about change (one's own and that of an 'other'). One can take the idea-aspects of the early Warhol films a step further; even reading about an eight-hour film alters one's capacity to respond to the three-minute one, let alone to one of eight hours' duration. Such facts have tremendous implications in terms of one's deculturalization, awakening one from bad (film-) habits, one's useless, demented, 'sane' reactions to what is different.

Part Four
Physical Nature Assigned to Classes and Held to Them by Rules

'Over a very large area the law is indifferent to sex.' Yet when property rights are transmitted by marriage the question of a legally valid bond becomes a matter of concern. It is no new thing for the law to be drawing the line between biological and social events, choosing the moment when a foetus is enough of a person to require legal protection, deciding when a marriage has been physically consummated, deciding on the definitions of death, rape, cruelty, indecency, a standard of living above starvation. At less public and weighty levels the same assessment and drawing of boundaries proceeds through the whole social process. Physical nature is masticated and driven through the cognitive meshes to satisfy social demands for clarity which compete with logical demands for consistency.

20 Mr Justice Ormrod

Sex

Excerpt from Mr Justice Ormrod's summing-up of the case *Corbett* v.
Corbett (*otherwise Ashley*), *The Law Reports*, Part 5, May 1971, Probate Division,
pp. 105–7.

It appears to be the first occasion on which a court in England has been called upon to decide the sex of an individual and, consequently, there is no authority which is directly in point. This absence of authority is at first sight surprising, but is explained, I think, by two fairly recent events, the development of the technique of the operation for vaginoplasty and its application to the treatment of male transsexuals, and the decision of the Court of Appeal in *S. Y.* v. *S. Y.* (*orse. W.*) [1963], p. 37, in which it was held that a woman suffering from a congenital defect of the vagina was not incapable of consummating her marriage because the length of the vagina could be increased surgically so as to permit full penetration. There are passages in the judgements which seem to go so far as holding that an individual, born without a vagina at all, could be rendered capable of consummating a marriage by the construction of an entirely artificial one. But for this decision the respondent would have had no defence to the prayer for a decree of nullity on the ground of incapacity. Until this decision, all matrimonial cases arising out of developmental abnormalities of the reproductive system could be dealt with as cases of incapacity, and, therefore, it has not been necessary to call in question the true sex of the respondents, assuming that it had occurred to any pleader to raise this issue. Now that it has been raised, this case is unlikely to be the last in which the courts will be called upon to investigate and decide it. I must, therefore, approach the matter as one of principle.

The fundamental purpose of law is the regulation of the relations between persons, and between persons and the state or community. For the limited purposes of this case, legal relations can be classified into those in which the sex of the individuals concerned is either irrelevant, relevant or an essential determinant of the nature of the relationship. Over a very large area the law is indifferent to sex. It is irrelevant to most of the relationships which give rise to contractual or tortious rights and obligations, and to the greater part of the criminal law. In some contractual relationships, e.g. life assurance and pensions schemes, sex is a relevant factor in determining the rate of premium or contributions. It is relevant also to some aspects of the law regulating conditions of employment and to various state-run schemes such as national insurance, or to such fiscal matters as selective employment tax. It is not an essential determinant of the relationship in these cases because there is nothing to prevent the parties to a contract of insurance or a pension scheme from agreeing that the person concerned should be treated as a man or as a woman, as the case may be. Similarly, the authorities, if they think fit, can agree with the individual that he shall be treated as a woman for national insurance purposes, as in this case. On the other hand sex is clearly an essential determinant of the relationship called marriage because it is and always has been recognized as the union of man and woman. It is the institution on which the family is built, and in which the capacity for natural heterosexual intercourse is an essential element. It has, of course, many other characteristics, of which companionship and mutual support is an important one, but the characteristics which distinguish it from all other relationships can only be met by two persons of opposite sex. There are some other relationships such as adultery, rape and gross indecency in which, by definition, the sex of the participants is an essential determinant: see *Rayden on Divorce*, 10th edn., 1969, p. 172; *Dennis* v. *Dennis* (*Spillett cited*) [1955], p. 153; and Sexual Offences Act [1958], ss. 1, 13.

Since marriage is essentially a relationship between man and woman, the validity of the marriage in this case depends, in my judgement, upon whether the respondent is or is not a woman. I think, with respect, that this is a more precise way of formulating the question than that adopted in paragraph 2 of the petition, in which it is alleged that the respondent is a male. The greater, of course, includes the less but the distinction may not be without importance, at any rate, in some cases. The question then becomes, what is meant by the word 'woman' in the context of a marriage, for I am not concerned to determine the 'legal sex' of the respondent at large. Having regard to the essentially heterosexual character of the relationship which is called marriage, the criteria must, in my judgement, be biological, for even the most extreme degree of transsexualism in a male or the most severe hormonal imbalance which can exist in a person with male chromosomes, male gonads and male genitalia cannot reproduce a person who is naturally capable of performing the essential role of a woman in marriage. In other words, the law should adopt in the first place, the first three of the doctors' criteria, i.e. the chromosomal, gonadal and genital tests, and if all three are congruent, determine the sex for the purpose of marriage accordingly, and ignore any operative intervention. The real difficulties, of course, will occur if these three criteria are not congruent. This question does not arise in the present case and I must not anticipate, but it would seem to me to follow from what I have said that the greater weight would probably be given to the genital criteria than to the other two. This problem and, in particular, the question of the effect of surgical operations in such cases of physical inter-sex, must be left until it comes for decision. My conclusion, therefore, is that the respondent is not a woman for the purposes of marriage but is a biological male and has been so since birth. It follows that the so-called marriage of 10 September 1963 is void.

I must now return briefly to counsel for the respondent's submissions. If the law were to recognize the 'assignment' of the respondent to the female sex, the question which would have to be answered is, what was the respondent's sex immediately before the operation? If the answer is that it depends on 'assignment', then if the decision at that time was female, the respondent would be a female with male sex organs and no female ones. If the 'assignment' to the female sex is made after the operation, then the operation has changed the sex. From this it would follow that if a fifty-year-old male transsexual, married and the father of children, underwent the operation, he would then have to be regarded in law as a female and capable of 'marrying' a man. The results would be nothing if not bizarre. I have dealt, by implication, with the submission that because the respondent is treated by society for many purposes as a woman, it is illogical to refuse to treat her as a woman for the purpose of marriage. The illogicality would only arise if marriage were substantially similar in character to national insurance and other social situations, but the differences are obviously fundamental. These submissions, in effect, confuse sex with gender. Marriage is a relationship which depends on sex and not on gender.

21 R. Hertz

The Hands

Excerpts from R. Hertz, *Death and the Right Hand*, translated by Rodney Needham, Cohen & West, 1960, pp. 90–93 and 104–9. First published in 1909.

It is not that attempts have been lacking to assign an anatomical cause to right-handedness. Of all the hypotheses advanced only one seems to have stood up to factual test: that which links the preponderance of the right hand to the greater development in man of the left cerebral hemisphere, which, as we know, innervates the muscles of the opposite side. Just as the centre for articulate speech is found in this part of the brain, so the centres which govern voluntary movements are also mainly there. As Broca says, 'We are right-handed because we are left-brained.' The prerogative of the right hand would then be founded on the asymmetric structure of the nervous centres, of which the cause, whatever it may be, is evidently organic.

It is not to be doubted that a regular connection exists between the pre-dominance of the right hand and the superior development of the left part of the brain.[1] But of these two phenomena, which is the cause and which the effect? What is there to prevent us turning Broca's proposition round and saying, 'We are left-brained because we are right-handed'? It is a known fact that the exercise of an organ leads to the greater nourishment and consequent growth of that organ. The greater activity of the right hand, which involves more intensive work for the left nervous centres, has the necessary effect of favouring its development. If we abstract the effects produced by exercise and acquired habits, the physiological superiority of the left hemisphere is reduced to so little that it can at the most determine a slight preference in favour of the right side.

The difficulty that is experienced in assigning a certain and adequate organic cause to the asymmetry of the upper limbs, joined to the fact that the animals most closely related to man are ambidextrous, has led some

1. Recent investigation has led to the finding by one anatomist that: 'Although there is a functional asymmetry of the brain, in that the main speech centres tend to be situated in the left cerebral hemisphere, it is extremely doubtful whether there is any significant difference in the mass of the cerebral hemispheres. The conclusion must, therefore, be reached that cranial and cerebral asymmetry are not associated with handedness. . . .' Scott, 1955) – translator's note.

authors to disclaim any anatomical basis for the privilege of the right hand. This privilege would not then be inherent in the structure of *genus homo* but would owe its origin exclusively to conditions exterior to the organism.

This radical denial is for the less bold. Doubtless the organic cause of right-handedness is dubious and insufficient, and difficult to distinguish from influences which act on the individual from outside and shape him; but this is no reason for dogmatically denying the action of the physical factor. Moreover, in some cases where external influence and organic tendency are in conflict, it is possible to affirm that the unequal skill of the hands is connected with an anatomical cause. In spite of the forcible and sometimes cruel pressure which society exerts from their childhood on people who are left-handed, they retain all their lives an instinctive preference for the use of the left hand. If we are forced to recognize here the presence of a congenital disposition to asymmetry we must admit that, inversely, for a certain number of people, the preponderant use of the right hand results from the structure of their bodies. The most probable view may be expressed, though not very rigorously, in mathematical form: in a hundred persons there are about two who are naturally left-handed, resistant to any contrary influence; a considerably larger proportion are right-handed by heredity; while between these two extremes oscillate the mass of people, who if left to themselves would be able to use either hand equally, with (in general) a slight preference in favour of the right. There is thus no need to deny the existence of organic tendencies towards asymmetry; but apart from some exceptional cases the vague disposition to right-handedness, which seems to be spread throughout the human species, would not be enough to bring about the absolute preponderance of the right hand if this were not reinforced and fixed by influences extraneous to the organism.

But even if it were established that the right hand surpassed the left, by a gift of nature, in tactile sensibility, strength and competence, there would still remain to be explained why a humanly instituted privilege should be added to this natural superiority, why only the best-endowed hand is exercised and trained. Would not reason advise the attempt to correct by education the weakness of the less favoured? Quite on the contrary, the left hand is repressed and kept inactive, its development methodically thwarted. Dr Jacobs tells us that in the course of his tours of medical inspection in the Netherlands Indies he often observed that native children had the left arm completely bound: it was to teach them *not to use it.* We have abolished material bonds – but that is all. One of the signs which distinguish a well brought-up child is that its left hand has become incapable of any independent action.

Can it be said that any effort to develop the aptitude of the left hand is doomed to failure in advance? Experience shows the contrary. In the rare cases in which the left hand is properly exercised and trained, because of technical necessity, it is just about as useful as the right; for example, in playing the piano or violin, or in surgery. If an accident deprives a man of his right hand, the left acquires after some time the strength and skill that it lacked. The example of people who are left-handed is even more conclusive, since this time education struggles against the instinctive tendency to 'unidexterity' instead of following and strengthening it. The consequence is that left-handers are generally ambidextrous and are often noted for their skill. This result would be attained, with even greater reason, by the majority of people, who have no irresistible preference for one side or the other and whose left hand asks only to be used. The methods of bimanual education, which have been applied for some years, particularly in English and American schools, have already shown conclusive results: there is nothing against the left hand receiving an artistic and technical training similar to that which has up to now been the monopoly of the right.

So it is not because the left hand is weak and powerless that it is neglected: the contrary is true. This hand is subjected to a veritable mutilation, which is none the less marked because it affects the function and not the outer form of the organ, because it is physiological and not anatomical. The feelings of a left-hander in a backward society are analogous to those of an uncircumcised man in countries where circumcision is law. The fact is that right-handedness is not simply accepted, submitted to, like a natural necessity; it is an ideal to which everybody must conform and which society forces us to respect by positive sanctions. The child which actively uses its left hand is reprimanded, when it is not slapped on the over-bold hand: similarly the fact of being left-handed is an offence which draws on the offender a more or less explicit social reproof.

Organic asymmetry in man is at once a fact and an ideal. Anatomy accounts for the fact to the extent that it results from the structure of the organism; but however strong a determinant one may suppose it to be, it is incapable of explaining the origin of the ideal or the reason for its existence.
. . .

The hands are used only incidentally for the expression of ideas: they are primarily instruments with which man acts on the beings and things that surround him. It is in the diverse fields of human activity that we must observe the hands at work.

In worship man seeks above all to communicate with sacred powers, in order to maintain and increase them, and to draw to himself the benefits o their action. Only the right hand is fit for these beneficial relations, since it participates in the nature of the things and beings on which the rites are to act. The gods are on our right, so we turn towards the right to pray.

A holy place must be entered right foot first. Sacred offerings are presented to the gods with the right hand. It is the right hand that receives favours from heaven and which transmits them in the benediction. To bring about good effects in a ceremony, to bless or to consecrate, the Hindus and the Celts go three times round a person or an object, from left to right, like the sun, with the right side turned inwards. In this way they pour upon whatever is enclosed in the sacred circle the holy and beneficent virtue which emanates from the right side. The contrary movement and position, in similar circumstances, would be sacrilegious and unlucky.

But worship does not consist entirely in the trusting adoration of friendly gods. Man would willingly forget the sinister powers which swarm at his left, but he cannot; for they impose themselves on his attention by their murderous blows, by threats which must be eluded, and demands which must be satisfied. A considerable part of a religious cult, and not the least important part, is devoted to containing or appeasing spiteful or angry supernatural beings, to banishing and destroying bad influences. In this domain it is the left hand that prevails: it is directly concerned with all that is demoniacal. In the Maori ceremony that we described it is the left hand that sets up and then knocks down the wand of death. If greedy spirits of the souls of the dead have to be placated by the making of a gift, it is the left hand that is specified for this sinister contact. Sinners are expelled from the Church by the left door. In funerary rites and in exorcism the ceremonial circuit is made 'in the wrong direction', presenting the left side. Is it not right that the destructive powers of the left side should sometimes be turned against the malicious spirits who themselves generally use them?

Magical practices proliferate on the borders of regular liturgy. The left hand is at home here: it excels at neutralizing or annulling bad fortune, but above all in propagating death. 'When you drink with a native [on the Guinea Coast] you must watch his left hand, for the very contact of his left thumb with the drink would suffice to make it fatal.' It is said that every native conceals under his left thumb-nail a toxic substance that possesses almost 'the devastating subtlety of prussic acid'. This poison, which is evidently imaginary, symbolizes perfectly the murderous powers that lie in the left side.

It is clear that there is no question here of strength or weakness, of skill or clumsiness, but of different and incompatible functions linked to contrary natures. If the left hand is despised and humiliated in the world of the gods and of the living, it has its domain where it is mistress and from which the right hand is excluded; but this is a dark and ill-famed region. The power of the left hand is always somewhat occult and illegitimate; it inspires terror and repulsion. Its movements are suspect; we should like it to remain quiet and discreet, hidden in the folds of the garment, so that its corruptive influence will not spread. As people in mourning, whom death has enveloped, have to veil themselves, neglect their bodies, let their hair and nails grow, so it would be out of place to take too much care of the bad hand: the nails are not cut and it is washed less than the other. Thus the belief in a profound disparity between the two hands sometimes goes so far as to produce a visible bodily asymmetry. Even if it is not betrayed by its appearance, the left still remains the cursed hand. A left hand that is too gifted and agile is the sign of a nature contrary to right order, of a perverse and devilish disposition: every left-handed person is a possible sorcerer, justly to be distrusted. To the contrary, the exclusive preponderance of the right, and a repugnance for requiring anything of the left, are the marks of a soul unusually associated with the divine and immune to what is profane or impure: such are the Christian saints who in their cradle were pious to the extent of refusing the left breast of their mother. This is why social selection favours right-handers and why education is directed to paralysing the left hand while developing the right.

Life in society involves a large number of practices which, without being integrally part of religion, are closely connected with it. If it is the right hands that are joined in a marriage, if the right hand takes the oath, concludes contracts, takes possession, and lends assistance, it is because it is in man's right side that lie the powers and authority which give weight to the gestures, the force by which it exercises its hold on things. How could the left hand conclude valid acts since it is deprived of prestige and spiritual power, since it has strength only for destruction and evil? Marriage contracted with the left hand is a clandestine and irregular union from which only bastards can issue. The left is the hand of perjury, treachery, and fraud. As with jural formalities, so also the rules of etiquette derive directly from worship: the gestures with which we adore the gods serve also to express the feelings of respect and affectionate esteem that we have for one another. In greeting and in friendship we offer the best we have, our right. The king bears the emblems of his sovereignty on his right side, he places at his right those whom he judges most worthy to receive, without polluting them, the precious emanations from his right side. It is because the right and the left are really of different value and dignity that it means so much to present the one or the other to our guests, according to their position in the social hierarchy. All these usages, which today seem to be pure conventions, are explained and acquire meaning if they are related to the beliefs which gave birth to them.

Let us look more closely at the profane. Many primitive peoples, when they are in a state of impurity – during mourning, for example – may not use their hands, and in particular they may not use them for eating. They must be fed by others putting the food into their mouths, or they seize the food in their mouths like dogs, since if they touched the food with their polluted hands they would swallow their own death. In this case a sort of mystical infirmity affects both hands and for a time paralyses them. It is a prohibition of the same order that bears on the left hand, but as it is of the same nature as this hand itself the paralysis is permanent. This is why very commonly only the right hand can be actively used at meals. Among the tribes of the lower Niger it is even forbidden for women to use their left hands when cooking, evidently under pain of being accused of attempted poisoning and sorcery. The left hand, like those pariahs on whom all impure tasks are thrust, may concern itself only with disgusting duties. We are far from the sanctuary here; but the dominion of religious concepts is so powerful that it makes itself felt in the dining-room, the kitchen, and even in those places haunted by demons and which we dare not name.

It seems, however, that there is one order of activity at least which escapes mystical influences, viz. the arts and industry: the different roles of right and left in these are held to be connected entirely with physical and utilitarian causes. But such a view fails to recognize the character of techniques in antiquity: these were impregnated with religiosity and dominated by mystery. What more sacred for primitive man than war or the hunt! These entail the possession of special powers and a state of sanctity that is difficult to acquire and still more difficult to preserve. The weapon itself is a sacred thing, endowed with a power which alone makes blows directed at the enemy effective. Unhappy the warrior who profanes his spear or sword and dissipates its virtue! Is it possible to entrust something so precious to the left hand? This would be monstrous sacrilege, as much as it would be to allow a woman to enter the warriors' camp, i.e. to doom them to defeat and death. It is man's right side that is dedicated to the god of war; it is the *mana* of the right shoulder that guides the spear to its target; it is therefore only the right hand that will carry and wield the weapon. The left hand, however, is not unemployed: it provides for the needs of profane life that even an intense consecration cannot interrupt, and which the right hand, strictly dedicated to war, must ignore. In battle, without actually taking part in the action, it can parry the adversary's blows; its nature fits it for defence; it is the shield hand.

The origin of ideas about right and left has often been sought in the different roles of the two hands in battle, a difference resulting from the structure of the organism or from a sort of instinct. This hypothesis, refuted by decisive arguments, takes for the cause what is really the effect. It is none the less true that the warlike functions of the two hands have sometimes reinforced the characteristics already attributed to them and the relations of one to the other. Consider an agricultural people who prefer peaceful works to pillage and conquest, and who never have recourse to arms except in defence: the 'shield hand' will rise in popular estimation while the 'spear hand' will lose something of its prestige. This is notably the case among the Zuñi, who personify the left and right sides of the body as two gods who are brothers: the former, the elder, is reflective, wise, and of sound judgement; while the latter is impetuous, impulsive, and made for action. But however interesting this secondary development may be, which considerably modifies the characteristic features of the two sides, it must not make us forget the primary religious significance of the contrast between the right and left.

What is true of military art applies also to other techniques; but a valuable account from the Maori enables us to see directly what makes the right hand preponderant in human industry. The account concerns the initiation of a young girl into the craft of weaving, a serious affair wrapped in mystery and full of danger. The apprentice sits in the presence of the master, who is both artisan and priest, in front of two carved posts which are stuck in the ground and form a sort of rudimentary loom. In the right post lie the sacred virtues which constitute the art of weaving and which make the work effectual; the left post is profane and empty of any power. While the priest recites his incantations the apprentice bites the right post in order to absorb its essence and consecrate herself to her vocation. Naturally, only the right hand comes into contact with the sacred post, the profanation of which would be fatal to the initiate; and it is the same hand that carries the thread, which is also sacred, from left to right. As for the profane hand, it can cooperate only humbly and at a distance in the solemn work that is done. Doubtless this division of labour is relaxed in the case of rougher and more profane pursuits. But none the less it remains the case that, as a rule, techniques consist in setting in motion, by delicate manipulation, dangerous mystical forces: only the sacred and effective hand can take the risk of initiative; if the baneful hand actively intervenes it will only dry up the source of success and vitiate the work that is undertaken.

Reference

SCOTT, G. B. D. (1955), 'Cranial and cerebral asymmetry and handedness', *Man*, vol. 55, pp. 67–70.

22 F. Steiner

The Head

Excerpt from F. Steiner, *Taboo*, Cohen & West, 1956, pp. 45–6.

In Polynesian belief, the parts of the body formed a fixed hierarchy which had some analogy with the rank system of society. Although it need not be stressed in a sociological context, it cannot be accident that the human skeleton was here made to play a peculiar part in this ascetic principle of mana-taboo. Now the backbone was the most important part of the body, and the limbs that could be regarded as continuations of the backbone derived importance from it. Above the body was, of course, the head, and it was the seat of mana. When we say this, we must realize that by 'mana' are meant both the soul-aspect, the life force, and a man's ritual status.

This grading of the limbs concerned people of all ranks and both sexes. It could, for example, be so important to avoid stepping over people's heads that the very architecture was involved: the arrangements of the sleeping-room show such an adaptation in the Marquesas. The commoner's back or head is thus not without its importance in certain contexts. But the real significance of this grading seems to have been in the possibilities it provided for cumulative effects in association with the rank system. The head of a chief was the most concentrated mana-object of Polynesian society, and was hedged around with the most terrifying taboos which operated when things were to enter the head or when the head was being diminished; in other words, when the chief ate or had his hair cut. Hair-cutting involved the same behaviour as actual killing, and the hands of a person who had cut a chief's hair were for some time useless for important activities, particularly for eating. Such a person had to be fed. This often happened to chiefs' wives or to chiefs themselves, and among the Maori these feeding difficulties were more than anything else indicative of exalted position. The hands of some great chiefs were so dangerous that they could not be put close to the head.

23 Mrs Humphry

The Laugh

Excerpts from Mrs Humphry, *Manners for Women*, James Bowden, 1897, pp. 11 and 13.

Miss Florence St John told the world once in the pages of a Sunday paper how she learnt to laugh. Mr Farnie, she says, took her in hand for the laughing scene in *Madame Favart*, and made her sing a descending octave staccato with the syllables Ha, ha! The actress rehearsed it over and over again, and on the night of the production found herself perfectly *au fait*. Any one who has ever heard Miss Florence St John's pretty laugh on the stage, will admit that it was worth taking some pains to achieve. A curious thing about laughing is that when it has really a hearty sound it often re-acts upon one, and though it is but an empty echo, it suggests the sense of mirth which ought properly to have inspired it. There are many reasons why the careful culture of the laugh should be attended to. [. . .]

Laughing should, if its expression does not come by nature, be carefully taught. Nor need there be any artificiality in this, for, after a while, it becomes as natural as the correct pronunciation of words after a series of elocution lessons, and, as everybody knows, distinct enunciation does not come by nature. But who could describe it as artificial? In the same way the pretty harmonious laugh is a second nature with many. The only thing to be guarded against is that the inculcated laugh is apt to grow stereotyped, and few things are more irritating than to hear it over and over again, begin on the same note, run down the same scale, and consequently express no more mirth than the keys of the piano.

There is no greater ornament to conversation than the ripple of silvery notes that forms the perfect laugh. It makes the person who evokes it feel pleased with himself, and even invests what he has said with a charm of wit and humour which might not be otherwise observed. There is in London artistic society a lady whose beautiful voice is generally admired. She laughs on two soft contralto notes, and, limited as they are, there is no more genuine or musical expression of mirth to be heard anywhere than hers.

24 S. J. Tambiah

Classification of Animals in Thailand

Excerpt from S. J. Tambiah, 'Animals are good to think and good to prohibit', *Ethnology*, vol. 8, no. 4, October 1969, pp. 424–59.

Two major issues are raised by the Thai data, and I shall use two frames of analysis to investigate them. The first is: what is the relation between dietary prohibitions concerning animals and the animal classification scheme? More specifically, what kind of fit is there between dietary taboos relating to certain animals and their position or location in the scheme of classificatory categories? The second issue is the relation between rules concerning the eating of animals and the rules pertaining to sex and marriage.

Although the first problem is in one sense more general in that it entails the description of the animal world as seen by the actors and therefore deserves prior attention, I shall begin with the second, because, having worked through the data, I find it holds essential clues for making sense of the first. The three series I shall correlate are marriage and sex rules, house categories, and a set of animals called *sad baan* (domesticated animals or animals of the house or village) and *sad paa* (animals of the forest), which are two of the three categories into which *sad* (animals) are subdivided. *Sad paa* and *sad baan* constitute for the villagers two opposed categories within a single related series. This assertion will be substantiated later. The middle series relating to house categories is spatial in that it relates to the ordering of the different parts of the villager's house and compound. This series in fact links the concepts relating to marriage and sex with those relating to animal edibility. In content this spatial series is different from that which appeared in Leach's essay, because in the Thai case the spatial ordering of the house is a domain of conceptualization which is closely related to their conceptualization of sex and dietary rules.

The village of Baan Phraan Muan

Baan Phraan Muan means village of Muan the hunter. It is located in northeastern Thailand between Udorn town and the Mekong River, which forms the boundary between Thailand and Laos. The name of the village is deceptive as a representation of present-day life, for the people we are concerned with are peasant rice growers. Their economy is a monoculture centered on rice, and hunting as such is of marginal interest. Villagers rear domestic animals such as buffalo, pig, duck, an chicken, and they derive a good part of their day-to-day animal food from the flooded fields, canals, and perennial swamps, which are significant landmarks in a dry country which depends on insecure monsoon rains.

Villages are clustered. The settlement (*baan*) is surrounded by fields and water sources; further out are patches of fast dwindling forest. The region is dotted with villages spaced out a few kilometers from one another. Settled agriculture of the kind described tends to make a village inward-looking, but villages have had traditional social contacts with each other through a network of marriages and by participating in both Buddhist festivals and regional cults. Most marriages, however, are made within the village.

The clustered village itself is residentially broken up into fenced compounds in which dwell closely related families. Since marriage is normally uxorilocal, the typical compound tends to be composed of the household of parents (and their unmarried children) and the family of the daughter who has most recently married, plus other households of older daughters previously married. A later stage of the domestic cycle would result in two or more households related by ties of siblingship (commonly sisters, or even brothers and sisters). In 1961 Baan Phraan Muan had a population of 932 persons constituting 182 families, 149 households, and some eighty compounds.

The concept of marriage ceremony (kin daung)

The words for marriage ceremony in Phraan Muan village explicitly allude to the connection between 'eating' and 'sexual intercourse', in the frequently encountered sense of the man being 'the eater' and the woman 'the eaten'. Villagers refer to the marriage ceremony as *kin daung*, which has the following range of meanings:

1. *Kin* means to eat; *daung* is an abbreviation of *kradaung* meaning tortoise (or turtle) shell.

2. *Daung*, tortoise shell, means female sexual organ. This is a slightly vulgar usage but by no means so vulgar that villagers are inhibited from using it in company. Thus *kin daung* means 'to eat the female sex organ', i.e. to have sexual intercourse.

3. *Kin daung* also means the marriage feast (at which many guests are present). Thus the most usual meaning of the concept is the marriage ceremony including the feast which ratifies the marriage.

Orthodox marriage transactions in the village follow this sequence. Old respected elders (*phuu thaw*) representing the groom visit the bride's parents, and, if the marriage is acceptable to the latter, the marriage payment (*khaa daung*, 'the price of the female sex organ') they would receive from the groom's parents is agreed upon. The *khaa daung* is the payment to the bride's parents for the transfer of the girl and can be claimed in whole or part by the husband under specified conditions if there is separation in which the blame rests with the wife or her parents.

In the evening preceding the marriage ceremony, relatives on both sides assemble separately in the respective parental houses, and they give money gifts to the parents. The gifts are called *phau daung* ('to help hold the marriage ceremony'). The next morning elders from the bridegroom's house go to the bride's, where they meet the elders representing her parents, and, after some ritual haggling, the *khaa daung* is counted and accepted. This is followed by the bridegroom's procession to the bride's house, the holding of the *sukhwan* ceremony to call the soul essences of the couple (see Tambiah, 1968) and the paying of respects by them to each other's parents and relatives (*somma phuu thaw*), who tie their wrists with cord and give them money gifts (*ngoen sommaa*). The ritual concludes with the marriage feast.

The implications of the concept of *kin daung* are not exhausted at this verbal metaphorical level, but appear in a ritual sequence connected with one kind of disapproved marriage which I shall discuss later. One of the objects used in the rite is the tortoise shell, and some additional linguistic facts need to be set out in order fully to interpret its role.

Mary Haas (1951) presents a number of names among northeastern Thai which sound vulgar or impolite in the Bangkok dialect (Central Thai). One such is *tâw* or *tàw*, which means 'tortoise or turtle' both in Bangkok and the northeast, and in Bangkok has as one of its further meanings 'vagina'. In this sense it is a very obscene word. It is noteworthy that the northeasterners also see in the tortoise or turtle a metaphor for vagina, but use part of the animal, the shell (*daung*), for it in this context; therefore, for them *tàw* as such is not obscene.

The categorization of human beings in relation to sex and marriage

People (*khon*) are differentiated in diverse ways. We are concerned here with the ordering of persons in respect to sexual accessibility and approved marriage.

The kinship system of the villagers is bilateral. The ordering of persons in this system is along two axes – the vertical generational and the lateral 'sibling'. Kinship terminology is widely applied, and the village population is arranged into generational strata: grandparents, parents, siblings, children and grandchildren. Within these generational hierarchized layers ranges of kind are distinguished by distance, especially within one's own generation.

Incest and marriage prohibitions are combined in different permutations in village thought. While marriage across generations and also marriage which breaks the rule of 'relative age' (the rule that the husband must be older than his wife) are prohibited, especially if the partners are close kinsmen, marriage and sex regulations are usually formulated on the lateral axis differentiating categories of persons in Ego's own generation. Kinsmen in one's own generation (including affines) divide into two categories, *phii* and *naung*, older and younger sibling, and the concept *yaad phii-naung* in its widest reference means 'kinsmen'. It is thus the *phii-naung* series, subject to further differentiation into named subcategories to which attach rules of sexual conduct and marriage, that is under consideration here. It is the series that closely reflects village formulation:

1. Phii kab naung (blood brothers and sisters, siblings). Sex relations (*see*) between siblings are forbidden. If they engage in them, they must be forcibly separated. Marriage (*aw kan*, 'to take') between them is impossible. These attitudes are axiomatic and are therefore not the focus of verbal elaboration. In short, both sex and marriage are prohibited with *phii kab naung*.

2. Luug phuu phii naung (first cousins). Sex relations between first cousins are forbidden; if they engage in them, they must be forcibly separated. Marriage is forbidden. The expressions used in discussing these prohibitions are worth mentioning: *Awkan baw dai* ('cannot marry') because *bau yuen pid booran* ('impermanent and against custom', 'impermanent' here meaning that one or the other partner will die); *haam gaad sum diawkan* ('strictly forbidden, descended from common ancestor'); *bau kam bau khun bor mang bau mee* ('they will not be prosperous, not rich'); *haa kin mai saduag, chibhaai, mai ram ruay* ('insufficient livelihood, ruin [lose possessions], not wealthy'). These attitudes simply deny that stable and prosperous marriage is possible between first cousins. It is axiomatic that a marriage ceremony cannot take place (*tham pithii baw dai*), and that if two first cousins live together, and refuse to be separated, they will be disinherited and disowned. Villagers appear to observe these rules strictly. No marriage between first cousins was encountered.

3. Phii-naung (classificatory siblings, second cousins). Second cousins, though not separated from third cousins by a special term, nevertheless comprise a special category in regard to sex and marriage, a transitional ambivalent category. Sex between second cousins is not a serious matter if of temporary duration. In this village, however, since sex usually follows courtship and courtship is a prelude to marriage (in fact ideally there should be no intercourse before marriage), sex relations between second cousins carries the possibility of marriage.

There are cases of the marriage of second cousins in the village, but they are infrequent. The attitude toward such marriages is ambivalent. *Tham prapheenii haam tae aw dai khaw chaub ragkan*; 'custom forbids but they can marry if they love each other.' They can be married ceremonially in the orthodox fashion, but if second cousins break the relative age rule (i.e. the woman is an 'older sibling' of the man), they must go through a certain ritual to overcome the effects of incest. In normal usage a husband can be referred to by his wife as *phii* (older sibling) and can refer to his wife as *naung* (younger sibling). Thus a marriage that contravenes relative age distinctions creates an unacceptable linguistic asymmetry between husband and wife.

In the corrective ritual the couple are made to eat rice from a tortoise shell. The symbolism is that it is dogs that commit incest and ignore relative age distinctions, and that eating in the fashion of dogs misleads the punishing moral agents into thinking that they are not humans but animals. *Riagwaa khaw pen maa cha dai yuu diawkan yuen*, 'they are called dogs so that then they can live long together.' The ritual not only invokes the dog but physically employs the tortoise shell (*daung*). It has already been indicated that *kin daung* means a marriage ceremony, and that *daung* linguistically and metaphorically means vagina. The words and metaphor which are normally associated with acceptable marriage are now used instrumentally in an unacceptable marriage. The ritual implies that the couple are eating from (born of) the same tortoise shell (the same vagina), and in thus themselves eating together (having sexual intercourse) they are behaving like incestuous dogs.

We may note two relevant features. At the range of second cousins, rules concerning marriage become ambiguous in terms both of closeness of kinship and of relative age and can be broken with the aid of proper ritual action. Second, the ritual cited reveals explicit connections between 'eating' and 'sex', tortoise and vagina, and dog-like behaviour and forbidden sex or marriage relations.

4. *Phii-nuang*, *yaad haang*. The second term means distant relatives. Third and more remote cousins fall into this category. Marriage is recommended or approved within this range, and sex relations are possible.

5. *Khon oeuen*, 'other people', i.e. nonkinsmen. Typically they are persons of other villages in the region. It is possible to marry them and thereby convert nonkin to kinsmen.

6. Finally, we come to the unknown 'outsider' who marks the limit of sex relations and marriage. He stands at the edge of the social universe, rather than constituting a special forbidden category. Outsiders may be superior,

powerful wealthy persons or inferior, unfamiliar strangers. Witchcraft is attributed to remote villagers. This category also includes the urban world to which power and wealth and also poverty and degradation belong. There is no single term for outsiders. There are, however, such named groups as Cheg (Chinese), Kaew (Vietnamese), Khaeg (Indians), and Farang (a word which denotes white-skinned foreigners and is derived from *farangseed*, the French).

The social significance of house categories

This section deals with a series of categories pertaining to the architecture and arrangement of space in a village house and compound.

The house categories which refer to the physical arrangement of the rooms and floor space have for the villagers a direct association with the human series already described and also a relevance for the manner in which the domesticated and forest animals are conceived. The architecture of the house thus becomes a central grid to which are linked categories of the human and animal world.

All village houses, with very few exceptions, are raised from the ground on wooden stilts or pillars. Access to the house (*baan*) is by a ladder. The space on the ground under the floor is used for keeping animals and storing household goods.

The village settlement (also called *baan*) breaks up ecologically into compounds. Physically a compound means a house or a collection of two or three houses enclosed by a fence with one or two entrances. The people who live within the same fence (*juu nai wua diawkan*) comprise a compound group. The village concept for compound is *baun baan* (the place where the house is) or *baun diawkan* (shared place). A compound typically takes its name from the oldest member, who may be a female if the male head is dead (e.g. *baun baan Phau Champee*).

The description of the physical layout of the house requires a preliminary statement of certain aspects of kinship, marriage, and residence. Bilateral kinship in the village is combined with certain residence customs. While inheritance of rice land is bilateral, residence and inheritance of house and compound follow different rules. First residence after marriage is usually uxorilocal. The son-in-law and married daughter spend a few years in the latter's parental house, until they are displaced by the second daughter's marriage. Commonly, the displaced daughter and husband then build their own house in the wife's parental compound. The youngest daughter and her husband usually remain as part of the stem family, looking after the parents in their old age and inheriting their house and an extra portion of rice land. Any house where parents have adult children is thus likely to include a son-in-law and married daughter.

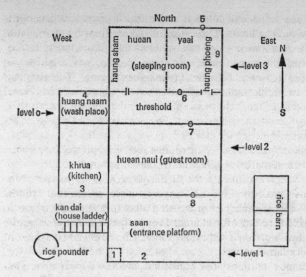

Key

1. hoan naam covered water pots for drinking
2. water pots for washing feet
3. fireplace
4. water pots
5. pillar called saaw haeg (1)
6. pillar called saaw khwan (1)
7. Pillar called saaw khwan (2)
8. pillar called saaw haeg (2)
9. shelf with Buddha statue

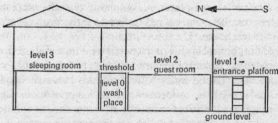

Figure 1   (a) House plan (living space on raised floor) ;
           (b) Profile of house showing levels

Figure 1a sets out the floor plan of an orthodox village house. The major features of the layout that concern us are the following. A ladder (*kan dai*) leads up to the *saan*, an unenclosed and roofless entrance platform which I call 'threshold'. From the entrance platform one enters the *huean naui* (little house) or *bawn rab khaeg* (place for receiving guests). This guest room is roofed and has walls, except on the side which gives onto the open entrance platform. The limits of the guest room are fixed by two pillars, *saaw haeg* and *saaw khwan* (*haeg* means 'first' and *khwan* refers to the 'spiritual essence' of a human being). From the guest room one enters the *huean yaai* (large house) or *baun naun* (place for sleeping). This sleeping room too has two important named pillars, *saaw khwan* and *saaw haeg* (their arrangement being the reverse of those in the guest room, so that both *saaw haeg* are at the extremities). The area between the two *saaw khwan* is the second 'threshold' in the house, separating the sleeping quarters from the guest room. The sleeping room is internally divided into *haung phoeng* (room of parents) and *haung suam* (room for son-in-law and married daughter), but this room has no actual partition, only an invisible one constituting the third 'threshold'. To the left of the guest room are the kitchen (*khrua*) and adjoining it the washing place (*haung naam*), an open platform on which are pots of water used for bathing and for cooking. It is a place for cleansing and is used by members of the household only.

Another major fact relating to the architecture of the house is that all the floors of the named divisions are on different levels (see Figure 1b). The washing place (*haung naam*) is the lowest in level (level 0). The entrance platform (*saon*) is at the next level (level 1); the kitchen is also on this level. The guest room (*huean naui*) is higher (level 2), and the sleeping room (*huean yaai*) is the highest level (level 3). These levels are not accidental but are symbolic of the various values assigned to the divisions of the house.

The directions and cardinal points indicated in Figure 1a have symbolic values. Ideally, a person entering the house would face north, and the entrance platform is at the southern end and the sleeping room at the northern end. The directions can be reversed, but never must the sleeping room be placed in the west. The kitchen and the washing place are always on the western half of the house. The four directions have the following values. East is auspicious, represents life, is sacred (the Buddha shelf of the house is always placed in the easterly direction), and is the direction of the rising sun. East is also, when one faces north, the direction of the right hand and represents the male sex. West is inauspicious and represents death, impurity, and the setting sun. It also represents the left hand and the female sex. North is auspicious and is associated with the elephant, an auspicious animal because of its size, its natural strength, and its associations with royalty and Buddhist mythology. South is of neutral value.

The sleeping room or 'large house' (*huean yaai*), the most sacred place in the house, is divided in two by an invisible partition. The *haung phoeng* (the parents' room) is always the eastern half, the *haung suam* (the room for son-in-law and married daughter) is always the western half. Thus the relation parents *vis-à-vis* son-in-law and married daughter in the house is expressed by values associated with east and west. The linguistic meaning of *phoeng* and *suam* is obscure. Villagers cannot tell what *phoeng* means (the dictionary meaning is 'lean-to'); they explain that *haung phoeng* is the parents' room. Similarly *suam* evokes no linguistic meaning except that *haung suam* is associated with son-in-law and married daughter. In the language of Central Thailand *suam* means lavatory. The villagers of Baan Phraan Muan are aware of this and are somewhat embarrassed by this connotation but explicitly deny that the association holds for them.

When the house is located in the ideal direction (*huean yaai* at the northern end), *haung phoeng* is, for a person facing it, on the right and *haung suam* on the left. We have seen that right in village formulation is auspicious and also associated with male; left is inauspicious and associated with female (in any assembly of both sexes, men ideally sit on the right and women on the left). There are always two doors leading into the *huean yaai* – one into the *haung phoeng* and the other into the *haung suam*.

The most conspicuous social feature of the division in the sleeping quarters is that a son-in-law must not enter the sleeping quarters through the doorway of the parents-in-law; furthermore, once inside the room he must never cross over into their 'room'. This taboo does not bear on children of either sex, including the married daughter. There is only one occasion on which the son-in-law ever enters through the doorway of his wife's parents. At his wedding ceremony, he is ceremonially led through that door by the ritual elders (*thaaw*) for the ritual of *sukhwan* (binding the soul essence to the body). This symbolizes that he is accepted into the house by the bride's parents and that he is legitimately allowed into the sleeping quarters as a son-in-law. There is no reciprocal taboo on parents-in-law crossing over into the *haung suam*. The taboo on the son-in-law represents an asymmetrical 'avoidance' with all its sex and incest connotations.

The sleeping arrangements inside the *haung yaai* emphasize further the precautions taken against incest and prohibited sex. Father and mother are so placed that the father sleeps at the right in the east with his wife beside him on the left. The male children sleep on the side of the father, the female on the side of the mother. When sons reach the age of adolescence they are sent out to sleep in the room outside (the *huean naui*); when daughters grow up they move to the western half of the room, the parents to the eastern half. This anticipates the arrangement when the daughters marry.

After the marriage of a daughter, the son-in-law would, in an ideally placed house, sleep in the western corner with his wife to his right, while the wife's father sleeps in the eastern corner with his wife to his left. These spatial arrangements readily convey the precautions taken against separating the junior and senior generations. Furthermore, while the father and mother keep the orthodox right–left position, the son-in-law is placed left in respect of his wife. This reversal symbolically places the son-in-law in an inferior position in the house. It should be noted that a man is strictly forbidden to have sex relations with his wife's sisters; by being put in the western end of the room he is spatially removed from them. While there is no social avoidance, he must not joke with them in any manner suggestive of sexual connotations.

Apart from the members of the household (normally parents, children and son-in-law) who sleep in the *haung yaai*, only siblings of parents (*phii kab naung*) and first cousins (*luug phuu phii naung*) are allowed to enter the *haung yaai*, though they are not permitted to sleep there. These two kin categories, as we have seen, are considered so close that sex and marriage with them are forbidden. These restrictions, which apply in everyday life, are not operative on ceremonial occasions like death, marriage, ordination, and merit-making ceremony in the house when monks are invited. On such occasions the ritual proceedings take place inside the sleeping room (*haung yaai*), and all guests can enter. Ritual occasions temporarily obliterate the restrictions of everyday life; marriage, for example, recreates and adds to the social structure of the house, whereas death disturbs and diminishes it.

The *huean naui* is the place for receiving and entertaining guests (*baun rabkhaeg*). Typically these guests are second and more distant cousins, neighbors and friends from the same village, and those from nearby villages. These categories (*phii-naung* and *yaad haang*) are eminently marriageable and sex partners. They are forbidden to enter the sleeping quarters (*huean yaai*), unless they enter into a marriage relationship with a member of the household. They are divided from the sleeping quarters by a threshold space represented by the two *khwan* pillars which stand between the two rooms.

The *haung naam* or wash place adjoining the kitchen is a platform with water jars. It is used for washing and bathing by family members only; it is considered unclean, but the dirt is 'private' and pertains to the family.

The kitchen (*khrua*) is not a particularly private or sacred space. Cooking, however, is normally a female task. Hence it is predictably placed in the west and to the left.

The *saan* or entrance platform as we have said, is another threshold, giving entry into the house proper. It is a place for washing one's feet before entering the house. Pots of water are placed on the floor (the boards of which are loosely spaced to permit water to flow through), and persons coming from the outside are normally expected to cleanse their feet. Only persons who are invited or are socially admissible can mount the ladder and step on the *saan*. *Khoen ouen* or 'other people' are normally excluded from entering the house, unless invited.

The compound fence marks the boundary of private property. Outsiders are not expected to enter the compound (*baun baan*).

We may conclude this section by noting the close correspondence between the marriage and sex rules pertaining to the human series and the house categories which say the same thing in terms of living space and spatial distance. The house and the kin categories are linked in turn to an animal series, which will now be outlined.

Animal series: sad baan and sad paa

Animals are classified into *sad baan*, animals of the house or village and *sad paa*, animals of the forest. They are listed in Table 1.

By *sad baan* the villagers mean animals that are reared or looked after (*liang*) by them. It is therefore appropriate to refer to them as domesticated animals. It should also be noted that, while domesticated and forest animals are opposed categories (which in turn are internally differentiated), there is also an overlap between them in the forest animals which villagers say are the 'counterparts of domesticated animals'.

Table 1 **Sad baan and sad paa**

Sad baan (domesticated animals)	*Sad paa (forest animals)*
	Wild counterparts of *sad baan*
Khuay (buffalo) edible with rules	*Khuay paa* (wild buffalo) edible
Ngua (ox) edible with rules	*Ngua paa* (wild ox) edible
Muu (pig) edible with rules	*Muu paa* (wild boar) edible
Maa (dog) not edible (taboo)	*Maa paa* (wolf) not edible
Maew (cat) not edible	*Chamod* (civet cat) edible (ambiguous)
Kai (chicken) edible	*Kai paa* (wild fowl) edible
Ped (duck) edible	*Ped paa* (wild duck) edible
Haan (goose) edible but rarely eaten	
	Other animals
	Kuang (deer) edible
	Faan (barking deer) edible
	Nuu paeng, nuu puk (forest rat) edible
	Kahaug (squirrel) edible
	Kadaai (hare) edible
	Ling (monkey) not edible
	Animals of the deep forest, rarely seen
	Saang (elephant) not edible
	Sya (tiger) not edible
	Sya liang (leopard) not edible
	Mii (bear) not edible

The domesticated animals (*sad baan*) *par excellence* in the village are the dog (*maa*), cat (*maew*), ox (*ngua*), buffalo (*khuay*), pig (*muu*), chicken (*kai*), and duck (*ped*). The goose (*haan*), though found in the village, is rare. The horse is not found in the village or surrounding villages as a domesticated animal, and will therefore be excluded from further discussion (like the elephant, it is associated with royalty and also appears in some episodes in the Buddha's life). Of the domesticated animals found in the house and compound, only the dog and the cat actually live together with human beings inside the house. This is consciously pointed out by villagers and sets them apart as a subcategory.

The village house, as already described, stands on pillars or stilts. The house categories – sleeping quarters, guest room, wash place, kitchen and entrance platform – pertain to the house floor above the ground. The house thus has space and ground underneath which is called *tai thun*, the subdivisions of which have no particular names but are referred to as ground under the entrance platform, sleeping room, etc. (see Figure 2). These spaces are demarcated on the ground by the pillars. The domesticated animals other than the dog and cat are housed, especially at night, underneath the house; this space is also used for storing certain kinds of property. There is a pattern in the arrangement of animals and property under the house, and the villagers have explicit ideas about it.

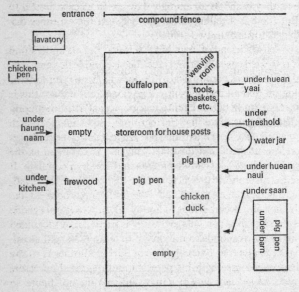

Figure 2 Space under the house (ground level)

A part of the ground under the sleeping quarters (*huean yaai*) is blocked off by posts and divided into three sections. In one is stored the weaving loom; weaving, a female activity, is done in this spot. In another section are usually stored baskets, agricultural equipment, and other miscellaneous property. The remaining and major portion of the space is used for tying up buffaloes, especially at night, and is considered the right place for them.

The pig pen is located in the space under the *huean naui*, the place for entertainment of guests. Chickens and ducks may also be housed there or elsewhere in the compound; they are never kept at night under the sleeping room.

During the day, buffaloes (and oxen) and pigs can be tied anywhere in the compound, but at night special precautions are taken. The spaces under the entrance platform (*saan*) and especially the wash place (*haung naam*) are regarded as dirty and wet, and one of the most inauspicious things that can happen to the house is for a buffalo or an ox to sleep there at night. Should the animal do so by accident, a ceremony for removing bad luck (*sia kraw*) must be conducted.

The spatial facts concerning the domesticated animals allow us to infer a gradation among them in the context of their association with the values attached to the house categories.

The dog (*maa*) and the cat (*maew*) enjoy almost human privileges in the freedom allowed them to move in and out of the house. They sleep in the house or outside as they wish. Of all animals they are in a sense closest to human beings. But there is a telling difference between the attitudes displayed by the villagers toward the two animals.

The dog is in one sense a friend of man, but it is not a 'pet' as understood by the English. It is treated casually, given great license and little care. It is, in fact, an animal that arouses paradoxical attitudes which are symptomatic of its close bearing on human relationships. The dog is not edible; this is not simply a neutral attitude but a definite taboo. Verbal attitudes represent the act of eating dog as revolting. Furthermore, this animal, though close to man, is viewed as a 'low creature' (*pen khaung tam*); it eats faeces (*khii*) and is therefore unclean and inedible. The dog is regarded as the incestuous animal *par excellence;* canine parents and children copulate. It is, as already noted, a metaphorical vehicle in the ritual by which the mystical dangers of a wrong marriage are nullified – the bride and groom eat like dogs from a turtle shell and become dogs to hoodwink supernatural agents. It seems clear that in Phraan Muan village the dog is treated as a 'degraded human'; its inedibility corresponds to notions of uncleanliness and incest. One of the strongest insults that one villager can hurl at another is to say that a dog has had intercourse with his paternal and maternal ancestors (*maa sii khood phau khood mae myng*). Other animals do not figure so effectively in insulting language.

The cat, objectively no different from the dog in its food habits or sex behavior, evokes none of the negative attitudes directed at the dog. The cat is not as frequent a village animal as the dog, and it, too, is not a 'pet' in the English sense. In fact, it is 'neutral' in its implications for man. The cat is also not eaten. Villagers say that there is no taboo on eating cat but that they do not eat it (*mai haam tae mai kin*). It is not eaten because it is useful to man; the Buddha created the cat in order that it may eat the rat, which is harmful to man because it gnaws his clothes. There is also an attitude – by no means elaborated into a theory – that the cat brings coolness to the house. Though I have not witnessed it, I am aware that a cat is used in rain-making ritual; the exposure of a cat to the sun or the washing of a cat attracts rain. It thus seems that the cat and dog, both of which live with man in the house, represent opposed values centering around a single problem. The dog is debased, unclean, tabooed as food, and incestuous; eating it is as repulsive as incest. The cat is clean, useful, and cools the house; its appearance in rain-making ritual also connotes valued fertility; not eating it appears to be associated with its positive metaphorical representation of proper and prosperous family relationships. This point is reinforced by statements made by villagers that they do not like the dog to enter the sleeping quarters (*huean yaai*). If it is seen in this room it is quickly expelled. The cat, on the other hand, is given full freedom to enter and sleep there.

The ox (*ngua*) and the buffalo (*khuay*) are not opposed animals; the same attitudes are expressed toward them. The ox, however, is rare in the village, whereas the buffalo is commonly found as a work animal. Since I am more familiar with the role of the buffalo, I shall largely confine my comments to it. Of all domestic animals, in fact, of all animals, the ox and the buffalo are differentiated most in terms of age and sex distinctions. For most domesticated animals, as well as their wild counterparts, distinctions are made between adult males, adult females, and young animals of either sex by adding to the name of the animal a second word meaning 'male', 'mother', or 'small', e.g. *maa puu*, *maa mae*, and *maa naui*, respectively, for dogs. Similar distinctions are made for the ox and the buffalo: *ngua thoeg*, bull; *ngua mae*, cow; *ngua naui*, calf; *khuay thoeg*, bull buffalo; *khuay mae*, cow buffalo; *khuay naui*, buffalo calf. However, two additional age and sex discriminations are made for the ox and buffalo alone, namely, *bag* (young adult male) for a bullock and *mae nang naui* (virgin or unmarried female) for a heifer, the very same words that are used to represent the comparable human statuses.

The ox – in the form of a cow and its calf – appears as the central character in a story of village origin that has wide circulation in the region in which Phraan Muan village is located:

This is the story of an ox called Hoo-Saparat. A rich merchant (*seethii*), who lived at the spot which is now the swamp (*bueng*) called Chuean, owned a pregnant cow. The rich man asked his servant Siang to take the cow out to graze. The cow disappeared. Siang and others tried to track it, and the place where they did this was called the village of Noon Duu (which means 'upland' and also 'to look'). The cow was not found there, and its tracks were followed until it was found at the village of Phakhoo (*pha* = meet; *khoo* = ox). The ox was then taken to graze at the village of Naam Suay ('beautiful water'). The herders stopped to eat and the cow disappeared again, because it wanted to find a place to calve. Siang then went to see a hunter called Muan to ask whether he had seen the cow. Muan was not able to help. Muan lived in the village that was called Baan Phraan Muan (village of Muan the hunter, the village described in this paper). The tracks of the cow were discovered again and followed; the cow was eventually found and its legs were securely bound at the village of Ngua Khong (*ngua* = ox; *khong* = rope to bind legs). The cow calved at this place, and Siang took the placenta to wash at the village of Naam Kun (*naam* = water/pond; *kun* = not clear/muddy). [It may be noted that the word used for placenta is *naung*, which is explicitly recognized as the same word as *naung*, meaning younger sibling. In the village the placenta is eaten and relished]. The cow and calf were taken back to the owner in Bueng Chuean.

All the villages mentioned in the story actually exist today, and the story links them in a regional complex by means of linguistic play, and by using the cow and its calf as its vehicles. The cow and calf, mother and child, are associated with the founding of human settlements, and we may well ask why in the Thai context the ox or the buffalo appropriately serve as effective vehicles for such an origin story?

The buffalo is of vital importance as a work animal in agriculture, especially for plowing rice fields. It is looked after with great care. A frequent sight is that of a buffalo pasturing, accompanied by a man (or less frequently a woman) or a young boy or girl as its protector, and I am tempted to say, its companion. By and large it is the task of young boys to graze the buffalo. They ride the animal and sleep on its back in the hot afternoons. The buffalo needs a human protector not only because it must be fed properly but particularly so that it may not stray and be stolen by strangers. It must be prevented from invading the fields during the time when paddy is growing there.

The buffalo's hardest work period is during the plowing season. Thereafter it is free of work, except to pull carts. So important is its economic role that it is the only animal that is included in religious ritual devoted to ensuring good crop yields. Before plowing starts, the village holds a ritual for its guardian spirit; the villagers ask for good health for themselves and their buffaloes and for generous yields. After harvest, there is a thanksgiving rite to the spirit for boons granted.

The close association of buffalo with human beings is also manifest in the fact that to the buffalo alone of all animals is attributed *khwan* (spiritual essence), a pre-eminently human possession (although *khwan* is also attributed to rice, the staple food). The buffalo also enters the realm of Buddhist religion; one of the taboos associated with the Buddhist sabbath (*wanphraa*) is that no plowing should be done on that day. It is said that this should be a day of rest for the buffalo as well and that it would be sinful (*baab*) to make it work. Here the buffalo is again singled out as a being toward which man must act ethically; it is in a sense assimilated to the human ethical code. However, there is no counter-assertion that the buffalo acts ethically toward man.

What is the attitude of villagers to the buffalo and the ox as a source of food? It is said that the buffalo is eminently a ceremonial food – the most appropriate food to be served at feasts. This statement is partly related to the fact that it is a big animal that can provide meat for a large number of guests, but its ceremonial appropriateness is more than this practical consideration. A buffalo or an ox is killed to provide meat for village Buddhist calendrical festivities such as Bun Kathin and Bun Phraawes (large-scale collective merit-making rites) and household and family rituals, e.g. house blessing, marriage, mortuary rites, and the ordination of a son of the household. The killing of the animal in these rites is not a sacrifice in the classical sense; it is simply the most appropriate food.

However, there are important ritual attitudes connected with the killing of buffalo and ox. Villagers claim that, in the case of a collective village ritual, no animal that belongs to the village may be killed; it must be acquired from another village. In the case of a family or household ritual, no animal reared in the house may be slaughtered; it must be acquired from another household in the village or in another village. If this norm is broken certain evil consequences will allegedly follow for the village or household: *chibhaai*, i.e. loss of animals through death and disease; *liang yaag*, i.e. difficulty in rearing animals, especially young ones; *phae luug*, i.e. infertility of animals in the sense that few calves will be born. These are the same words and concepts used by the villagers to describe the consequences of breaking marriage and sex taboos.

The attitudes toward the buffalo and ox in respect to their killing and eating thus show a correspondence to the attitudes relating to proper marriage and sex relationships among human beings. Sex relationships within the *baan* (house) are legitimate if the marriage partner comes from another *baan* and is outside the range of prohibited kin; marriage is the event that initiates this desirable state of affairs. The buffalo and the ox that belong to the house must not be killed and eaten (paralleling prohibited marriage and sex); killing and eating the buffalo and ox in an approved manner corresponds to the rules of correct exchange in marriage and sex relations. It might be said that the food taboo concerning the dog parallels negative attitudes to sex and incest, whereas the ritual attitude relating to the killing and eating of the buffalo and ox parallels positive attitudes concerning marriage and sex. The buffalo, like the dog, appears in verbal insults with sexual connotations, e.g. *ii naa hua khooi*, 'your face is like the head of my penis.' *Khooi* here sounds like *khuay* (buffalo) and is a pun. However, compared with the incest insult in which the dog appears, this insult is mild and innocuously Freudian. Can we say that the insulter is here saying that he has procreated the insulted? Beef or buffalo meat can be eaten on ordinary as well as ritual occasions. Villagers, however, rarely eat beef; their normal protein needs are provided by animals of the water (*sad naam*). Nevertheless, they can buy meat in the town or from other villagers if an animal has been killed, though this rarely occurs in the village except for ceremonial purposes. Under conditions of protein scarcity, as when there are no fish in the ponds and swamps, the villagers may kill a buffalo and share the meat or sell it in the village, but these facts do not negate the everyday ritual attitudes.

Attitudes toward the pig are similar to, but weaker than, those that the villagers show toward the buffalo and ox. Whereas the latter are housed under the sleeping room the pig is usually kept under the room for entertaining guests. Though sharing none of the quasi-human attributes of the buffalo and ox, the pig is nevertheless the focus of the same attitudes in connection with killing and eating. Pork is also a ceremonial meat, though only as a second preference. If a pig is killed for feasting the same rules apply as those concerning the buffalo and ox. Hence the same interpretation holds of the relation between marriage and sex on the one hand and killing and eating on the other. Unlike the buffalo and ox, however, the pig is reared chiefly for commercial purposes, to be sold to middlemen for slaughter. The pig does not figure in verbal abuse.

The duck and the chicken are the commonest feathered creatures. Technically they are not 'birds' (*nog*); the villagers do not invest them with the same values. The duck is, in fact, associated with negative ritual attitudes which contrast with those toward the chicken on the one hand and the buffalo on the other. Like pigs, ducks are reared to be sold in the marketplace. Like other domestic animals, they are rarely eaten as ordinary food. But unlike other edible domesticated animals, duck should not be eaten at feasts – occasions at which the eating of buffalo or ox or pig is appropriate. Villagers say that duck must not be served to assembled guests because if they eat it they will not come together again; they will lose interest in one another (*bya kan*). Duck should not be served at marriage feasts or the marrying couple is likely to separate. This prohibition is explained thus.

The duck lays eggs but it ignores them and does not bother to hatch them; it is lazy. A hen must then be made to sit on the eggs and hatch them. Thus the duck is compared to a lazy wife and mother, the hen to a responsible wife and mother, and their behavior is seen as appropriate for making metaphorical statements about human relationships. The avoidance of eating duck at marriage transmits the message that husband and wife should not separate but must be a responsible pair as spouses and parents. In situations of emergency, if duck must be served, its beak and legs are cut off and buried (in village ritual burial has the implication of neutralizing ritual danger and pollution). There is no prohibition about killing a duck that belongs to the house. No ritual prohibitions are associated with the chicken. It can be eaten as ordinary food and can be served at feasts to supplement other more desirable meat.

The dog and the cat are not sacrificial animals. The village of Phraan Muan, apart from Buddhist rites, observes a cult addressed to the village guardian spirits and also rites to appease malevolent spirits (*phii*). In the appeasement of malevolent spirits, who act capriciously, part of the offering usually consists of cooked chicken or duck. The village guardian spirits are propitiated in two contexts: (1) in collective rituals held twice a year, to request a good harvest and as thanksgiving after the harvest, at which occasions, ideally, a whole cooked chicken must be offered; (2) in individual rites of affliction, where gifts of food are offered to the guardian spirits that they may withdraw their usually righteous anger. In cases of the latter type the offerings are graduated according to the severity of the offense committed and may range from a chicken for a minor fault to a pig's head in serious instances. The buffalo is sacrificed on only one occasion – in connection with the practice of the one major regional cult – when the guardian spirit of the largest swamp in the region (Bueng Chuean) is propitiated with a buffalo sacrifice before the plowing season in order to ensure good rains. Many villages participate in this sacrifice, and they all contribute money for the purchase of the buffalo. If, in the communication of man with the supernatural, animals can be considered as acting as sacrificial intermediaries and as substitutes for the sacrificer, we can observe their gradation on a scale of increasing values: chicken and duck, pig, buffalo. This gradation corresponds to their ideal spatial location in the house compound.

Animals of the forest (*sad paa*) are opposed in village thought to domesticated animals in terms of their habitat and of man's relations to them. The latter live in the village and are cared for by man; the former live in the forest and are wild. As a class, forest animals have a greater variety of members than the domesticated category. In village classification, however, there is an important overlap between them which can serve as a starting point for the discussion of the edibility of forest animals. Villagers say that every domesticated animal has its forest counterpart: the wild buffalo, the wild ox, the wild boar, the wolf (called *maa paa*, 'forest dog'), the civet cat (called *chamod* or *maew paa*, 'forest cat'), wild fowl, and wild ducks.

The rules regarding the edibility of these forest counterparts are guided by the rules relating to the corresponding domestic animals. All are edible except the wolf, which resembles the house dog and is therefore obnoxious, and the civet cat, about which there is some ambivalence. We have noted that the house cat, though not eaten, is not rejected on the same grounds as those advanced for the degraded and incestuous dog; the civet cat is eaten by the villagers but is forbidden to pregnant women. Furthermore, the civet cat attacks domestic fowl and such attacks are considered inauspicious. When it leaves the forest and enters the village, it is an animal out of place. One major difference between the wild and domestic species, however, must be noted: all the edible forest counterparts can be hunted, killed and eaten at any time without ritual restriction. A wild buffalo or pig is consequently not the same as its domestic counterpart.

There is a range of other forest animals that are perfectly edible and can be hunted at will. Examples are the deer, barking deer, forest rat, forest squirrel, and hare. One point of interest is that the forest rat becomes edible by virtue of being a forest denizen, even though it is recognized as a kind of rat (*nuu*) which, when found in the house or in the field, is not recognized as desirable food.

There is another class of animals of the deep forest which are considered inedible. They are the elephant, tiger, leopard, lion and bear. These animals represent to the villagers the power, danger, and might of the forest as opposed to human settlement, and they are viewed with admiration and awe and fear. Villagers hardly ever encounter them in their wild state, and hence they seem almost mythical to them. Inedibility here simply refers to their existence in a world remote from the human. All except the bear are included in the list of Buddhist food taboos. However, or perhaps because of their special status, they are used as vehicles for expressing certain ideas and values. The elephant, tiger, and lion, together with mythological creatures such as the mythical sky bird (*krut* or *garuda*) and the mythical water serpent (*naag* or *nāga*), appear in astrological charts; the elephant stands for inherited size and strength (*waasaana maag*), the tiger has natural power (*amnad*), and the lion is said to hide away in the deep cavern. The elephant and the tiger are singled out for further elaboration. The elephant, when caught and domesticated, becomes a royal animal and is then an animal useful to man. 'It also helped Lord Buddha to subdue Phaya Maan' (Mara). In the astrological chart the tiger (*sya*) is opposed to the domesticated ox, representing the antithesis of forest *v.* village, of wild beast *v.* man. It is thus appropriate that *sya* (tiger) is the title given to gangsters and bandits (Wijewardene, 1968). Philanderers are also called *sya phuuying*.

The attitude of the villagers toward the monkey is intriguing and suggests that the villagers see in some of the forest dwellers an imitation of themselves. Eating monkey is forbidden in the village, and the taboo is said to derive from Buddhism. Interestingly, the monkey is not avoided as food because it is a 'friend of man' (*ling pen sieow manud*); it is 'descended from man' (*ling maa chag khon*). This inversion of the Darwinian evolutionary theory is formulated in a story:

There is a story called *Nang Sibsaung*, i.e. a woman with twelve children. This woman with so many children was too poor to support and feed them. The children therefore had to go into the forest in search of food, and they ate the wild fruits there. In the course of time hair grew on their bodies and they became monkeys.

Monkeys are thus in a sense lost and degenerate human beings; their affinity to humans makes them improper food. Yet it is whispered in the village that some people do eat them. Their animal and semi-human status is a bar to open 'cannibalism'.

Relationship between the three series (human, animal, house categories)

I have spelled out marriage and sex regulations as a scale of social distance, house categories as a scale of spatial distance with social implications, and rules that apply to the eating of domestic and forest animals as a scale of 'edibility distance'. The three series are in general, if not in a very precise manner, homologous or isomorphic. I have summarized in Table 2 the main features of the three series. Each row read horizontally states the distance gradient; each column read vertically states the pattern of metaphorical equivalence between the three series. Some of the nuances in the text cannot, of course, be included in the table, but the kind of equivalent statements that can be read from it are:

1. Incest between siblings; a son-in-law crossing over into the wife's parents' sleeping quarters; a buffalo leaving its place and wallowing in the mud of the washroom; eating dog.
2. Marriage of first cousins; persons allowed to enter the sleeping room abusing the privilege and sleeping there; slaughtering a buffalo reared in the house for a wedding feast.
3. Recommended marriage; entertaining kin in the guest room; feasting on buffalo reared by another household.

Table 2 Relationship between three series: marriage and sex rules, eating rules, and rules of etiquette concerning house categories

	Blood siblings	*First cousins (second cousins are ambiguous)*	*Classificatory siblings beyond second cousins*	*Other people*	*Outsiders*
Human series Marriage and sex rules	Incest taboo	Marriage taboo; sex not condoned	Recommended marriage (and sex)	Marriage and sex possible	No marriage
House categories Rules relating to house space	*Haung phoeng and haung suam* Sleeping rules separating parents from son-in-law and married daughter	*Huean yaai* (sleeping room) Rights of entry but not sleeping	*Huean naui* (guest room) Taboo to cross threshold into huean yaai	*Saan* (platform) Visitors wash feet if invited in	*Compound fence* Excludes outsiders
Animal series Eating rules	*Domestic animals that live inside the house* Inedible and taboo	*Domestic animals that live under the house (and have been reared there)* Cannot be eaten at ceremonials	*Domestic animals belonging to other households* Eminently edible at ceremonials	*Animals of the forest: counterparts, deer, etc.* Edible	*1. Powerful animals of the forest, 2. Monkeys* Inedible and taboo

4. Marriage with nonkin (other people); visitors entering the house and cleansing their feet on the house platform; eating edible animals of the forest.
5. Outsider; compound fence; powerful or degraded forest animals.

As long as we say that the three series imply correspondence, or that each series makes statements that have their equivalents in the other series, we are on safe ground. But the price of security is formalism. If, adopting Lévi-Strauss' terminology, we say that the three series 'constitute codes making it possible to ensure, in the form of conceptual systems, the convertibility of messages appertaining to each level', so that the realm of men's relations to each other becomes in some manner related to the seemingly different realm of man's relations with nature (animals), we are faced with the following questions: what is the relationship between the two realms and what is the logic and basis of the conversion of the message from one realm to the other? We must reserve consideration of these questions until after we have examined the classification of animals.

Animal classification, unaffiliated classes and anomalous animals

The villagers of Baan Phraan Muan have a scheme of six major categories into which they spontaneously place living creatures. The six are *khon* (people), *maeng* (insects), *nog* (birds), *sad naam* (water animals), *sad baan* (animals of the house and village, i.e. domesticated), and *sad paa* (forest animals). There are other named classes of animals which are not placed in any of these major categories; these I shall hereinafter refer to as 'unaffiliated' (or unique) classes.

Although I use the words 'living creatures', this does not represent an explicit head term in the local language, though the sense can be conveyed discursively. But there are linguistic usages which clearly distinguish human from nonhuman living beings and posit a common characteristic for all forms of the latter. An important linguistic marker is the use of classifiers with nouns, chiefly as complements and for stating numerical quantities, in the Thai-Lao language (see Haas, 1964, for the rules).

Khon means people or human beings and is also the classifier for them. This classifier is never used for any other being, whereas a single common classifier, *tua*, is used for all other living creatures (*sad*, *nog*, *maeng*, and the 'unaffiliated' types). A primary meaning of *tua* is 'body'. This shows that in one respect all nonhuman living creatures are equated in a single universe; however, *tua* as a classifier is not used solely in respect to them.[1] The

1. *Tua* is also a classifier for some inanimate objects, like tables, chairs, trousers, and coats, and it could perhaps be plausibly argued that this usage represents an extension from the primary meaning to things that have characteristics analogous to those of

English labels which I have given in parentheses for the categories of non-human living creatures which share the classifier *tua* should not be construed by the reader to be equivalents. They are given to aid the non-Thai speaker, but the reader is advised to think in terms of the Thai categories, for these show some startling discrepancies when matched with English folk usage.

Maeng (insects)

A large number of individual species (ant, bee, mosquito, butterfly, cockroach, etc.)[2] are placed in the class of *maeng*. For the villager, *maeng* by and large connotes animals that are not eaten, but I have encountered two exceptions: *tak taen* (grasshopper) is eaten, and one kind of red ant (*mod daeng*) is crushed to make a vinegary sauce.

Nog (birds)

The individual birds are described in terms of characteristics such as feathers, wings, or two legs, but from the point of view of the villagers an important semantic load carried by the word *nog* is that 'all *nog* are edible'. The habitat of *nog* varies and is not a principle that enters into the definition of the class. Linguistic usage unambiguously identifies *nog* by using it as a prefix before individual names. In the list of *nog* familiar to the villagers that I collected,[3] all were said to be edible with one exception, the owl, whose distinctive properties (e.g. that it is active and moves around at

living beings, e.g. arms and legs. However, *tua* is also a classifier for such other things as numeral digits and letters of the alphabet to which the same logic cannot be applied. The classifier for people in general is *khon*, but there are certain exceptions where differences in status or rank are involved. Thus the classifier for royal personages and monks is *ong*, and degraded noun usages for human beings, e.g., *man* (an inferior person), have the classifier *tua*, indicating clearly that such a term reduces them to animal status.

2. Examples of *maeng* are: *maeng saab* (cockroach), *maeng mum* (black spider), *maeng pueng* (honeybee), *maeng thau* or *thaan* (wasp), *maeng mot* (ant, further differentiated into red, white, and black ants), *maeng wan* (fly, housefly), *maeng haw* (louse), *maeng yung* (mosquito), *maeng ngam* (crab), *maeng phii sya* or *ka bya* (butterfly), *maeng bong kue* (millipede), and *maeng kee kep* (centipede). The grasshopper (*tak taen*), which is edible, interestingly does not take the prefix *maeng*. In general, *maeng* may be said to comprise insects and a few aquatic invertebrates, of which a good example is the crab. The crab, which is eminently edible, has another appellation, *puu naa*, which virtually removes it from the class of *maeng*, most but not all of whose members are inedible.

3. Examples of *nog* are: *nog kaew* (parrot), *nog caug* (sparrow), *nog khiilab* (pigeon), *nog yaang* (crane), *nog khaukaag* (stork), *nog khaw* (dove), *nog kiano* (flamingo), *nog huug* or *nog khaw maew* (owl). The class *nog* may be said to consist of all feathered bipeds with the exception of domesticated fowl, their wild counterparts, and those whose names have the prefix *ii*, e.g. crow (*ii kaa*) and vulture (*ii haeng*). Most but not all *nog* are edible.

night) are conveyed in its names, *nog khaw maew* (bird like a cat) and *nog huug* (bird that makes the sound '*huug*').

For someone operating with English classificatory usages, it will come as a surprise that domesticated ducks and chickens and their wild counterparts are not classed as *nog* but as *sad*. More spectacularly, the vulture (*ii haeng*) and crow (*ii kaa*) are not only not defined as *nog* but are not affiliated with any major first-order category. Their unique prefix (*ii*) sets them apart linguistically.

What place do *nog* have in the diet of the villagers? Although 'all *nog* are edible', they are not part of the common diet, since the villagers rarely engage in hunting or trapping activities. *Nog* are a delicacy but they are not served, even if available, on ceremonial occasions. Though not taboo, they are simply not an appropriate ceremonial food. Finally, there are no special rules regulating the eating of *nog*. By and large, in village dietary rules, *maeng* are inedible, and *nog* are edible, and thus in a sense they comprise two opposed, though peripheral domains, in the universe of living creatures.

Sad baan, sad naam, and sad paa

The word *sad* is rendered in dictionaries as 'sentient being', 'beast', 'animal creation' (McFarland, 1944), and as 'animal', 'beast' (Haas, 1964). The villagers are firm and clear in their use of the word. *Maeng* (insects) and *nog* (birds) are definitely not *sad*. By scrutinizing the variety of creatures which are called *sad*, one might say that they include all mammalian quadrupeds, the majority of aquatic animals, and domesticated poultry and their wild counterparts.

The three classes which bear the prefix *sad*, namely, *sad baan* (animals of the house or village), *sad naam* (animals of the water), and *sad paa* (animals of the forest), are based on three distinct ecological realities – the village settlement, water, and the forest.[4] Water is in an important sense associated with the rice fields, and the village settlement is separated from the forest by the intermediate ecological features of field, canal, and swamp. Just as

4. Central Thai vocabulary, as reported for the northeastern villages, has an elaborate set of words for describing special features of the members of the *sad* class. Haas (1964) and McFarland (1944), for example, list such usages as *sad kinnom* (mammal), *sad kinnya* (carnivore), *sad lyajkhlaan* (reptile), *sad saungthaaw* (biped) and *sad siithaaw* (quadruped). It is possible that many of these expressions are not traditional but have been devised in recent times under the influence of Western biological concepts. The subdivisions of *sad* that I list, also given in the dictionaries, are the important operative ones in the village being described as well as the major classes traditional to Thailand: *sad nam* (water animals), *sad bog* (land animals), *sad baan* (domesticated animals), and *sad paa* (forest animals). In any case, the welter of intermediate distinctions, which are largely absent for *nog* and *maeng*, indicate a focus on *sad* as the animals of greatest interest to the Thai.

the rice fields provide the villager with his staple cereal, it is water (and the fields) that provide him with his everyday protein food. There is a well-known Thai saying: 'There is fish in the water and rice in the fields.' What follows is an amplification of this statement.

In the village during the monsoon rains and for some time afterwards, when the rice is growing, the paddy fields are full of water, and, bordering the fields are a large canal and several subsidiary ditches which drain off the excess water. When the fields are transformed into a sheet of water they teem with multiple varieties of fish (*plaa*), shrimp (*kung*), crab (*puu*), and frogs (*kob*), which constitute highly appreciated food. There is another ecological feature in the region which is a perennial source of food – the permanent swamps (*bueng*) which, especially in the harsh hot dry season, a time of water scarcity, have become symbols of rain and are associated with rain-making ceremonies. In the dry season fishing in the swamp is a major seasonal activity for both men and women.

While the vast majority of water animals[5] are eaten, there are interesting exceptions. The water leech is considered inedible because it sucks human blood; the villagers used the word *khiidied* (hate) to describe their reaction to this animal. The crocodile (*khee*) is inedible because of a Buddhist taboo – largely theoretical because crocodiles are not present in the area. The most important prohibition is associated with the otter (*naag*), which is tabooed on two grounds: one linguistic and the other its resemblance to the house dog. The word *naag* ordinarily denotes the mythical water serpent which dwells in the swamps and rivers and is associated with rain; it appears in Buddhist mythology as a servant and protector of Buddhism and in rain-making ritual and mythology as an opponent of human beings. I have discussed *naag* or *nāga* symbolism elsewhere (Tambiah, 1968); it is a multivalent symbol representing rain and fertility, as well as enmity and benevolence towards man. The second objection to the otter is its resemblance to the dog (*maa*), which is strongly tabooed. From our previous discussion of the dog we can appreciate the vehement assertions of hatred (*khiidied*) which villagers direct toward this truly strange-looking creature of the water.

The tortoise (*taw*) poses problems. We have already noted that the tortoise shell (*daung*) is associated with the female sex organ, whereas the word *taw* does not carry the vulgar connotation of vagina as it does in Central Thai. The tortoise is normally edible in Phraan Muan village, but one variety is tabooed. It is called *taw phii* ('tortoise belonging to the spirit,'

5. Examples of water animals are: *plaa* (fish, subdivided into various species), *gung* (shrimp), *haui* (oyster), *kop, kiad*, and *huag* (kinds of frogs), *puu naa* (field crab), *lan* (eel), *taw* (tortoise or turtle), *kee* (crocodile), *naag* (otter), *ping* (water leech). Most *sad naam*, but the crocodile, otter, and water leech are exceptions.

i.e. the turtle associated with the guardian spirit of the swamp and also by extension with the guardian spirit of the village), or alternatively *taw san lang diaw* (tortoise with a single stripe on its shell). Tortoises with more than one stripe are edible, whereas villagers say that the *taw phii* is specially forbidden by the intermediary (*cham*) of the guardian spirit whose animal it is. As a water creature and by virtue of its association with the swamp spirit, the tortoise symbolizes water. I am unable to suggest why it is particularly associated with the swamp spirit, or whether sexual symbolism has anything to do with one of its varieties being tabooed as food.

Among water animals, the otter and the tortoise can be viewed as a related and opposed pair: the otter, which is dog-like and shares the same name as the mythical and sacred water serpent and perhaps represents its negative features, and the sacred tortoise, which represents perennial water (and perhaps also female sexuality) and is associated with the guardian spirit of the swamp.

The other two categories with the *sad* prefix – *sad baan* (domesticated animals) and *sad paa* (animals of the forest) – have already been discussed in detail. The status of these three classes *vis-à-vis* the major classes *maeng* and *nog* presents an analytical problem from the point of view of formal classification theory which apparently is not unique to the Thai situation (as pointed out to me by Brent Berlin in a personal communication).

From a formal standpoint, we might suppose that the villagers first divide nonhuman beings (distinguished by the classifier *tua*) into three major classes – *sad*, *maeng*, *nog* – and then subdivide *sad* into two categories, *sad bog* (land animals) and *sad naam* (water animals) and the former of these again into two subclasses, *sad baan* and *sad paa*. But the perceptual field of the villagers is somewhat different. Although at a certain level *sad* as a generic term may be contrasted with *khon* (roughly 'beasts' versus 'men'), yet from their own spontaneous statements it is clear that for them *sad baan*, *sad naam*, and *sad paa* are basic major classes of the same order as *maeng* and *nog*. It would appear that the various classes of *sad* are of major interest to them (far more than other kinds) and that, whatever the formal logical operations and the place of classes in the scheme for the classification theorist, the actors assign different weights to divisions of the natural world on the basis of relative interests, so that their own perceptual field collapses certain parts of this scheme and magnifies or upgrades the place of certain logically lower order categories to the status of others of a logically higher order. For these reasons I shall hereinafter refer to *maeng*, *nog*, *sad baan*, *sad naam*, and *sad paa* as 'major classes', although a formal elucidation of the scheme may state things slightly differently.

The formal scheme based on the explicit and implicit ideas of the actors (but subject to the limitations discussed) is represented in Figure 3 and can

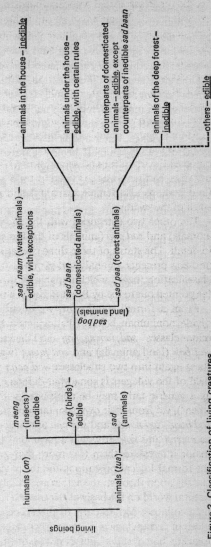

Figure 3 Classification of living creatures

be elucidated as follows. All living creatures divide into two basic categories: human beings (*khon*) and nonhuman beings (characterized by the classifier *tua*). The world of nonhuman living creatures is first divided into three major categories: *sad*, *nog*, and *maeng*. *Maeng* are largely inedible, *nog* are largely edible; they are differentiated off at this level of classification.

At the next level of differentiation, although a contrast between land animals (*sad bog*) and water animals (*sad naam*) may be invoked in certain situations, it is more often perceptually and verbally overriden by another formulation. All *sad* are divided, on the basis of three ecological locations (house and village, water and fields, forest), into *sad baan*, *sad naam*, and *sad paa*, the water animals being separated off and declared edible with some important exceptions. Although water animals are further subdivided (into kinds of fish, frogs, etc.) they are not grouped into higher-level kinds attributed to domestic and forest animals.

Domesticated animals divide implicitly into those that live in the house together with humans (inedible) as opposed to those that are reared apart from them under the house (edible with special rules). Forest animals divide into those that are counterparts of domestic animals (edible without rules except for counterparts of inedible domestic animals) and animals of the deep forest credited with extraordinary properties (inedible). There is a residue of animals like deer and forest rat which are all edible.

One problematic fact emerging from this classification is that the *sad* categories are not constructed around a single dimension of edibility as is largely true of *maeng* (insects) and *nog* (birds). This is especially so of domesticated and forest animals, from our discussion of which we have drawn the conclusion that edibility rules concerning domestic and forest animals cannot be meaningfully considered apart from their relation to other social facts, such as concepts of social distance, marriage rules, and house categories, i.e. to other systems of human classification.

But does the concordance between the three series established earlier help us to understand the logic of the dietary rules which apply to creatures which are neither domesticated animals (*sad baan*) nor forest animals (*sad paa*)? I think that it does, but must first set out the problem.

Unaffiliated classes and anomalous animals

I have used the term 'unaffiliated classes' for the types of animals that the Thai villagers do not include in what they conceive to be the major categories of *maeng*, *nog*, and the threefold division of *sad*. Table 3 presents some examples, together with their position as regards edibility.

These unaffiliated classes are problematic in two ways. From a formal point of view the snake (*nguu*), vulture (*ii haeng*), rat (*nuu* . . .), etc. are classificatory categories of the same order as *nog*, *maeng*, etc., but clearly

Table 3 **The edibility of unaffiliated classes of animals**

Giant lizard (*khapkae*)	medicinal food for children
Lizard (*khiikiam*)	not eaten, but no aversion to it; too small to constitute food
House rat (*nuu sing*)	'only small children eat'; possibly eaten by adults but not admitted
Chameleon (*chiikapom*)	medicinal food
Field rat (*nuu thaung khaau*)	'only small children eat'; adults eat privately
Monitor lizard (*laeng*)	edible, but dangerous to mothers after childbirth
Water monitor (*hia*)	inedible (aversion)
Snake (*nguu*)	inedible (aversion)
Toad (*khan khaag*)	inedible (aversion)
Vulture (*ii haeng*)	inedible (aversion)
Crow (*ii kaa*)	inedible (aversion)

the villagers do not see them as of the same magnitude as the major classes. These animals are also problematic in respect to their edibility, as indicated in Table 2. A second type of dietary problem is posed by the animals, like the owl and the otter, that are inedible members of a largely edible class. For my purposes I propose to call both types anomalous, the first being a kind of classificatory anomaly in that it is neither placed in a major class nor given an equivalent major status, the second being anomalous within its class. I shall try to demonstrate that the problems they pose can be discussed in terms of a single theoretical framework. To account for the observed facts, I shall put forward a theory in the form of a series of related propositions. The theory relates classification or conceptual order, dietary attitudes, and omens or inauspicious signs in one scheme of ideas which represents an adaptation and extension of ideas propounded by Leach and Douglas.

Proposition 1: an animal that is not placed in an ordered system of major classes receives further signification as ambiguous food. To find out the exact dietary signification given to it we must investigate to what named major class it is penumbral and what dietary value is given to that class. Creatures like the giant house lizard (*khapkae*, *tukae* in Central Thai), the house lizard (*khiikiam*, *chingchaug* in Central Thai), and the house rat (*nuu sing*) are not placed in any major class. Villagers say that these animals are found in the house, and therefore resemble *sad baan* (domestic animals), but that they are not reared by people, so they are not *sad baan*. Thus they are penumbral to *sad baan*, with which they share one property (location) but not the other (human care). Moreover, they live inside the house like the dog and cat, and these animals are tabooed as food. What is the status of these creatures as food? The house rat, though it is sometimes eaten, is not relished, nor do villagers like to admit to eating it. They state that young children, being what they are, are allowed a laxity that is not respectable in adults. It is interesting that throughout Thailand children are addressed as *nuu*. The giant lizard is likewise not ordinary food but is considered a medicinal food for children. The small lizard is definitely not eaten. There appears to be an analogy between creatures that are small and marginal to the house and unsocialized children. On the whole, our proposition holds in regard to these creatures which live in the house but are not of the house.

Much the same attitudes concerning edibility are exhibited toward the chameleon (*chiikapom*) and the field rat (*nuu thaung khaau*). These animals live on land (*sad bog*) and are found in the compound, in the village, and in the fields, but they are also not domesticated animals. The chameleon is said to be eaten only for medicinal purposes. While villagers are known to eat the field rat, they publicly say that it is the young children (*deg num num*) who eat it. The idiosyncratic status of these animals again corresponds to their ambiguity as food objects.

We now come to a set of animals which the villagers say are unplaced in the major classes because they share charactcristics of two ecological categories, water (*naam*) and land (*bok*). The monitor lizard (*laeng, takuad* in Central Thai) and the water monitor (*hia*) are remarkable examples of such anomalous animals. The *laeng*, a land animal, is normally regarded as edible, but is sometimes forbidden to postparturient mothers because it is considered poisonous and may cause illness or dry up the mother's milk. It is found in the peripheries of the village, in the forest. The *hia* is regarded as physically uglier than the *laeng* and is considered altogether inedible; it is, moreover, the focus of intense emotional attitudes of hatred. Both the *laeng* and the *hia* pose classificatory problems to the villagers. When asked why they do not assign them to a major category, they reply that, while the land and water monitors are physically similar, one lives in the water and the other on land. Moreover, the tabooed and hated *hia* moves on land as well as in the water and thus straddles both ecological habitats. In Central Thai, *sad khrueng naam khrueng bog* – 'animals partly water partly land' – expresses their anamolous properties. This expression, though known in Northeast Thailand, is not used there.

Proposition 1 to some extent accounts for their ambiguous status as food, but the *hia* (water monitor) is the focus of attitudes which require a further proposition to account for them. The *hia* is both inedible and hated. To call a person *hia* is one of the worst insults possible, though perhaps not as extreme as calling him or her a dog (*maa*). Finally, the *hia* is an animal of bad omen: its appearance in the village and entry into the compound is a highly inauspicious event, which in some instances may require a ceremony to dispel bad luck, It is an animal 'out of place' (see Proposition 2 below).

Snakes, distinguished by the class name *nguu*, parallel the case of the monitor lizard. When asked why they do not belong to a major category, the villagers answered that there are both land snakes and water snakes. Snakes are considered entirely inedible, however, and this cannot be fully explained by our proposition. The villagers regard snakes as enemies, as poisonous and injurious to man, which is objectively true for a number of them.

Proposition 1 does not account for the special attitudes of the villagers toward such unaffiliated animals as the toad, water monitor, vulture, and crow. It must be supplemented with a second idea, which I derive from Douglas's statement that 'dirt is matter out of place' but apply in a new manner in the form of a second proposition.

Proposition 2: an unaffiliated animal, if it is seen as capable of leaving its location or habitat and invading a location or habitat of primary value to man, will be the focus of strong attitudes expressed in the forms of (1) a food taboo and (2) a bad omen or inauspicious sign. In the case of our villagers, the habitat of primary value is their village settlement and home (*baan*).

Like the water monitor, the toad (*khan khaag*) has no place in the major classes and arouses positive attitudes of hatred among the villagers, who consider it ugly. (Linguistically, hatred and ugliness are coupled, the words being *sang* and *naa sang;* an alternative word for hatred is *kiidied*.) The villagers resist linking the toad with the edible frog, and point out that it is a land animal. Their 'aversion' for the toad is linked to the fact that one of the most inauspicious things that can happen to a house and its members is the entry of a toad into the house. If this happens, a special ceremony must be held to get rid of the bad luck (*sia kraw*). A toad that steps over the threshold is thus an animal out of place and a bad omen. It is the supreme symbol of the unwanted and unclean outsider entering the house. The appearance of a snake in the house is similarly interpreted.

The vulture (*ii haeng*) and the crow (*ii kaa*) are not considered *nog* (birds) – one of the surprises of the classification scheme to an outside observer – and they are both inedible. Their names carry the prefix *ii*, which has implications of abuse, insult, and lower social status.[6] On the vulture are focused

6. Mary Haas (1964) elucidates the following usages of the prefix *ii* (presumably in Central Thailand): (a) it is a bound element in names of birds and animals, e.g. crow, barking deer, vulture, palm civet, oyster, and swallow; (b) it is a derogatory title used with the first names of women; formerly used for female slaves, it is now applied as an insult to women criminals and prostitutes (as an exclamation, *ii* expresses dislike, repulsion, and aversion); (c) it is also apparently a colloquial term freely used in reference to objects and persons regardless of sex and without special connotation.

The use of the prefixes *aj* and *ii* in North Thailand is the subject of an interesting analysis by Wijewardene (1968). Some of the points he makes have relevance for my

attitudes very similar to those relating to the toad. It arouses aversion, and if a vulture alights on the roof it is an inauspicious invader of the house, and a *sia kraw* ceremony must be held forthwith. Vultures, which are common in Northeastern Thailand, behave quite differently from *nog*. They fly very high, soar in the sky, and swoop down to eat carrion, dead cattle, and dogs. In alighting on the roof of a house they are very conspicuously out of place.

The crow is not edible, but it does not evoke 'aversion'. It is a scavenger and an unwanted but everyday intruder and therefore too common to attract ritual attitudes centering around bad luck. The vulture and the crow are not only unaffiliated to *nog* but are also inedible. The former brings bad luck by virtue of its rare but unwelcome invasion of the village and house. The latter, though not rare, is simply not food and not *nog*.

The same kind of logic works with animals which are affiliated with a major class but which can at times be out of place and thus viewed as signals or omens of misfortune. The ominous significance of the buffalo which leaves its appointed place in the house at night to wallow in the mud of the wash place has already been noted. This event requires a rite to dispel bad luck. Another inauspicious sign – though not one which requires a ritual – is the crossing of a civet cat from its forest habitat into the village. A modification of the two propositions already stated will allow us to express the attitude toward animals which, although firmly placed in the major classificatory classes, are yet anomalous within their class.

Proposition 3: an animal that is placed in a class because it shares certain dominant properties of that class may yet be seen as exceptional or anomalous

theme. *Ii* is used as a prefix for a number of animals which are intermediate between (foolish) domestic and (wise) remote wild forest animals, e.g., the monkey, gibbon, squirrel, iguana, and civet cat. *Ai* and *ii* are legitimate terms of address for younger relatives (male and female respectively) and younger members of Ego's circle of familiar social relations. The terms are insulting if used outside this field, for they imply lower social status. One of the puzzles probed by Wijewardene is why parents are addressed as *ii-pau* and *ii-mae*. Finally, the prefixes *ai* and *ii* appear as strong terms of abuse in conjunction with dog and monkey (*ai-*(*ii*) *maa, ai-*(*ii*) *wauk*).

It is perhaps premature to generalize for Thailand as a whole because there appear to be regional and local variations in linguistic usage. In the Northeastern village of my acquaintance the prefix *ii* was used, as far as I know, only in conjunction with the vulture and crow. It appears to be used more widely for animals in Northern Thailand, but it is interesting that the majority of animals listed by Wijewardene and Haas are also 'intermediate' or 'anomalous' animals in the Northeast. It is in Central Thailand that the prefix has the widest range of application, which apparently includes a number of birds. It is not a distortion to say that there, too, the prefix, when used in relation to human beings, implies abuse, insult, lower social status, and also understandably familiarity between equals. It is possible that the logic by which the prefix is used for some animals and birds may be similar to the one I have expounded.

and therefore ambiguous as food or inedible (even if other members of its class are edible) if it shares one or more characteristics with animals of another class which carries strong values and is considered inedible. In the Thai case, the strong values in question relate to domestic animals of the inedible class – the dog and cat. The proposition applies to the animals of the forest (*sad paa*) which are viewed as counterparts of the domestic dog and cat, namely, the wolf and the civet cat. It also applies to the hated otter, which, though clearly an animal of the water, so obviously resembles the dog. The owl, too, though in one sense clearly *nog*, is yet one of the exceptional inedible *nog* because it is a night bird and is recognized as resembling the domestic cat, which also sees at night. It is, in fact, called 'cat bird'. The owl is inauspicious because it is thought to steal the *khwan* (spirit essence) of the inmates of the house which it approaches; more intriguingly, it is viewed as the representation of the *khwan* of an inmate of the house who is wandering outside at night.

Proposition 4: an animal that belongs to a class that is edible and positively valued, if it also shares one or more characteristics with a member of another positively valued and edible class, qualifies as an auspicious and eminently edible animal. This permutation of the previous proposition, though it has no manifestation in Phraan Muan village, deserves to be stated to make the scheme complete. Such an animal may even be considered unique and a multi-faceted symbol, as in the celebrated case of the pangolin among the Lele (Douglas, 1957). Perhaps positive mediators are compounded of such stuff. Unique classes or creatures of a different sort, on the other hand, may perhaps be generated from a cluster of characteristics which combine the positive features of an edible class and the negative features of an ambiguous or inedible class, thereby becoming the foci of restrictive rules of eating surrounded by ritual precautions. The Karam cassowary (Bulmer, 1967) is an apt illustration.

Our discussion indicates that Douglas's theory of classificatory anomalies and their relationship to dietary rules is inadequate as it stands. Propositions 2 and 3 are needed as additional principles to explain the Thai facts. A further lesson we can draw is that simple intellectual deductions from a society's formalized scheme of animal categories will not take us far unless we can first unravel the core principles according to which people order their world and the valuations they give to the categories (see also Bulmer, 1967). In the present analysis the core principles lie in the domain of primary social interests and values connected with the ordering of kin, incest and marriage, and conceptions of social distance. This is why an exposition of the nexus between the three series (human sex and marriage discriminations, spatial categories of the house and compound, and the internal differentiation of domesticated and forest animals) was found critical for unraveling problems posed by the formal system of ordered categories (classification). It also has implications for the more general problems we posed at the beginning: man's relationship to the animal world and the role of dietary regulations in the ordering of social relations.

Conclusion

The Thai village I have described is not a totemic society. Therefore the totemic controversy in the strict sense does not apply to it. But in so far as this controversy has also focused on dietary rules relating to animals and ritual or religious attitudes toward animals, I must relate my ethnography and its implications to the larger theme. Hence, in these concluding comments, Lévi-Strauss comes back on stage.

By and large this essay has affirmed the Lévi-Straussian approach in that the attitudes toward animals as expressed in dietary rules do not make total sense in terms of Radcliffe-Brown's narrow notion of social or utilitarian value, but that they represent a systematic mode of thought that corresponds to other systematized conceptual systems in the society. But the question is: Is it enough to show correspondence or homologies between relational sets, or resemblances between systems of differences, and go no further?

If, as Lévi-Strauss accepts, there is a general connection of a metaphorical nature between sex and marriage rules and eating prohibitions, and if both are sets of ethical rules, we need to investigate why human beings find it apt to make this particular connection, why the killing and eating of an animal is a focus for representing sex relations? Lévi-Strauss has appreciated that totemism is more than a system of signs in that dietary rules relating to totemic animals have ethical and normative behavioral implications. He has, in fact, raised and tried to answer the question: if totemic representations amount to a code, why are they accompanied by rules of conduct?

His answer is disappointing because he either by-passes the question or resorts to the argument of the lowest common denominator. He counters the problem that totemic media of representation are frequently associated with eating prohibitions on the one hand, and with rules of exogamy on the other, by arguing that these are not necessary relations for any one of them can be found without the others, and any two of them without the third. He argues that dietary prohibitions are not intrinsic to totemism since food prohibitions either do not always coexist with totemic classifications or are found in the absence of totemism. Therefore they are either extra- or para-totemic (Lévi-Strauss, 1966) or logically subordinate (Lévi-Strauss, 1966). Moreover, 'Eating prohibitions and obligations . . . seem to be theoretically equivalent means of "denoting significance" in a logical system some or all of whose elements are edible species' (Lévi-Strauss, 1966). Finally, the most radical conclusion is that the rationale why some species are permitted and others forbidden lies in the concern to introduce a distinction between 'stressed' and 'unstressed' species. Prohibiting some species is merely one of several ways of singling them out as significant, but the logic can work in terms of practical rules of behavior or in terms of images. The two modes are analogous and of equal weight. In fact, taboos regarding death names, sex rules, and dietary prohibitions are all analogous modes for stressing significance. They can be redundant, supplementary, or complementary. An impoverishment of semantic content in the interest of form is thus accomplished.

Lévi-Strauss is evasive and even begs the question, for it is precisely the nature of the 'significance' denoted that is never established. It could be said that his treatment of totemism is concerned with a single polemic – the demolition of those anthropologists who have seen dietary prohibitions as an intrinsic element and as symbolizing man's sense of identity, affinity, or participation with animals. The classic question of Radcliffe-Brown (1922, 1952) as to why man should have a ritual attitude toward animals still remains as a haunting problem.

The inability of Lévi-Strauss to deliver the complete answer is, one suspects, linked to the position he has taken in regard to the question of the relation of man to animal. In *Totemism* (1962), when discussing man's 'triple passage (which is really one) from animality to humanity, from nature to culture, and from affectivity to intellectuality', he says: 'It is because man originally felt himself identical to all those like him (among which, as Rousseau explicitly says, we must include animals) that he came to acquire the capacity to distinguish *himself* as he distinguishes *them*, i.e. to use the diversity of species as conceptual support for social differentiation.' While no doubt justifiably criticizing those anthropologists who have conceived the relation between man and animal to be of only a single kind – identity, affinity or participation – Lévi-Strauss places this sense of identity of man with animal sometime in the historic past when man for all time made his passage from nature to culture. Thus he phrases the process in sequential terms: 'The total apprehension of men and animals as sentient beings, in which identification consists, both governs and *precedes* the consciousness of oppositions between, firstly, logical properties conceived as integral parts of the field, and then, within the field itself, between "human" and "non-human"' (Lévi-Strauss, 1962). It is because man is seen as once and for all having made the passage from affinity with the animal to separation from it, which state is equated with the primacy of the intellect, that Lévi-Strauss can see in nutritional prohibitions a refusal by men 'to attribute a real animal nature to their humanity'. Thus these prohibitions are interpreted as symbolic characteristics by which humans distinguish different animals which then provide a natural model of differentiation for human beings to create differences among themselves.

While *Totemism* and the earlier chapters of *The Savage Mind* are addressed to the devaluation of man's sense of identity with animals as expressed in dietary rules, it is intriguing and gratifying that Lévi-Strauss (1966) adopts a quite different conception of man's relation to animals when he discusses French conventions regarding the naming of animals. Happily for him, dietary prohibitions do not enter into this issue.

This scintillating analysis of the logic of French naming of birds, dogs, cattle, and racehorses is conducted with the aid of two concepts, metaphorical and metonymical relations based on principles of contiguity and resemblance. I have myself (Tambiah, 1968), taking a hint from Jakobson, used the concepts metaphor and metonym in a slightly different manner to decode the logic of Trobriand magic. This magical system postulates metaphorical or symbolic similarities (usually verbally in the spells) and simultaneously uses material parts of the symbol metonymically and realistically in the rite to achieve a transfer both in thought and deed. I shall use these concepts once again to sum up the Thai situation.

The Frenchman's relation to animals is discussed by Lévi-Strauss in the following terms. Birds are separated from human society, yet they form a community that is homologous to or resembles human society. The world of birds is thus a metaphorical human society, and the procedure for naming them is metonymical in that human Christian names are given them. The relation of bird names to human names is that of part to whole. Birds are metaphorical human beings.

The dog is the exact reverse. Dogs do not constitute an independent society but are, as domestic animals, a part of human society, although they are accorded a low position in it. The relation of dogs to human society is metonymical, and they are given metaphorical stage names drawn from the paradigmatic chain of language since it would cause uneasiness or mild offense to give them human names. Dogs are metonymical human beings.

The social position of cattle is metonymical since they form part of the technical and economic system of man, but different from that of dogs in that they are treated as objects. Cattle are thus metonymical inhuman beings and are given descriptive names from the syntagmatic chain of speech (metonymical).

Racehorses are metaphorical inhuman beings. They are products of human industry but lead the desocialized existence of a private society. They are disjoined from human society and lack intrinsic sociability. Their names are vigorously individualized and are metaphorical, drawn from the syntagmatic chain of speech and transformed into discrete units.

We note that, in this analysis, Lévi-Strauss is dealing with the complex relation between the Frenchman and the animal world, which involves principles of contiguity and similarity (negative and positive), of symbolic relations as well as participation (why else is dog meat tabooed?), and of exchange of similarities and differences between culture and nature.

I submit that the Thai villagers' relation to the animal world shows a similar complexity which expresses neither a sense of affinity with animals alone nor a clear-cut distinction and separation from them, but rather a coexistence of both attitudes in varying intensities which create a perpetual tension. And I submit that dietary regulations are intrinsic to this relationship. They provide a clue to the ritual attitude toward animals, to linking eating rules with sex rules, to man on the one hand drawing nature into a single moral universe and also at the same time vigorously separating nature from culture.

A backward glance at the ethnography reported will illustrate. If we look at the first-order classificatory categories we see first that *maeng* (insects) and *nog* (birds) are separated off into inedible and edible categories; they are at the same time declared distant to man. The next process of elimination is applied to creatures of the water (*sad naam*), which by and large constitute the everyday animal diet, with some conspicuous exceptions whose logic of exclusion lies in the next level of differentiation.

It is in respect to the universe of land animals – domestic and wild – that the Thai villager thinks and feels in a complex fashion; it is in respect to them that attitudes of affinity and separation, opposition and integration fuse to produce the complex correspondence of sex rules, house categories, and animal distinctions.

The dog, by virtue of the fact that it lives in the house and has a close association with man, has a metonymical relation to human society. The taboo on eating dog has a metonymizing role; it cannot be physically eaten and incorporated because it is in a sense incorporated into human society. But at the same time the dog is considered degraded and incestuous and thus stands for the antithesis of correct human conduct. This degradation to a subhuman status is used by the villager to perform a metaphorical transfer on the basis of an analogy. Man imposes on the behavior of the dog the concept of incestuous behavior, thereby attributing a human significance to the sexual behavior of dogs. This then allows man to copy the behavior of dogs metaphorically, e.g. eating food from a tortoise shell, in order to correct the moral consequences of his own improper incestuous marriage.

The ox and the buffalo have a metonymical relation to man that is, unlike the relation to the dog, highly valued in a positive sense. The metonymizing behavioral acts that express this relation are that humans must act ethically towards them (e.g. not working them on the Buddhist sabbath), and that concepts of human statuses are applied to them. These metonymizing acts are man-made and are possible because there can be no real confusion of man and animal. The ox and buffalo are not 'human'; they do not reciprocate in a human idiom. They are edible with rules.

The ox and the buffalo have a metaphorical significance for man, different from that of the dog, by virtue of their positive valuation. There is almost a precise reversal in the ritual idiom. An impure act of an ox or buffalo, e.g. straying into the dirt of the wash place at night, has by a direct metaphorical transference a bad consequence for humans (e.g. bad omen that has to be dispelled by ritual). It corresponds to improper sexual relations on the part of the inmates of the house. Again the taboo on eating the meat of the ox or buffalo of the house at a marriage feast is a metaphorical statement of proper marriage, which conjoins eating with sex and marriage regulations.

The domestic pig partakes, in a somewhat weaker fashion, of the attitudes towards the ox and buffalo. The duck has only a marginally metonymical relation to man. The avoidance of eating duck at a marriage feast is a metonymizing act which expresses a metaphorical significance of a negative kind (e.g. the human wife should not behave like the unmotherly duck).

The wild animals of the forest have a different significance for the Thai villager. The elephant and the tiger have no physical relationship with man (nonmetonymical), but their attributes have strong metaphorical significance for him. They provide the imagery for the uncommon man, royalty and bandits, the social and anti-social heroes. That they are considered inedible is a statement of their extreme distance and difference from man.

The anomalous animals derive their significance either as recognizable imitations of domestic animals (or even man himself) or as inauspicious intruders into the ordered life of home and village. The otter resembles the dog physically, but has no metonymical relation to man. Hence it is doubly hated and rejected as food. It is anomalous within the class of water animals which is eaten by man.

The vulture, the toad, and the snake do not belong to any major class. They are unplaced at this level of classification. But they are prone to leave their normal habitat and intrude into the habitat of man. In doing so, they are seen as performing metonymizing acts that establish unwanted contact with man, thereby bringing bad luck and misfortune. They are negatively valued sacred things that threaten to be out of place and to attack the established order of the universe. In a less dramatic way the civet cat presents the same threat, and the crow represents an unwanted association with man that has to be lived with.

The monkey as a creature of the forest has little contact with man (non-metonymical). But it is seen as bearing a metaphorical resemblance to man and portraying his descent into savagery. The taboo on eating it represents this physical and social rejection.

Thus, in sum, animals are effective vehicles for embodying highly emotionally charged ideas in respect to which intellectuality and affectivity cannot be rigidly separated as representing human and animal modes of conduct. If we are to answer adequately the question why man has a ritual attitude to animals, why values and concepts relating to social relations are underpinned to rules about eating animals, we have to inquire for the society in question why the animals chosen are so appropriate in that context to objectify human sentiments and ideas. Lévi-Strauss has nobly defended the primitive as capable of contemplating nature independently of the rumblings of the stomach and of using natural models of differentiation to express social relations; he has at the same time substituted for crude utilitarian needs the nebulous concept of 'interest' as dictating that contemplation. In the event, this interest turns out to be man's need to express and order social relations, to forge a system of moral conduct, and to resolve the problem of man in nature.

Between Lévi-Strauss' message and sign-oriented intellectualism, represented in the statement that natural species are chosen not because they are good to eat but because they are good to think, and the actor-oriented moralism of Fortes, (1967), represented in the statement that animals are good to prohibit because they are good to eat, lies scope for an imaginative reconstitution and reconciliation of the structural properties of symbolic systems *qua* systems and the effectiveness of symbols to bind individuals and groups to moral rules of conduct. Cultures and social systems are, after all, not only thought but also lived.

References

BULMER, R. (1967), 'Why is the cassowary not a bird? A problem of zoological taxonomy among the Karam of the New Guinea Highlands', *Man*, n.s., vol. 2, no. 1, pp. 5–25.

DOUGLAS, M. (1957), 'Animals in Lele religious symbolism', *Africa*, no. 27, pp. 46–57.

DOUGLAS, M. (1966), *Purity and Danger*, Routledge, & Kegan Paul; Penguin, 1970

FORTES, M. (1967), *Totem and Taboo*, Proceedings of the Royal Anthropological Institute of Great Britain and Ireland, 1966, pp. 5–22.

HAAS, M. (1951), 'Interlingual word taboos', *Amer. Anthrop.*, vol. 53, pp. 338–44.

HAAS, M. (1964), *Thai–English Student's Dictionary*, Stanford University Press.

LEACH, E. (1964), 'Anthropological aspects of language: animal categories and verbal abuse', in E. J. Lenneberg (ed.), *New Directions in the Study of Language*, MIT Press.

LÉVI-STRAUSS, C. (1962), *Totemism*, Beacon Press.

LÉVI-STRAUSS, C. (1966), *The Savage Mind*, Weidenfeld & Nicholson.

MCFARLAND, G. B. (1944), *Thai–English Dictionary*, Stanford University Press.

MAYER, A. C. (1960), *Caste and Kinship in Central India*, University of California Press.

MEGGITT, M. L. (1963), *The Lineage System of the MaeEnga of New Guinea*, University of Chicago Press.

MIDDLETON, M. L., and TAIT, D. (1958), *Tribes Without Rulers, Studies in African Segmentary Systems*, Routledge & Kegan Paul.

RADCLIFFE-BROWN, A. R. (1922), *The Andaman Islanders*, Cambridge University Press.

RADCLIFFE-BROWN, A. R. (1952), *Structure and Sanction in Primitive Society*, Free Press.

RAJADHON, P. A. (1958), *Five Papers on Thai Custom*, Data Paper 28, Southeast Asia Program, Cornell University.

TAMBIAH, S. J. (1968), 'The magical power of words', *Man*, n.s., no. 3, pp. 175–208.

WIJEWARDENE, G. (1968), 'Address, abuse and animal categories in Northern Thailand', *Man*, n.s., no. 3, pp. 76–93.

25 R. Bulmer

Why the Cassowary is not a Bird

R. Bulmer, 'Why is the cassowary not a bird? A problem of zoological taxonomy among the Karam of the New Guinea Highlands', *Man*, new series, vol. 2, no. 1, March 1967, pp. 5–25.*

The Karam people of the upper Kaironk Valley in the Schrader Mountains of New Guinea place in the taxon *yakt*[1] all the 180 or so kinds of flying birds and bats they recognize and name. Cassowaries, which are large ostrich- or emu-like birds, are not included in *yakt* but constitute the contrasting taxon, *kobtiy*. Why, to the Karam, is the cassowary not a bird? This is a simple question, but the conclusion I shall arrive at is that there is no simple, single answer to it apart from the very general statement, 'The cassowary is not a bird because it enjoys a unique relationship in Karam thought to man.' The same difficulties appear in attempting to find answers to other, similar, questions such as why the dog is not grouped taxonomically with any other kind of creature by the Karam but also occupies a position on its own.

Speakers of the Karam language number about 13,000 and occupy the eastern sector of the Schrader Range and a little of the western fringes of the Bismarck Range in the Territory of New Guinea. The particular communities with which I have been working are Kaytog and Gobnem whose members, numbering approximately 350, occupy territory in the upper Kaironk and upper Aunjang (or Aunje) Valleys at altitudes between 5000 and 8600 feet.[2] This territory includes, in actuality and in Karam thought,

* This is a revised version of a paper read at the Royal Anthropological Institute on 27 October 1966. I undertook ten months' fieldwork among the Karam of the upper Kaironk Valley in 1960, 1963–4 and 1965–6 as part of a continuing programme of linguistic and social anthropological studies in this region conducted by the Department of Anthropology, University of Auckland. Grateful acknowledgement is made for financial support from the US Public Health Service (M.H. 07957–01), the New Zealand University Research Grants Committee, and the Golden Kiwi Lotteries Fund Scientific Research Committee of New Zealand. I must also thank my companions in the field, Bruce Biggs, Andrew Pawley, Graham Jackson and Inge Riebe, for their indispensable collaboration, Edmund Leach and Marilyn and Andrew Strathern for helpful comments on an earlier draft of this paper, and Meyer Fortes for characteristically insightful suggestions made in informal discussion of my field material.

1. Spelling of Karam words follows the phonemic orthography of Biggs (1963).
2. Aufenanger (1964) has published ethnographic notes on two other Karam communities of the upper Kaironk Valley. Reports on other Karam-speaking groups include

two contrasting ecological zones. The Kaironk Valley bottom and sides between 5000 and 6500 to 7000 feet are *mseŋ*, 'open country', consisting of grasslands interspersed with currant gardens, groves of casuarina trees and a little rather poor, naturally regenerating, bush-fallow. *Ytk*, 'forest' or 'bush', is applied to the ridges flanking the Kaironk Valley where, above about 7000 feet, fairly extensive tracts of tall forest trees remain, and to the entire upper section of the Aunjang Valley, which has undergone much less deforestation than the Kaironk. However, for the past two generations, and possibly for a longer period, some gardens have been cut in the forest at altitudes up to 8000 feet, and at Gulk in the upper Aunjang Valley there is an area of about one square mile of continuous clearing between 6900 and 8000 feet.

Like other New Guinea Highlanders Karam are horticulturalists with a wide range of crops. Their main subsistence crop is sweet potato, *Ipomoea batatas*. Their main ceremonial crop is taro, *Colocasia esculenta*. Pig husbandry is important to them. Hunting and collecting are significant subsidiary aspects of their economy.

Karam settlement pattern is of dispersed homesteads which shift with the cycles of land use and ceremonial activities. The largest Karam houses may contain, at least for a few months at a time, up to thirty people.[3] Territorial groups are small – none in the upper Kaironk Valley appears to have more than 160 members – and somewhat fluid in their composition, with many people enjoying rights to dwell and use land with more than one group. Although Karam distinguish between paternal and maternal kin, and post-marital residence is normally virilocal, the genealogical framework of their local groups is ambilateral. They may be said to have shallow segmentary ramages, but not lineages.

Karam zoological taxonomy is conveniently approached at two levels, or from two angles. One can look at the broadest groupings, what I call the 'primary taxa', and try to see what sense these make as a set, and it is with part of this problem that I am concerned in this paper. Or one can look at the smallest units which Karam discriminate, the 'terminal taxa', and with them the rather few intermediate taxa present in the system, and see what kinds of discriminations are there being made. This is a task outside the scope of the present essay. Here I need only say that at this level Karam show an enormous, detailed and on the whole highly accurate knowledge of natural history, and that though, even with vertebrate animals, their terminal taxa only correspond well in about 60 per cent of cases with the

those of Moyne and Haddon (1936) on the people living near Mount Aiome and of Gusinde (1958) on the people of the lower Asai Valley.

3. Aufenanger (1964) describes houses in the upper Kaironk Valley.

species recognized by the scientific zoologist, they are nevertheless in general well aware of species differences among larger and more familiar creatures. The general consistency with which, in nature, morphological differences are correlated with differences in habitat, feeding habits, call-notes, and other aspects of behaviour is the inevitable starting point for any system of animal classification, at the lowest level.

At the upper level of Karam taxonomy, however, objective biological facts no longer dominate the scene. They are still important, but they allow a far greater, almost infinitely varied, set of possibilities to the taxonomist. This is the level at which culture takes over and determines the selection of taxonomically significant characters. It is not surprising that the result shows little correspondence either to the taxonomy of the professional zoologist, which reflects the theory of evolution, or, for that matter, to our modern western European folk-taxonomies. Thus, as can be seen from Table 1, mammals are split up between six different Karam primary taxa, some being thrown in with birds and others with frogs. There are no Karam taxa corresponding to 'reptile', 'lizard', 'snake' and so forth.

In elucidating the principles which underlie Karam taxonomy at this level one of the problems is that Karam appear to take a great deal of this very much for granted, in much the same way that one takes the grammar or the phonology of one's mother-tongue for granted. It is only where distinctions are patently rather difficult to maintain, as where morphologically extremely similar small furred animals are divided among three different taxa, or where they know some other people classify creatures differently, as with cassowaries and birds,[4] that they have ready-made explanations. However, largely by inference, a simple logic can be constructed which makes reasonably good sense if imposed upon these categories. Initially, two kinds of factors need to be taken into account: firstly, gross morphological similarities and differences; secondly, habitat.

Thus, if we take morphological factors, all of which, even if somewhat arbitrarily selected, can be simply defined in the Karam language, we can, by dividing creatures up into boney versus boneless; winged versus wingless; bipedal versus quadrupedal versus multipedal versus limbless; elongated versus not elongated; and large versus medium-sized versus small, arrive at a table (Table 2) which only leaves a small number of distinctions still to be made.

If we then look at habitat we find that with the aid of two dimensions, horizontal and vertical, the former with the forest at one pole and the homestead at the other, with open country and gardens lying in between, the

4. Pidgin-speaking Karam know that New Guineans from some other areas and Europeans regard cassowaries as 'birds'.

Table 1 **Karam zoological taxonomy***

	Primary taxa	Content	No. of intermediate taxa	No. of terminal taxa	Edibility
1.	*kobtiy*	Cassowaries	1	3 (1†)	Restricted
2.	*yakt*	Flying birds and bats	23	181 (33†)	3 t.t. not eaten; 2 restricted; others unrestricted
3.	*kayn*	Dogs	0	2	Not eaten
4.	*kaj*	Pigs	0	2	Normally unrestricted
5.	*kmn*	Larger marsupials and rodents	2	37 (14†)	2 t.t. restricted; others unrestricted
6.	*kopyak*	Rats from homesteads and gardens	0	2	Not eaten
7.	*as*	Frogs and small marsupials and rodents other than *kopyak*	2	35 (2†)	1 t.t. not eaten; others restricted
8.	*yn*	Skinks	1	11 (1†)	1 t.t. not eaten; others restricted

* Taxa as applied in identification or discussion of individual creatures. In most contexts in which collectivities of animals are being discussed, e.g. in statements concerning human diet, primary taxa applied to vertebrate animals constitute the same mutually exclusive set, but in discussion of collectivities of smaller creatures there are some simplifications. Thus, although in the identification of insects the term *joŋ* (15) can only be applied to grasshoppers and crickets, in general discussion of human diet it can be applied to all edible insects and spiders; similarly in answer to such a question as 'what does this bird eat?' *joŋ* can be taken to refer to insects and similar small creatures in general.

28 of the 94 primary taxa recorded are subdivided into mutually exclusive sets of 'secondary taxa', most of which are also 'terminal taxa' (t.t.), i.e. cannot be subdivided into standardly named groups. However, 28 secondary taxa are further subdivided into mutually exclusive tertiary taxa, which in all but two recorded cases are terminal taxa, these two (both birds) being subdivided into pairs of quaternary terminal taxa. 'Intermediate taxa' enumerated in this table are the secondary and tertiary taxa which are internally subdivided.

The larger primary taxa (*yakt, kmn, as*) are also subdivided internally in alternative and cross-cutting ways which are not referred to in this table: by habitat, size, plumage (of birds), cleanness or uncleanness as food, and to some extent as 'families' (*kñŋ*), though these lack standard names and definitions. Karam also relate certain taxa as developmental stages (e.g. *awleg* and certain *as*: 'tadpoles' and some 'frogs') or, among birds, as sexual pairs, without necessarily including the forms they thus relate within a single named group.

† = not present in upper Kaironk Valley, above 5000 feet.

Table 1 – *continued*

	Primary taxa	Content	No. of intermediate taxa	No. of terminal taxa	Edibility
9.	*wowiy*	Small gecko	0	1	Not eaten
10.	*aypot*	Agamid lizard	0	1	Restricted
11.	*ñom*	'Dangerous' snakes	1	6 (4†)	Not eaten
12.	*klŋan*	Small python	0	1	Restricted
13.	*tok*	Eels	0	2	Restricted
14.	*awleg*	Tadpoles	0	3	1 t.t. not eaten; others restricted
15.	*joŋ*	Grasshoppers and crickets	0	20	7 t.t. not eaten; others restricted
16.	*kogolok*	Weevils	0	6	Restricted
17.	*kaŋ*	Timber-boring larvae of certain beetles and moths	0	6	Restricted
18.	*yabol*	Earthworms	0	2	Not eaten
19.	*gogaj*	Snails	0	3 (1†)	1 t.t. not eaten; 1 restricted
20.	*kuymol*	Leeches	0	3 (1†)	1 t.t. restricted; others not eaten
	74 other primary taxa have been recorded, 6 applied to reptiles and fish not present in the upper Kaironk Valley, 68 applied to invertebrates. 63 of these, like *wowiy* (9), cannot be subdivided, i.e. are also terminal taxa.		0	95 (10†)	Approx. 40 t.t. restricted; others not eaten
Totals (94 primary taxa)			30	422 (67†)	Of t.t. applied to local creatures, 166 are unrestrictedly edible; approx. 120 restricted; approx. 69 not eaten.

† = not present in upper Kaironk Valley, above 5000 feet.

Table 2 Possible classification of Karam primary taxa by gross morphological features

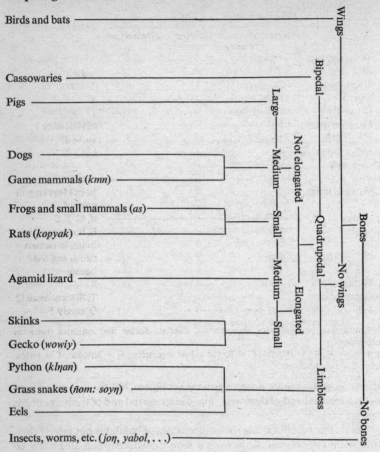

latter ranging from aerial through arborial, terrestrial and aquatic, to subterranean, we can elucidate nearly all the remaining distinctions, as can be seen from Table 3.

Further, we find that taxa already marked off discretely on morphological grounds alone can in most cases be assigned a characteristic position on one or both of the two axes of habitat. Thus birds and bats, while they span the whole horizontal dimension from forest to gardens and homesteads, are marked off in the vertical dimension by the fact that they fly in

Table 3 Classification of Karam primary taxa by habitat
(morphologically similar creatures are linked by brackets)

	Horizontal axis*				Vertical axis†
	Forest	Open country	Gardens	Homesteads	
Birds and bats	————————————————————————				A, B, C, some Q, some T
Cassowaries	———				T
Pigs	- - - - -		————————————		T
⌈ Dogs	————————————————————————				T
⌊ Game mammals	———— - - - -				Mainly B or T, some S
⌈ Frogs and small mammals	——————————————— - - - - -				C, Q, T, S
⌊ Rats			—————————————		T, S
Agamid lizard		- - - - -			B, but lays eggs in ground
⌈ Skinks		—————————————————————			B, C, T, S
⌊ Gecko			—————————————		B, but especially found in banana palms and old houses
⌈ Python	- - - - - - - - - - - - - -				B
⌈ Grass snakes		———			T, S, sometimes Q
⌊ Eels	- - - - - - - - - - - - - -				Q, rarely T

* Continuous line indicates characteristic habitat: dotted line indicates restricted occurrence.
† A = aerial; B = arboreal; C = found in low vegetation; Q = aquatic; T = terrestrial; S = subterranean.

the air: cassowaries are not merely wingless bipeds, but they are unambiguously terrestrial and of the forest; pigs are terrestrial and of the homesteads and gardens.

The justification for using these dimensions of habitat is not merely that, like the morphological distinctions I have drawn, they can all readily be expressed linguistically in Karam and that they seem to make sense of distinctions that are awkward to draw in purely morphological terms, but that Karam use them both, explicitly, in accounting not so much directly for their taxonomy as for the status animals enjoy in their system of dietary regulations. Thus Karam explain that they do not eat 'rats' (*kopyak*), certain small birds, and indeed almost any other creatures found around the homesteads except the domestic pig,[5] on the grounds that these eat or are

5. Men of some Karam communities, including Kaytog, now keep domestic fowls (*bojp*, *klokl*, or *yuyu*, placed in the primary taxon *yakt*), mainly for sale of birds and

otherwise associated with excrement, unclean foods and female dirt, and with the corpses which are exposed in open, fenced graves near the houses in the first stage of the disposal of the dead. They also distinguish between the mainly arboreal creatures hunted by men, which belong in the two big taxa *yakt* and *kmn* ('birds and bats' and 'game mammals'), most of which are unrestricted foods for everybody, and the smaller creatures mainly found on or under the ground or in low vegetation, *as, yñ, joŋ* etc. (frogs and small mammals, skinks and their eggs, grasshoppers and crickets and most other kinds of edible insects), which are mainly collected by women and children and which are forbidden foods for certain categories of males, notably boys during their rites of passage and adult men in their prime who practise sorcery.

The picture I have presented, though over-simplified is, I hope, on the whole coherent. But, having done this, what is the status of Tables 2 and 3 when combined? Is this a 'real' taxonomy or is it just a 'key', useful for deciding where things have to go, once the categories are *given*? Does it tell us all we need to know about how the categories really relate to each other? In the rest of this paper I in part demolish this pattern, or rather try to show that it is not so much wrong as inadequate for indicating the significance which certain of these animals have in Karam thought. What I have so far constructed is thus a temporary scaffolding for a structure which may look quite different when completed, whose salient features alone I can sketch in at present.

To return to the cassowary, why is this really not a bird? We may look first more closely at the objective physical and biological differences between the cassowary and other birds and bats, as these may be perceived at the level of common-sense natural history:

1. As we have seen, the cassowary is flightless: other birds and bats all fly.

2. The cassowary is virtually wingless; the wings are invisible without close inspection, and have no feathers, only a few bare quills: other birds and bats all have wings.

3. It follows from the above that the cassowary is exclusively terrestrial: other birds and bats not merely fly, but with a few exceptions perch at least sometimes on trees, bushes, rocks and other elevated places.

4. The cassowary is very much larger than any other bird, or bat, in the Karam domain. Although the local mountain species (*Casuarius bennetti*)

---

eggs to Europeans. They say they kept no fowls before European contact. I do not know the circumstances in which Karam themselves eat these creatures. Tame cockatoos, kept for their plumes, are not eaten, though wild ones are.

is a pygmy cassowary, much smaller than the species in lowland New Guinea and northern Australia, adults probably weigh fifty pounds or more, at least six times as much as the harpy eagle (*Harpyopsis novae-guineae*), the largest flying bird in the region. It is in fact the largest creature in the New Guinea mountains other than man and the pig. With size goes strength. While the wild cassowary is in no sense ferocious, being timid and avoiding man as far as possible, it has powerful legs and extremely sharp claws and can inflict serious wounds with these if, cornered (cf. Mayr and Gilliard, 1954).

5. Unlike birds, or any other local creatures, the cassowary has heavy, strong and very human-like leg bones, which are used to fashion jabbers or splitters for marita fruit, *Pandanus conoideus*.

Now, in case it might be thought that merely on its objective, common-sense, natural history there is sufficient reason to place the cassowary in a special category, we must note that some other New Guinea Highlanders, who have just as much common sense and just as much knowledge of casso-waries, nevertheless place them in the same taxon as other birds.[6]

Let us therefore ask what Karam themselves say if one enquires why a cassowary is not a bird. I must admit that I did not ask this question as often as I should have done, one problem being that by the later stages of my enquiry my regular informants knew that I knew some of the things to be explained below, and it was therefore understood between us that the question had complicated answers. But the first simple answers to the question simply and naïvely put were as follows:

1. 'It's not a bird because it doesn't have plumes (*slp*, *bog*), it just has "hair"' (*kas*).[7] Now it is a noticeable feature of the cassowary that it lacks conventional feathers with a stiff quill or midrib, but has wispy, soft hair-like plumage. This is technologically significant: there are special techniques for making cassowary plumes into headdresses and other ornaments, which are unlike those used in preparing ornaments from the plumes of other birds. But, if one pauses to think, this is not entirely a logical answer, since bats also lack plumes, their surface covering being also described as 'hair' by Karam, but they are nevertheless *yakt*.

6. E.g. the Melpa of the Mount Hagan area (according to information kindly provided by A. J. Strathern) and their neighbours the Kyaka Enga (according to my own records). However, Diamond (1966) reports that the Fore of the Eastern Highlands District, like Karam, do not classify cassowaries with other birds.

7. *Kas* has a wide range of referrents: hair, fur, feathers (in general), foliage. *Slp* is applied to the shoots, buds and in some cases blossom of plants, and to the elongated, thin tail feathers of certain birds. *Bog* is applied to relatively broad wing and tail plumes of birds, and also to wooden boards and to the walls and partitions of houses.

2. 'The cassowary's head is all bone: it has no brain (*jn-mok*),[8] not like a bird.' This answer took me aback at first. To us birds are, well, 'bird-brained', and it took some adjusting to assimilate the idea of a creature with less brain than a bird. But my informant was making a statement which was anatomically quite sensible. The adult cassowary has a large bony casque on the top of its skull: most birds have rather fragile, light skulls. Furthermore, proportionately it could be that for the size of a cassowary's skull there is a disappointingly small amount of brain, as compared with smaller birds. Karam eat bird and mammal brains so they should know about these things. But even though it is a valid taxonomic distinction in this case, I do not think we could really use it as a sufficient reason in itself for the special taxonomic status which the cassowary enjoys, unless cranial structure and bone–brain ratios could be shown to be of general relevance in Karam taxonomy, and I have no evidence that they are. I recorded no other cases where categories of creatures were separated out on this basis.

However, we can see that there are at least five ways in which cassowaries can be marked off as a distinct class of creatures by morphological characters alone: size; absence of wings or other visible upper limbs; heavy human-like leg-bones; unique pelage; and unique cranial structure. There are probably other features which Karam could point to if they were pressed for additional information. At the same time, to point to these features does not explain *why* the cassowary should enjoy special taxonomic rank. To understand this I would argue that we must consider the cassowaries' relationship to man: how, when and by whom they are hunted; how they are used; how their hunting and utilization are regulated.

When making enquiries on these points I soon learned that hunting cassowaries was quite a different kind of activity from what it had been among the Kyaka Enga of the north slopes of Mount Hagen, among whom I had previously worked. There, as far as I could gather (though I was not at that time concerned to enquire deeply into the subject), almost any kind of hunting was acceptable: individual hunting with snares or by stalking with bow and spear, capture of live chicks for domestication, mass drives by men armed with the weapons of war and of the hunt. For Karam, by contrast, hunting cassowaries is hedged around with rules and prohibitions.

Before I got into these I should perhaps note that cassowaries are not

8. *Mok* or *muk* is applied to the viscous sap or resin of certain plants and to the body-fluids, milk (*tiy-mok* – 'breast-*mok*'), semen (*waɲ-mok* – 'penis-*mok*') and brain (*jn-mok* – 'head-*mok*'). Bone-marrow, however, is *slom*, not *mok*, as is nasal mucus. Karam relate semen and brain and consider the brain of game mammals (*kmn*) and birds (*yakt*) to be strengthening foods.

common in the upper Kaironk Valley. The forest edge kin-group of about twenty adult men with which I lived killed on average one or two a year at the most, and men living in valley settlements probably get hardly any. In over thirty day-trips into the forest I never saw one. They are, however, on the evidence of their droppings and spoor, well distributed in the mountain forest from its lower limit in the Kaironk Valley at about 7000 feet right up to the ridge crest at 8600 feet. This is in contrast to what one finds in forest at this altitude in many parts of the Highlands, where the bird has been eliminated. Most Highlanders have to go down-hill, to less densely populated lower-lying areas, to get cassowaries, and not upwards. The way in which cassowary hunting is regulated by Karam may be a factor in accounting for the survival of the bird in their immediate territory.

The most important rules governing Karam cassowary hunting are as follows:

1. Men hunting cassowaries must 'practise avoidance' (*ask . . mosk g-*), meaning in this context that they must not use the everyday vocabulary for a very large number of objects and activities, but must use the alternative terms of the 'language of avoidance', known as *ask mosk mnm* or *alŋaw mnm* ('pandanus language' – see below).[9]

2. The blood of the living cassowary must not be shed. Thus, arrows and spears may not be used against it; it can only be captured in snares or despatched with a blunt instrument.

3. The hunter who has killed a cassowary should eat its heart.

4. People who have killed or eaten cassowary are *asŋ*, that is, in a ritually dangerous state, and should not plant taro or go near growing taro crops for one month.

5. Cassowary should be cooked and eaten in the forest or near the forest edge, and the apparatus used in hunting and in cooking cassowary should not be brought into settlements which are near taro gardens. The only exception to this rule appears to be that cassowaries were formerly sometimes brought into settlements for cooking and consumption at the *smiy* festivals, described below.

6. Live cassowaries must not be brought into homesteads and gardens. If they are, pigs, taro and bananas will not flourish. Thus the bird cannot be

9. One also 'practises avoidance' (*ask mosk g-*) in relations with affines and with cross-cousins of one's own sex, meaning in these contexts that one may not say their names. If such a relative has a name which is also the word for some animal, plant or object, this word must also be avoided in these other contexts and a synonym used. Many of these synonyms are the standard terms in 'pandanus language'.

domesticated. This is in marked contrast to the practice in many New Guinea Highlands societies where cassowary chicks are captured and tamed or semi-tamed and, when adult, used either live or dead in ceremonial gift exchange and ultimately eaten.

None of these rules applies to the hunting and consumption of *yakt* (flying birds and bats) with the possible partial exception of *alp* (large fruit-bats), which I briefly refer to below, and *duk*, the harpy eagle, about which my information is limited and contradictory.

Before going into the explanations which can be offered for these rules, both those of the Karam and the more extended and fanciful ones of the ethnographer, let me note two practical consequences they have. Firstly, they restrict cassowary hunting to an activity by one or two men alone, as in almost all other Karam hunting, rather than allowing it to be a group activity. Since the cassowary is a powerful bird, this introduces an element of personal duel into the hunt. Considerable prestige comes from successful hunting, and men tell good stories about the wrestling matches which ensue when one or two men attempt to despatch a cassowary using only the blunt butt end of an axe or some similar weapon. Secondly, the rules prevent communities which are growing taro from eating cassowary during the planting season (August to November) and for several months thereafter while the crop is growing and needs tending, and they discourage individual men of such communities from hunting cassowary during the same period. If a hunter from a community with growing taro does kill a cassowary, he cooks and shares it with kin elsewhere who are not handling this crop.

Logically, the next questions to be asked are, 'what is the significance of taro to the Karam?' and, 'what else besides cassowaries may not be killed or cooked or eaten by persons who are growing taro?'.

Taro (*m*) is a very special plant to the Karam. Although they live at an altitude which is marginal for its cultivation, and although sweet potato is their staple crop, taro is the cultivated vegetable food they value most highly.[10] The best garden land is reserved for taro, and they systematically encourage casuarina trees as fallow cover in the taro gardens, so that the splendid casuarina groves one sees in the upper Kaironk Valley are all fallow taro gardens. Sweet potato gardens, by contrast, lie fallow under grass or anything else that will grow there.

However, these taro and casuarina gardens are only found up to about 6500 feet. A little taro is grown in forest edge swiddens higher up the hill,

10. Over 40 named varieties of *Colocasia esculenta* are said to be grown in the upper Kaironk Valley. Approximately the same number of named varieties of sweet potato have been recorded. However, many sweet potato varieties are said to have been introduced within living memory, whereas this is true of only a small number of varieties of taro.

but it does not do well. Karam say taro flourishes at the base of the casuarinas; it does not flourish at the base of the *kamay*, the small-leafed southern beech, *Nothofagus* species, which dominates the mountain forest in this region above about 7500 feet. Presumably the reasons are climatic. Sweet potato still does very well in forest swiddens, up to 8000 feet. But the important point is that there is an opposition, as Karam see it, between taro cultivation and the mountain forest.[11]

The second point is that taro, unlike sweet potato, is a seasonal crop. Planted at the commencement of the wet season, August to November, the greater part of the crop is harvested at the end of the dry season, in June and July, and the same early months of the wet season, August to November, in the following year. It is available only in negligible quantities from January to May.

Apart from being the preferred root crop to the Karam, taro is also essential to the celebration of the festivals called *smiy* which provide the ceremonial element in Karam life. The seasonality of the crop determines the timing of the *smiy*. In the years in which a particular community holds this festival it can perhaps be seen as, among other things, a ritualized adjustment of the annual horticultural calendar, marking the division between the harvest and the new planting. Roots are harvested and stored in raised shelters (*abañ*) for up to two months before they are used in the *smiy*. After this period in storage the taro is rather soapy in texture, but Karam like it like that even better than fresh, and it has thrown a new shoot which is then cut off and planted.

Smiy festivals, then, are held between August and November, while the taro is being both harvested and planted. A *smiy* is held by the leader of an extended family or local ambilateral kin group. Its main overt function is as a rite of passage for youths, including the sons and nephews of the holder, who have their nasal septa pierced and stay in seclusion in a rear chamber of the ceremonial house for a period of from three to five days. But it is also an occasion when pigs are slaughtered, propitiations are made to the dead, gifts of pork, vegetables, shell-valuables and axes are made to affines, and a spectacular all-night dance is held to which all are welcome, provided that they are not in a state of blood-feud with the hosts. Lastly, adolescent girls also have their nasal septa pierced, but with little ceremony. A man's, and his group's, prosperity and prestige are indicated by the scale of their *smiy*, and it seems probable too that the number of social ties publicly activated

11. Bananas, which rank next after taro in importance as a ceremonial crop and which are mainly grown in the same gardens, are also said not to flourish in forest clearings and at the forest edge. A similar but rather less elaborate antithesis between bananas and the things of the forest to that presented here for taro is postulated by Karam.

there is an indication of the support they can raise in other contexts, notably when they need allies to assist in vengeance killings.

Much planning goes into a successful *smiy*. Taro gardens have to be planted, pigs have to be husbanded, a very large ceremonial house has to be built (which may afterwards be converted into a residence for the kingroup) together with other smaller structures for the accommodation of dancers and spectators, and then taro and other vegetables have to be harvested and placed in the special stores outside the ceremonial house, and very large quantities of firewood have to be amassed for cooking-fires and for the fires which will illuminate the dancers and warm the other guests.

Taro is thus essential to the ceremonial life of the Karam. Understandably there is great concern that the crop should flourish; much care goes into its cultivation and a great deal of minor ritual is associated with this. The taro garden itself is in a sense a holy place. At the centre of a large taro garden there is normally a small spring associated with the ancestors who first cleared the garden and only their descendants, the present owners of the garden, should approach it and wash the roots they have harvested in it.

Turning to the plant itself, we find that taro is said by Karam to die (*kum-*), the same verb being used as in reference to men and animals; of other plants it is merely said, they rot (*kuy g-*) or wither (*mlep g-*). Also, the suckers which some kinds of taro throw and which, together with the decapitated heads and shoots from harvested roots, are used for seed, are referred to as its 'daughters' (*m pañ*). It is not too fanciful, perhaps, to suggest that taro may be seen as having the same kind of life and tenuous continuity that human populations do. This is consistent with the fact that shoots and suckers of the most highly valued and ritually significant varieties, known as *m kls-tmel* ('taro strong no-good' or 'dangerously strong taro'), are acquired from one's blood relatives, and it is these that are planted near the spring in the centre of the taro garden. So, if the continuity of taro can be seen as related to the continuity of kin groups, this is an additional reason why it should be husbanded carefully so that the stock increases and does not die out.

At the same time, as we have seen, only a limited area of the Karam domain will support taro gardens. The crop does not grow well above about 6500 feet, and even below that altitude much of the land will not support it. This has interesting sociological implications. Population pressures mean that some people have to live, at least for part of the time, where taro will not grow. The Karam settlement pattern is one of dispersed homesteads which shift, or circulate, with cultivation and fallow of land over cycles of very approximately fifteen years in time, and of up to ten miles in linear distance and 3000 feet in altitude between the most distant homesteads of the same family. While a family lives up the hill, at the forest edge or in forest clearings, most of its taro has to be left in gardens to which its members commute somewhat irregularly, and where other people, close kin and their spouses, will help in looking after it. Normally a group only holds its *smiy* festivals while it is resident in one of the lower-altitude sections of its territory, but one can hold a *smiy* in a forest settlement if one can get enough support with taro cultivation from kin and affines living lower down the hill. The dependence of forest dwellers on valley kinsmen, and particularly of men on their sisters and sisters' husbands, which taro imposes, is possibly important to an understanding of the failure of Karam society to develop segmentary, ideologically patrilineal local descent groups, such as are found in much the greater part of the New Guinea Highlands.

To return to the question of why there is an antithesis, a required separation, between cassowaries and the taro crop, we can see that in the first place the cassowary is the prime game of the forest, and the taro is the key element in horticulture, or, in civilization. If we turn to the other things which have to be kept away from growing taro, we find that a number of these too can be seen to exemplify the same opposition.

Let me take first the fact that to shed the blood of a cassowary makes a man ritually dangerous, or unclean. Here the cassowary is not unique. If one kills a man or a dog one is similarly *asŋ*, and to a lesser degree this is true if one kills marsupials of two particular species, *madaw* (the terrestrial cuscus, *Phalanger ?gymnotis*) and *blc* (the striped possum, *Dactylonax palpator*).[12] As to the eating of cassowary, dogs are not eaten at all, and men are only eaten by witches (*koyb*). Terrestrial cuscus and striped possum are eaten, but on the same terms as the cassowary: having done so one is *asŋ* and may not go near growing taro for one month. Some informants say that eating *alp* (large fruit bats or 'flying foxes', especially the spinal

12. I am grateful to Dr Hobart Van Deusen of the American Museum of Natural History, New York, Mrs Dorcas MacClintock of New Haven, and Mr Basil Marlow of the Australian Museum, Sydney, for identifying mammal specimens. To Dr Van Deusen I owe the tentative identification of the 'terrestrial cuscus', from my account of Karam statements concerning its habits, as *Phalanger ?gymnotis*. Among locally known cuscuses (*Phalanger* spp.) and the superficially similar ring-tail possums (*Pseudocheirus* spp.), this species is singular, according to Karam lore, in characteristically having its lair in a rock-crevice or under the roots of a tree, and in spending much of its time on the ground, whereas the other morphologically similar species are essentially arboreal. The striped possum (*Dactylonax*) is remarkable, in the opinions both of professional zoologists and of the Karam, for the long digits of its fore-feet, and particularly for its very long fourth toe, which is used to extract wood-boring insects or insect larvae. The terrestrial cuscus is identified in Karam mythology with the ghosts of the dead, its subterranean lair being an entrance to the underworld. The striped possum is one of the creatures Karam associate particularly with witchcraft, on account of its very elusive habits and probably also because of its distinctive black and white markings.

winged bat, *Dobsonia moluccensis*) and *aypot* (an agamid lizard, *Goniocephalus binotatus*) should place one under the same restriction, but there is no general agreement about these creatures.[13] Terrestrial cuscus and striped possum, like cassowary, are certainly forest animals. So, in spite of its domestication, is the dog, since in Karam eyes this is a *wild* beast which they partially domesticate; I shall have more to say about this later. Also identified with the forest is the only vegetable food the eating of which renders one dangerous to growing taro. These are the nuts of the mountain pandanus palms. These are important and entail a second ethnobotanical digression.

There are many species of pandanus palms or screw-palms in the New Guinea mountains, and several of them are of considerable economic and ritual significance. The best known, the red- or yellow-fruiting *Pandanus conoideus*, known as marita in New Guinea, is cultivated up to about 5000 feet in the Schrader Mountains and is not what we are concerned with here. To Karam, two of the three local species of nut-bearing pandanus are much more important.[14] One, *gudiy*, which grows between 5500 and 7500 feet, has foliage which provides the roofing for houses; its nuts have rather small kernels which make only a minor contribution to diet. A second, *kumiy*, which grows locally between about 6500 and 8000 feet, is mainly important for its nuts, which are harvested casually and in any month of the year when they happen to be ripe; it is not very plentiful. The third, *alŋaw* which is the ritually important species, only grows locally above 7500 feet, but it is very common in the mountain forest and its nuts are very highly prized.

The first point about *alŋaw* is that it is highly seasonal in its cropping. It produces ripe nuts in May and June,[15] that is, during the dry season when weather conditions are optimal for forest hunting expeditions and also just at the right time in terms of the cycle of taro cultivation, since these are the months when most of the taro is almost full-grown but the crop does not require much further attention. So, in May or June family groups camp in the forest to harvest and cook pandanus nuts, and to hunt. Nuts are cooked in earth-ovens, and as with game cooked in the forest, the nature demons (*kcekiy*) who reside there are propitiated. During nut harvest prohibitions are observed on sexual intercourse (at other times there is no restriction on

13. *Alp, aypot* and also *klŋan* (a small arboreal python, probably *Chrondropython viridis*) are also foods which certain people cannot eat because they were forbidden and avoided by their ancestors, either paternal or maternal.

14. Botanical identifications of these palms have not been obtained. For brief further notes see R. Bulmer (1964, p. 148).

15. Individual palms do not fruit every year, and there is said to be considerable annual fluctuation in the size of the general harvest. Palms are keenly examined, some months ahead of harvest-time, to see if nuts are forming.

marital intercourse in the forest, and no restriction on entering the forest for hunting or other purposes by men or women after they have had intercourse),[16] and, as when cassowary hunting, on using everyday words for all sorts of objects and actions. As we have seen, the second, ritual language which has to be used is called *alŋaw mnm*, 'pandanus language'.[17] It is said that if this language is not used the kernels of the nuts will be soft and watery when they are removed from the earth-ovens. After cooking, some of the nuts are carried back to the homesteads, where they may be eaten or offered in hospitality to guests over a period of several weeks.

Pandanus nuts are very oily, nutritionally doubtlessly very valuable, and of some economic importance, possibly more so in the recent past, two generations or so ago, than now. But there is more to *alŋaw* than this. The palms are individually owned and their ownership not only conveys the right to dispose of the nuts (I recorded an account of a murder in revenge for theft of *alŋaw* nuts), but also conveys exclusive rights to certain birds of paradise and other valued game in the areas which these palms, together with cordyline shrubs and with such natural features as streams and ridge-crests, mark off into individual forest holdings.

Significantly, whereas rights to garden land can be acquired through either parent (and, as we have seen, seed taro is acquired from both parental groups also), in Karam dogma pandanus palms can only be inherited in the male line. Although it is perfectly acceptable for a man's sisters' sons to occupy his gardens as residual heirs, if he has no sons or brothers' sons and, indeed, to occupy these even if there are agnatic heirs, provided that these give their consent, it would be unthinkable for a man to claim his mother's brother's *alŋaw*, even if there were no sons or brothers' sons to inherit them. To do so would show a lack of sorrow or proper feeling for this relative.

The implications of this seem clear, although I must add that no Karam has put them to me in these terms. Firstly, if pandanus palms were only acquired by inheritance, forest holdings ought to give one a most wonderful spatial representation of agnatic relationships and agnatic groupings, which would be quite the opposite of the overlapping, inter-locking and

16. Some informants say that married couples usually abstain from sexual activity while making and planting taro gardens, and that it is usual for them to commence the period of regular and frequent intercourse which is deemed necessary to provide enough semen to form a child after the hard work of garden making is over.

17. In 'pandanus language' *yakt* are known as *wjblp*; *kmn* as *wŋbek*; *kobtiy*, the cassowary, as *wŋbek nmey*, 'mother of game mammals'. This designation may be taken as figurative. There are other instances in Karam taxonomy where one kind of creature is named as the 'mother' of another similar but much smaller kind. However, it does indicate clearly that cassowaries are seen as allied to other kinds of terrestrial and arboreal game, rather than to flying birds.

somewhat transitory ambilateral or cognatic groups which actually exist in settlement areas. Secondly, the frictions between cross-cousins (a man's sons on the one hand and his sister's sons on the other) which can occur over right to dispose of women in marriage and to receive bridewealth for them,[18] and among their descendants, over rights in garden land, should be eliminated in the forest through the rule of exclusive agnatic inheritance.

However, it is obviously impossible in practice for the forest to remain as a sort of living archive of purely agnatic genealogy; people migrate, and some families flourish and others die out. The solution to these problems of demographic readjustment is provided by two other rules and a dogma which again present forest conditions as a sort of reverse image of what prevails in 'civilization'. Unlike garden crops, all three nut-bearing pandanus palms, *alŋaw*, *gudiy* and *kumiy*, are said never to be planted by men. Karam say that if men planted them they would not grow, and anyway it would be unthinkable to try. They know perfectly well that palms grow from seed, from the nuts which they eat. But if one asks who plants the nuts, the first answer is that the nature demons do. Subsequently one learns that certain game mammals, particularly *gudiy-ws* (one of the giant rats, *Anisomys imitator*), which also eat the nuts, bury some of these and that the cassowary also propagates *gudiy*, like a host of other forest trees, by defecating undigested nuts which it has swallowed. Thus the original human owner of a pandanus palm cannot be the man who planted it. Rather, the owner is the man who first finds a young palm growing and puts his mark on it. It would be unthinkable for an unrelated man to claim young palms in the immediate vicinity of groves with known owners who are continuing to harvest these. But where an owner is dead or has no heirs, or where a man, through force of circumstance, ceases to visit his groves, it is easy enough for new palms growing among his old trees to be acquired by other

18. Kinship categories are applied to cognates of Ego's generation according to (1) sex of relative, (2) whether relative is of same or different sex to Ego, and (3), if of same sex as Ego, whether their parent(s) and Ego's parent(s) are cognates of same or opposite sex. Thus *mam* = brother or male parallel cousin (man or woman speaking) or cross-cousin (woman speaking); *ay* = sister or female parallel cousin (m. or w.s.) or female cross-cousin (m.s.); *ñbem* = male cross-cousin (m.s.); *pañbem* = female cross-cousin (w.s.). A man cannot marry any *ay* for whom he has 'made gardens', i.e. who has lived in the same homestead as himself, or for whose marriage he may claim to receive part of the bridewealth. In practice this makes all first cousins unmarriageable, and certain second and third cousins also, depending on residence and on whether or not contributions to their parents' marriage-payments have led to continuing claims on their own bridewealths. Male first cross-cousins are said to have particularly strong interests in the marriage arrangements of each others' sisters, and these appear to be most pronounced in the case of a man's claim on his mother's brother's daughter, since, it is said, his mother's brother received the bridewealth for his own mother. As indicated above, *ñbem* and *pañbem*, like affines, may not say each others' names.

people. So, gradually, over time the whole complex of forest holdings can, and does, change.[19]

I hope I have said enough to indicate that there is a real antithesis between uncultivated things and wild game, whose prime elements, cassowary and pandanus palm, are not merely undomesticated but *may not be* domesticated, on the one hand, and civilization, centering on the cultivation of the taro, on the other; and to suggest that this must be understood in evaluating the status of the cassowary and also the statuses of the other creatures of the forest which share some of the same attributes: the dog, terrestrial cuscus and striped possum.

However, we have also seen that to slay these creatures is in some sense equated with killing a man. To kill a man makes one *asŋ*, ritually dangerous, in just the same way as to kill a cassowary or a dog. Killing a cassowary is like committing homicide in yet another respect. If one kills a cassowary one must eat its heart (*mdmagl*). If one kills a human being one doesn't eat one's victim's actual heart, but as soon as possible one kills and cooks a pig and eats its heart instead. The term *mdmagl* is applied both to the heart and to the 'spirit' or 'life-force' which survives after death as the *cp-kawnan*, 'body-shade' or 'ghost', and by eating the pig's heart one prevents one's victim's ghost from following one. When one eats the heart of the cassowary, people say, one ensures that its spirit goes back to the forest, and will not prevent one from killing more cassowaries in future.[20]

So, a cassowary is in a sense equated with a man. Can we refine this and say what sort of man? One clue already exists in the rules of cassowary hunting, but before I draw attention to this I want to retrace the chronology of my field enquiry and let Karam mythology come to my aid.[21]

19. It is also said that the ownership of pandanus palms does not carry any continuing claim to land if it should be taken under cultivation. I do not know if disputes arise between men wishing to clear forest and owners of pandanus in the intended clearings. But informants were emphatic that once land had been cleared it could be disposed of by the clearer or his descendants without regard to the ownership of pandanus which might still stand on it. In fact there appears to be little if any regeneration of *gudiy* or *alŋaw* groves in garden areas, though individual *gudiy* palms survive for some decades and grow, in these circumstances, to heights of sixty feet or more.

20. Informants agree that men, dogs, cassowaries and birds (*yakt*) have *mdmagl* which survive after death, but disagree as to whether pigs and game mammals (*kmn*) do.

21. Karam distinguish two classes of stories, *sosm*, which are traditional tales referring to events outside the experience of living persons or specific remembered ancestors, and *kesm*, which are narratives relating the putatively true experiences of known people. Some *sosm* are at least in a broad sense 'myths', providing or reflecting accepted explanations for features of the natural universe, for certain human institutions and for human fate after death. Others are accepted as no more than fairy-tales, remembered and recounted merely for their entertainment value.

The relevant myth was the first one that I recorded, and it has been repeated to me in a number of versions.

A very long time ago a brother and a sister lived at Abmaj (in Kopon territory in the middle Kaironk Valley). One day in the dry season the brother went hunting, leaving the sister to weed their garden, and first telling her to burn the rubbish and not throw it into the nearby river. She disobeyed him and threw the rubbish into the stream, and it floated down and was seen by a cannibal man who was sharpening his axe at the water's edge at the confluence of the Kaironk and Mundmbul Rivers. The man followed the Mundmbul until he came to the garden, crept up on the girl and grabbed her by the neck as she bent down to weed the crops. She struggled and cried out and her brother heard her, hurried back and shot her assailant, so that he fell down dead by the water-course. The brother and sister cooked the game animals the brother had obtained with taro and other vegetables from their garden, and they butchered the man and cooked his head, limbs and guts in three separate ovens. They then made a trail of stakes along the water-course and put small pieces of human flesh and guts on these. The dead man's family came and found the meat and ate it. The brother then taught the sister to shoot with bow and arrows, and when the dead man's kin, realizing they had eaten their father, returned to take revenge, the pair slew them all, and also the relays of reinforcements that followed them. Then the two killed pigs and exchanged gifts, but though the sister gave the brother greensnail shells and axes and other good gifts, the brother only gave the sister very poor things.

After this the brother and sister competed to see who could shoot arrows the furthest [a game Karam boys play, walking along a track and firing arrows ahead of them as they go]. The brother moved on ahead of the sister, and when he came to a wallaby pit-trap on the track, he covered it up with leaves, and the sister, running after him, fell into this. The brother went to make a shelter [of the kind used by hunters when they sleep or cook game in the forest], and when he returned to the wallaby pit, the sister had turned into a cassowary and laid a clutch of eggs which in due course hatched. The brother made a *gawb* [bamboo jew's harp] and hung it in a tree so that the wind would make it sound and the cassowary-sister, hearing this, would stay nearby.

Later, two sisters from another settlement were in the forest to collect edible leaves for cooking at the *smiy* and they heard the jew's harp. Being curious as to what was making the noise, one of them climbed the tree, found it and broke it. The cassowary followed the girls back to their settlement, and when the people there saw it, the men pursued it with bows and arrows, and after a long chase and wounding it many times, killed and ate it. The brother revenged himself on them by taking away the two girls and when the rest of their kin-group followed, by cutting a tall *spiy* tree (*Albizzia ?fulva*) so that it fell on them and killed them all. He kept the two girls as his wives.[22]

22. Free and abbreviated translation of the story as tape-recorded in Karam by Bos, 13-year-old boy of Gobnem, prompted and corrected by several older youths of the same kin-group, on 21 November 1963. In another version the two women whom the cassowary follows home are already the wives of the brother, and at the settlement the cassowary kicks down the walls of her brother's ceremonial house.

My informants did not explicitly justify the way that cassowary hunting is regulated by reference to this myth; in fact, some of them say that this myth is really of the Kopon people of the middle and lower Kaironk Valley and specifically relates to Kopon initiation ceremonies, where small boys dance in cassowary plume head-dresses. But the myth does nevertheless suggest the appropriate metaphor for the relationship of cassowary to man, as Karam see it. Cassowaries are sisters, cross-cousins (i.e. father's sister's children), and their descendants, to men. This is really very appropriate. Brother and sister are mutually dependent, but the sister is under the brother's control, is married out (usually to the brother's advantage), and is in a sense dispossessed of much that she would have enjoyed if she had been a male. Your cross-cousins are the people with moral claims on you which you are nevertheless sometimes quite reluctant to meet: and whose names you should not say. You cannot keep your real cross-cousin out of your inheritance, or out of your taro gardens, at least not unless and until you are beginning to suspect witchcraft and consider homicide. How appropriate that you should treat your metaphorical cross-cousins, the cassowaries, with due respect when you kill them, and make entirely sure that they never come anywhere near your taro.

When I first heard the cassowary myth I said, the light suddenly dawning, 'do you mean that the cassowaries are cross-cousins of men?' To which my interpreter replied, 'if we are in the forest and see a group of cassowaries we say, "there are (our) sisters (*ay*) and cross-cousins (*ñbem*) over there"'.[23]

We may now return to the rules governing cassowary hunting, and in particular to the prohibition on using bow and spear. Karam explain this by saying that to do so would mean that one would shed its blood, and thus adversely affect the taro crop, and also that it would be useless in any case, since the cassowary's heart or spirit is too strong for it to be killed readily in this way. However, it seems relevant that to Karam, as to many other New Guinea Highlanders, sharp weapons of war – spear, arrow and axe-blade – are appropriate to fights between unrelated or distantly related people, whereas if one must fight with close people, one's kin, one should in theory do this only with blunt weapons, sticks or perhaps the butt end of an axe.

23. *Ay*, as indicated in note 18, applies not only to a male's sisters and female parallel cousins but also to his female cross-cousins. Another informant said that cassowaries were the *ñbem*, *mam* and *ay* of men. This is not inconsistent with the argument I advance, in so far as the children of cross-cousins refer to each other by sibling/parallel cousin terms if their linking parents were of same sex. Miss Riebe has, at my request, recently attempted to check this information. She tells me that only one of seven informants she consulted would confirm it, and he did so in so far as, he said, cassowaries were referred to as *ñbem* when they were trapped, though not in general contexts.

To recapitulate: to understand the cassowary's special status we must know:

1. That it is a forest creature, the prime game of the forest, and that there is an elaborate antithesis in Karam thought between forest and cultivation, based on the special value they attach to taro on the one hand and to *alŋaw* pandanus nuts on the other, and facilitated by the seasonal cropping of both these plants.

2. That the forest–cultivation antithesis is also linked to very basic concerns with kinship roles and kinship rights, and in particular to the problems of brother–sister relationships and of relationships between cross-cousins. These may in part be shared by many other societies but are perhaps particularly acute in a very small-scale society where segmentary groups, unlineal or otherwise, have not developed in such a way that they can bring collective weight to bear in solving problems of personal duty and personal interest.

3. Lastly, I would argue that to look for an explanation of the cassowary's special taxonomic status in purely taxonomic terms, by reference to objective features of its appearance and behaviour alone, could be to miss the point. Certainly it is a strange beast in many ways, and using only characters of which Karam are well aware one can isolate it as a separate taxon in any one of several different ways: as a terrestrial biped, as a hairy egg-layer, as a thick-skulled brainless monster and so on. But equally well, and still using characters which Karam are well aware of, one could fit it in with the birds (as many other New Guinea Highlanders do) or even perhaps with wild pig and wallaby in a class of 'big game animals'. So, for me at least, 'special taxonomic status' is a function of something broader, a special status in culture, or cosmology, at large.

I turn now to discuss, more briefly, the dog and the pig. Dog, *kayn*, has in some ways a more complicated position than the cassowary. Taxonomically it is harder to sort it out by size, morphology or behaviour from mammals in the *kmn* class, which are very varied, including wallabies, tree-kangaroos, bandicoots, possums, the carnivorous 'native cat' (*Satanellus*), giant rats and water rats, than it is to extract cassowary from the birds. The two anatomical features of the dog which Karam comment on in a number of contexts are its mouth and its prominent male genitalia. But cosmologically the dog is very special: a wild forest animal which ought by rights to be kept far away from homesteads and gardens, but which Karam nevertheless tame and use to help them hunt other animals and which, when it is in human settlements, manages to eat filth, get into graves, and do quite a lot of material and social damage by stealing food and killing piglets, both its owner's and other people's. Thus dogs break two kinds of boundaries, those between forest and cultivation, and those which attempt to separate the clean and the unclean (male and female, live and dead, kin and non-kin) within human settlements. It is not surprising that there is a complete prohibition on killing forest dogs, that domestic dogs must be killed without shedding their blood and must not be eaten, and that people who kill a dog, handle a dead dog, or handle a bitch which has newly littered, are all ritually dangerous for a month.[24] Like cassowaries, dogs are believed to have spirits which survive after death, and these are thought to be capable of bringing great harm to humans if provoked. Myth and folklore assign to dogs their own society, analogous to human society, and in one myth men stole women married to dogs and made them their own wives. Both in myth and in reality domestic dogs are the adopted children of their owners, adoptees of a special class for which there is a human parallel, taken as foundlings from distant places and unrelated people.[25]

Pigs, in contrast, are to the Karam rather domestic animals which sometimes run wild and 'go bush' than indigenous forest creatures, and considerable effort is made to prevent them getting away into the real forest.[26] Karam folk tradition, which presents the pig not as something which has always been there but as an acquisition in ancestral times from a neighbouring people, the Maring, is consistent with this assertion. Karam also say that intensive pig husbandry is really very recent among them, within the last two to three generations, and ethnological evidence lends some support

24. Dogs' teeth, like those of the larger *kmn* mammals, are strung in necklaces. They are said to have been an important valuable in gift exchange in earlier times. Teeth could be removed from a dead dog after the flesh had decomposed, without making one *as ŋ*: this parallels treatment of human corpses, which are considered to be especially contaminating until the flesh has decomposed and the bones have been cleaned for the second stage of the disposal of the dead.

25. In the past six years a few domestic cats (*ksiy*) have been obtained by mission employees in the Kaironk Valley, and one or two of these have become feral. Karam are in doubt as to whether cats should be regarded as *kmn* or *kayn*, but majority usage at present appears to be to consider them as dogs and refer to them as *kayn ksiy*.

26. Neither dog nor pig is indigenous to New Guinea. I am not aware of any good evidence as to the possible date of the dog's introduction. Pig bone has been found in archaeological deposits at Chuave, Eastern Highlands District, dated by C14 to between 3000 and 4000 B.C. (Bulmer, 1967). Feral dogs (*Canis familiaris ?hallstromi*) have been reported from Mount Giluwe, Mount Wilhelm and other parts of the Highlands. Feral pig is widely distributed in New Guinea, though mainly, it seems, at altitudes below 5000 feet Kaironk Valley Karam know of the extensive wild pig population in the lower-lying Jimi Valley to their south, but say that there are no real wild pig in the higher altitude forests flanking the upper Kaironk Valley itself, only occasional escaped beasts from domestic stock.

to this view.[27] They hardly figure at all in mythology, except in incidental references to their being cooked and eaten, but the one *sosm* we have collected which is specifically about them is worth reporting. It is very brief.

A man's younger brother died, so they say. He put three fences round the corpse. The first day he went to look at the corpse there were maggots on it. The second day he went to look at the corpse there were piglets on it. The third day he went to look at the corpse there were grown pigs. This was the origin of pigs. He looked after them and ate one. It was sweet. He bred them. This was in the Maring area.[28]

The sense of this seems plain. Pigs, which live with us and share our food, even share our women's milk (for Karam women, like women in many other parts of New Guinea, sometimes suckle piglets), also eat our excrement (though we try to stop them) and eat our corpses (though we try to prevent that too). And we eat them. Given the disgust which Karam evince for eating rats and birds which are associated with corpses and with excrement, and also for the witches who are believed to break into graves to eat human flesh, it is astonishing that they can bring themselves to eat pork at all. But they do (with very evident enjoyment, one must add), and they get round the pig's insalubrious habits by letting only women eat pigs' tongues and intestines, which are considered to be the most contaminated parts. In the case of pigs which are known to have broken into human graves, it is said that women and old men eat the whole beast. Karam explain this, as also the long list of other animal and vegetable foods which women can eat at all times but which are prohibited to certain categories of males, by saying that women are stronger than men. But underlying this there does seem to be an analogy between the relationship of men to women, or perhaps of men to their wives and female affines, and the relationship of humans to pigs. Women are always potentially dangerous because of their childbearing capacities and menstrual activities, but you have to live with them. Pigs are also filthy creatures, but you have to live with them, too.

Lastly, unlike cassowaries and dogs, pigs are not seen as having an independent spiritual existence. Those informants who say that they have spirits (*mdmagl*) which survive after death say that these, like human ghosts, follow the watercourses down to the underworld where, as spirit pigs, they join the herds of the human dead.

27. They say that the introduction within the last two generations of new, heavy-cropping varieties of sweet potato which grow well at high altitudes has enabled them to make larger gardens and thus maintain larger numbers of pigs. Earlier, pigs were not used in the *smiy*, but *kmn* mammals were smoked and stored for one or two months for this, though at least one live *kmn* had to be captured and killed and cooked at the festival. If available, cassowaries were also used at the *smiy*.

28. Narrated in Pidgin English by Gi, 19-year-old youth of Skow, 4 September 1965.

I hope it is not too fanciful to sum up by saying that if cassowaries and dogs are quasi-humans, cassowaries the metaphorical cognates of men and dogs the distant potential affines and adopted children, pigs are not quasi-humans with a separate society of their own, but sub-human or non-human members of the human family: like women, only more so.

The reader may wish to disregard my metaphorical statements about the relationships of these three special beasts to human beings: they are largely based on inferences, perhaps unsystematic, rather than on explicit formulations by Karam themselves. Nevertheless, I hope I have demonstrated that the statuses which these creatures occupy in the totality of Karam activities and thought are complex, and that to understand both their special taxonomic rank and the particular rules which govern their slaughter, handling, and consumption, one has to take an extensive body of ethnography into account. One cannot, I think, be satisfied with simple explanations of such things as dietary status in terms of taxonomy, or taxonomy in terms of dietary status.

There is of course a considerable literature on these problems, including notably Radcliffe-Brown's discussion of taboo (1952) and of ritual attitudes towards animals (1922, 1952) and the more recent contributions of Professor Lévi-Strauss (1966), Dr Leach (1964), Dr Mary Douglas (1966), and Professor Fortes in his recent Presidential Address to the Royal Anthropological Institute. Though I have not made explicit reference to any of this work, some of my debts will be apparent.

However, I shall conclude by referring – over-briefly – to the discussion in Dr Douglas's very interesting recent book (1966) of the status of two particular animals; the pig, as one of the abominations of the Ancient Hebrew, and that most interesting creature, the pangolin, among the Lele of the Congo. If I may somewhat unfairly remove her argument from its full context, Dr Douglas tells us that the pig was an unclean beast to the Hebrew quite simply because it was a taxonomic anomaly, literally, as the Old Testament says, because like normal domestic animals it has a cloven hoof, whereas unlike other cloven-footed beasts, it does not chew the cud (Douglas, 1966). And she pours a certain amount of scorn on the commentators of the last 2,000 years who have taken alternative views and drawn attention to the creature's feeding habits, the quality of its flesh, the moral virtues with which it is or is not endowed, and so on. Without pretending to having any knowledge of Hebraic or Semitic studies, I would myself regard the brief statements in Leviticus and Deuteronomy as taxonomic rationalizations, made by very sophisticated professional rationalizers, to justify the prohibition of a beast which there were probably multiple reasons for avoiding. It would seem equally fair, on the limited evidence available, to argue that the pig was accorded anomalous taxonomic status because it was unclean as to argue that it was unclean because of its anomalous taxonomic status. In any case, Dr Douglas's argument does not concern itself with the reasons why the pig, originally prohibited by a tribe of pastoralists, has remained such a questionable beast right through from Old Testament times to the peoples of the Middle East, the Islamic world, and many western Europeans. Here I find Dr Leach's discussion (1964) very much to the point. The commensal association of pig and man does seem to be the nub of the matter, and the fact that the pig was probably not a commensal associate of the Ancient Hebrew itself perhaps requires more explanation. If the archaeologists could tell us whether or not it was commensally associated with the neighbouring worshippers of heathen idols, this could be relevant.

However, when Dr Douglas leaves the pig and considers the pangolin, which is an animal of great ritual importance to a people for whom the ethnographic record is in many ways more adequate, I find her analysis much more satisfying. Here we are told not merely the many reasons why the beast is taxonomically anomalous (a forest mammal with scales like a fish, which only produces one offspring at a time, and which curls up in a ball when in danger rather than fleeing from the hunter), but also something of the multiple dimensions or contexts of Lele thought and activity in which these anomalies become relevant (Douglas, 1957, 1966).

I am impressed by Dr Douglas's general theory of pollution, that this is associated with things that are out of place in terms of the order which a society seeks to impose upon itself and on the universe it occupies. But the trouble is that things can be out of place in so many different ways, in terms of so many different, even if linked, dimensions. The first problem, operationally, seems to me to be to ensure that the ethnographic record is comprehensively enough recorded and presented. I hope that this presentation of the Karam ethnography will at least indicate the complexity of the ethnographic task.

References

AUFENANGER, H. (1964), 'Auf der Kultur der Simbai – Pygmaen im Schrädergebirge Neu-Guineas', *Ethnos*, no. 29, pp. 141–74.

BIGGS, B. G. (1963), 'A non-phonemic central vowel type in Karam, a 'Pygmy' language of the Schrader Mountains, Central-New-Guinea', *Anthrop. Ling.*, no. 5, pp. 13–17.

BULMER, R. (1964), 'Edible seeds and prehistoric stone mortars in the highlands of east New Guinea', *Man*, no. 64, pp. 147–50.

BULMER, S. (1967), 'Pig bone from two archaeological sites in the New Guinea highlands', *J. Polyn. Soc.*

DIAMOND, J. (1966), 'Zoological classification system of a primitive people', *Science*, no. 151, pp. 1102–4.

DOUGLAS, M. (1957), 'Animals in Lele religious symbolism', *Africa*, no. 27, pp. 46–57.

DOUGLAS, M. (1966), *Purity and Danger*, Routledge & Kegan Paul; Penguin, 1970.

GUNSIDG, M. (1968), 'Die Ayom-Pygmäen auf Neu-Guinea', *Anthropos*, no. 53, pp. 497–574, 817–63.

LEACH, E. (1964), 'Animal categories and verbal abuse', in E. H. Lenneberg (ed.), *New Directions in the Study of Language*, MIT Press.

LÉVI-STRAUSS, C. (1966), *The Savage Mind*, Weidenfeld & Nicolson.

MAYR, E., and GILLIARD, E. T. (1954), 'Birds of central New Guinea', *Bull. Am. Mus. Nat. Hist.*, no. 103, pp. 311–74.

MOYNE, LORD, and HADDON, A. C. (1936), 'The pygmies of the Aiome mountains, mandated territory of New Guinea', *J. R. Anthrop. Inst.*, no. 66, pp. 269–90.

RADCLIFFE-BROWN, A. R. (1922), *The Andaman Islanders*, Cambridge University Press.

RADCLIFFE-BROWN, A. R. (1952), *Structure and Function in Primitive Society*, Cohen & West.

Part Five
The Limits of Knowledge

Already the Readings so far make Wittgenstein's remarks less enigmatic. There was a dialogue that he might not have relished but which could quite properly have taken place between himself and the sociologists and linguists listed in Bernstein's contribution given here. Their reply to him would have been that it is not enough to announce that the limits of my world are my language, for speech is a social activity. Therefore the next question concerning the limits of knowledge is to ask how many kinds of social restraints there are on speech and knowledge.

26 E. Husserl

The Possibility of Cognition

Excerpt from E. Husserl, *The Idea of Phenomenology* (lectures given in 1907),
Martinus Nijhoff, The Hague, 1964, pp. 13–17. First published in 1950.

The natural attitude of mind is as yet unconcerned with the critique of cognition. Whether in the act of intuiting or in the act of thinking, in the natural mode of reflection we are turned to the objects as they are given to us each time and as a matter of course, even though they are given in different ways and in different modes of being, according to the source and level of our cognition. In perception, for instance, a thing stands before our eyes as a matter of course. It is there, among other things, living or lifeless, animate or inanimate. It is, in short, within a world of which part is perceived, as are the individual things themselves, and of which part is contextually supplied by memory from whence it spreads out into the indeterminate and the unknown.

Our judgements relate to this world. We make (sometimes singular, sometimes universal) judgements about things, their relations, their changes, about the conditions which functionally determine their changes and about the laws of their variations. We find an expression for what immediate experience presents. In line with our experiential motives we draw inferences from the directly experienced (perceived and remembered) to what is not experienced. We generalize, and then apply again general knowledge to particular cases or deduce analytically new generalizations from general knowledge. Isolated cognitions do not simply follow each other in the manner of mere succession. They enter into logical relations with each other, they follow from one another, they 'cohere' with one another, they support one another, thereby strengthening their logical power.

On the other hand, they also clash and contradict one another. They do not agree with one another, they are falsified by assured cognition, and their claim to be cognition is discredited. Perhaps the contradictions arise in the sphere that belongs to laws governing the pure predicational form: we have equivocated, we have inferred fallaciously, we have miscounted or miscomputed. In these cases we restore formal consistency. We resolve the equivocation and the like.

Or the contradictions disturb our expectation of connections based on past experience: empirical evidence conflicts with empirical evidence. Where do we look for help? We now weigh the reasons for different possible ways of deciding or providing an explanation. The weaker must give way to the stronger, and the stronger, in turn, are of value as long as they will stand up, i.e. as long as they in turn do not have to come into a similar logical conflict with new cognitional motives introduced by a broader sphere of cognition.

Thus, natural knowledge makes strides. It progressively takes possession of a reality at first existing for us as a matter of course and as something to be investigated further as regards its extent and content, its elements, its relations and laws. Thus the various sciences of the natural sort (*natürlichen Wissenschaften*) come into being and flourish, the natural sciences (*Naturwissenschaften*) as the sciences of physics and psychology, the sciences of culture (*Geisteswissenschaften*) and, on the other side, the mathematical sciences, the sciences of numbers, classes, relations, etc. The latter sciences deal not with actual but rather with ideal objects; they deal with what is valid *per se* and for the rest with what are from the first unquestionable possibilities.

In every step of natural cognition pertaining to the sciences of the natural sort, difficulties arise and are resolved, either by pure logic or by appeal to facts, on the basis of motives or reasons which lie in the things themselves and which, as it were, come from things in the form of requirements that they themselves make on our thinking.

Now let us contrast the natural mode (or habit) of reflection with the philosophical.

With the awakening of reflection about the relation of cognition to its object, abysmal difficulties arise. Cognition, the thing most taken for granted in natural thinking, suddenly emerges as a mystery. But I must be more exact. What is taken for granted in natural thinking is the possibility of cognition. Constantly busy producing results, advancing from discovery to discovery in newer and newer branches of science, natural thinking finds no occasion to raise the question of the possibility of cognition as such. To be sure, as with everything else in the world, cognition, too, will appear as a problem in a certain manner, becoming an object of natural investigation. Cognition is a fact in nature. It is the experience of a cognizing organic being. It is a psychological fact. As any psychological fact, it can be described according to its kinds and internal connections, and its genetic relations can be investigated. On the other hand cognition is essentially cognition of what objectively is; and it is cognition through the meaning which is intrinsic to it; by virtue of this meaning it is related to what objectively is. Natural thinking is also already active in this relating. It investigates in their formal generality the *a priori* connections of meanings and postulated meanings and the *a priori* principles which belong to objectivity as such; there comes into being a pure grammar and at higher stages a pure logic (a whole complex of disciplines owing to its different possible delimitations), and there arises once more a normative and practical logic in the form of an art of thinking, and, especially, of scientific thinking.

So far, we are still in the realm of natural thinking.

However, the correlation between cognition as mental process, its referent (*Bedeutung*) and what objectively is, which has just been touched upon in order to contrast the psychology of cognition with pure logic and ontology, is the source of the deepest and most difficult problems. Taken collectively, they are the problem of the possibility of cognition.

Cognition in all of its manifestations is a psychic act; it is the cognition of a cognizing subject. The objects cognized stand over and against the cognition. But how can we be certain of the correspondence between cognition and the object cognized? How can knowledge transcend itself and reach its object reliably? The unproblematic manner in which the object of cognition is given to natural thought to be cognized now becomes an enigma. In perception the perceived thing is believed to be directly given. Before my perceiving eyes stands the thing. I see it, and I grasp it. Yet the perceiving is simply a mental act of mine, of the perceiving subject. Likewise, memory and expectation are subjective processes; and so are all thought processes built upon them and through which we come to posit that something really is the case and to determine any *truth* about what is. How do I, the cognizing subject, know if I can ever really know, that there exist not only my own mental processes, these acts of cognizing, but also that which they apprehend? How can I ever know that there is anything at all which could be set over against cognition as its object?

Shall I say: only phenomena are truly given to the cognizing subject, he never does and never can break out of the circle of his own mental processes, so that in truth he could only say: I exist, and all that is not-I is mere phenomenon dissolving into phenomenal connections? Am I then to become a solipsist? This is a hard requirement. Shall I, with Hume, reduce all transcendent objectivity to fictions lending themselves to psychological explanation but to no rational justification? But this, too, is a hard requirement. Does not Hume's psychology, along with any psychology, transcend the sphere of immanence? By working with such concepts as habit, human nature, sense-organ, stimulus and the like, is it not working with transcendent existences (and transcendent by its own avowal), while its aim is to degrade to the status of fictions everything that transcends actual 'impressions' and 'ideas'?

But what is the use of invoking the specter of contradictions when *logic itself is in question* and becomes problematic. *Indeed, the real meaning of logical lawfulness*, which natural thinking would not dream of questioning, now becomes *problematic* and *dubious*. Thoughts of a biological order intrude. We are reminded of the modern theory of evolution, according to which man has evolved in the struggle for existence and by natural selection, and with him his intellect too has evolved naturally and along with his intellect all of its characteristic forms, particularly the logical forms. Accordingly, is it not the case that the logical forms and laws express the accidental peculiarity of the human species, which could have been different and which will be different in the course of future evolution? Cognition is, after all, only *human cognition*, bound up with *human intellectual forms*, and unfit to reach the very nature of things, to reach the things in themselves.

But at once another piece of absurdity arises. Can the cognitions by which such a view operates and the possibilities which it ponders make any sense themselves if the laws of logic are given over to such relativism? Does not the truth that there is this and that possibility implicitly presuppose the absolute validity of the principle of non-contradiction, according to which any given truth excludes its contradictory?

These examples should suffice. The possibility of cognition has become enigmatic throughout. If we immerse ourselves in the sciences of the natural sort, we find everything clear and comprehensible, to the extent to which they have developed into exact sciences. We are certain that we are in possession of objective truth, based upon reliable methods of reaching (objective) reality. But whenever we reflect, we fall into errors and confusions. We become entangled in patent difficulties and even self-contradictions. We are in constant danger of becoming sceptics, or still worse, we are in danger of falling into any one of a number of scepticisms all of which have, sad to say, one and the same characteristic: absurdity.

The playground of these unclear and inconsistent theories as well as the endless quarrels associated with them *is the theory of knowledge*, and *metaphysics* which is bound up with it historically and in subject matter. The task of the theory of knowledge or the critique of theoretical reason is, first of all, a critical one. It must brand the well-nigh inevitable mistakes which ordinary reflection makes about the relation of cognition, its meaning and its object, thereby refuting the concealed as well as the unconcealed sceptical theories concerning the essence of cognition by demonstrating their absurdity.

27 L. Wittgenstein

The Limits of my Language mean the Limits of my World

Excerpt from L. Wittgenstein, *Tractatus Logico-Philosophicus*, Routledge & Kegan Paul, second edition of new translation, 1971, pp. 115–17. First published in 1921.

5.6 The limits of my language mean the limits of my world.

5.61 Logic pervades the world: the limits of the world are also its limits.

So we cannot say in logic, 'The world has this in it, and this, but not that.'

For that would appear to presuppose that we were excluding certain possibilities, and this cannot be the case, since it would require that logic should go beyond the limits of the world; for only in that way could it view those limits from the other side as well.

We cannot think what we cannot think; so what we cannot think we cannot *say* either.

5.62 This remark provides the key to the problem, how much truth there is in solipsism.

For what the solipsist *means* is quite correct; only it cannot be *said*, but makes itself manifest.

The world is *my* world: this is manifest in the fact that the limits of *language* (of that language which alone I understand) mean the limits of *my* world.

5.621 The world and life are one.

5.63 I am my world. (The microcosm.)

5.631 There is no such thing as the subject that thinks or entertains ideas.

If I wrote a book called *The World as I Found It*, I should have to include a report on my body, and should have to say which parts were subordinate to my will, and which were not, etc., this being a method of isolating the subject, or rather of showing that in an important sense there is no subject; for it alone could *not* be mentioned in that book.

5.632 The subject does not belong to the world: rather, it is a limit of the world.

5.633 Where *in* the world is a metaphysical subject to be found?

You will say that this is exactly like the case of the eye and the visual field. But really you do *not* see the eye.

And nothing *in the visual field* allows you to infer that it is seen by an eye.

5.6331 For the form of the visual field is surely not like this

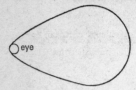

5.634 This is connected with the fact that no part of our experience is at the same time *a priori*.

Whatever we see could be other than it is.

Whatever we can describe at all could be other than it is.

There is no *a priori* order of things.

28 B. Bernstein

The Limits of my Language are Social

Excerpt from B. Bernstein, *Class, Codes and Control*, vol. 1, Routledge & Kegan Paul, 1971, pp. 122–5.

Hoijer, one of the major interpreters of Whorf, states that 'the fashions of speaking peculiar to a people, like other aspects of their culture, are indicative of a view of life, a metaphysics of their culture, compounded of unquestioned and mainly unstated premises which define the nature of the universe and man's position within it'.

This is not the place to follow the many twists and turns of the controversy these writings give rise to, or to examine the empirical support for the theory. This thesis had repercussions for psychology and has been an important factor in bringing about a relationship between linguistics and psychology. One of the many difficulties associated with it is that it focuses upon *universal* features of the formal patterning of language. Although Whorf insists that 'the influence of language upon habitual thought and behaviour does not depend so much on *any one system* (e.g. tense or nouns) within the grammar as upon ways of analysing and reporting experience which have become fixed in the language as integrated "fashions of speaking" which cut across the typical grammatical classifications, so that a "fashion" may include lexical, morphological, syntactic, and otherwise systematically diverse means co-ordinated in a certain frame of consistency'. These fashions of speaking, the frames of consistency, are not related to an institutional order, nor are they seen as emerging from the structure of social relations. On the contrary, they are seen as determiners of social relations through their role in shaping the culture. In Whorf's later writings, and in the writings of his followers, it is certain morphological and syntactic features of the *language* made psychologically active through the fashion of speaking which elicit habitual and characteristic behaviour in the speakers. In other words, the link between language, culture and habitual thought is *not* mediated through the social structure.

The view to be taken here is different in that it will be argued that a number of fashions of speaking, frames of consistency, are possible in any given language and that these fashions of speaking, linguistic forms, or codes, are themselves a function of the form social relations take. According to this view, the form of the social relation or, more generally, the social structure generates distinct linguistic forms or codes and *these codes essentially transmit the culture and so constrain behaviour*.

This thesis is different from that of Whorf. It has more in common with some of the writings of Mead, Sapir, Malinowski and Firth. Whorf's psychology was influenced by the writings of the *gestalt* school of psychology whereas the thesis to be put forward here rests on the work of Vygotsky and Luria. In a sense the Whorfian theory is more general and more challenging; although, perhaps, it is less open to empirical confirmation, for it asserts that owing to the differential rates of change of culture and language *the latter determines the former*. The thesis to be developed here places the emphasis on changes in the social structure as major factors in shaping or changing a given culture through their effect on the consequences of fashions of speaking. It shares with Whorf the controlling influence on experience ascribed to 'frames of consistency' involved in fashions of speaking. It differs and perhaps relativizes Whorf by asserting that, in the context of a common language in the sense of a general code, there will arise distinct linguistic forms, fashions of speaking, which induce in their speakers *different* ways of relating to objects and persons. It leaves open the question whether there are features of the *common culture* which all members of a society share which are determined by the specific nature of the general code or language at its *syntactic* and *morphological* levels. It is, finally, more distinctly sociological in its emphasis on the system of social relations.

To begin with, a distinction must be made between language and speech. Dell Hymes (1961) writes: 'Typically one refers to the act or process of speech, but to the structure, pattern or system of language. Speech is a message, language is a code. Linguists have been preoccupied with inferring the constants of the language code.' The code which the linguistic invents in order to explain speech events is capable of generating n number of speech codes, and there is no reason for believing that any one language or general code is in this respect better than another, whether it is English or whether it is Hopi. On this argument language is a set of rules to which all speech codes must comply, but which speech codes are generated is a function of the system of social relations.[. . .]

The particular form a social relation takes acts selectively on what is said, when it is said, and how it is said. The form of the social relation regulates the options which speakers take up at both syntactic and lexical levels. For example, if an adult is talking to a child he or she will use a speech form in which both the syntax and the vocabulary is simple. Put in another way, the consequences of the form the social relation takes are often transmitted in terms of certain syntactic and lexical selections. Inasmuch as a social relation does this, then it may establish for speakers principles of choice, so that a certain syntax and a certain lexical range is chosen rather than another. The specific principles of choice which regulate these selections entail from the point of view of both speaker and listener planning procedures which guide the speaker in the preparation of his speech and which also guide the listener in its reception.

Changes in the form of certain social relations, it is argued, act selectively upon the principles controlling the selection of both syntactic and lexical options. Changes in the form of the social relation affect the planning procedures used in the preparation of speech and the orientation of the listener. The speech used by members of an army combat unit on manoeuvres will be somewhat different from the same members' speech at a padre's evening. Different forms of social relations can generate quite different speech-systems or linguistic codes by affecting the planning procedures. These different speech-systems or codes create for their speakers different orders of relevance and relation. The experience of the speakers may then be transformed by what is made significant or relevant by the different speech-systems. This is a sociological argument, because the speech-system is taken as a consequence of the form of the social relation or, to put it more generally, is a quality of the social structure.

As the child learns his speech or, in the terms used here, learns specific codes which regulate his verbal acts, he learns the requirements of his social structure. The experience of the child is transformed by the learning which is generated by his own apparently voluntary acts of speech. The social structure becomes the substratum of his experience essentially through the consequences of the linguistic process. From this point of view, every time the child speaks or listens the social structure of which he is a part is reinforced in him and his social identity is constrained. The social structure becomes the developing child's psychological reality by the shaping of his acts of speech. Underlying the general pattern of his speech are, it is held, critical sets of choices, preferences for some alternatives rather than others, which develop and are stabilized through time and which eventually come to play an important role in the regulation of intellectual, social and affective orientations.

The same process can be put rather more formally. Individuals come to learn their roles through the process of communication. A role from this point of view is a constellation of shared learned meanings, through which an individual is able to enter into persistent, consistent and recognized forms of interaction with others. A role is thus a complex coding activity controlling the creation and organization of specific meanings *and* the conditions for their transmission and reception. Now, if it is the case that the communication system which defines a given role behaviourally is essentially that of speech, it should be possible to distinguish critical roles in terms of the speech forms they regulate. The consequences of specific speech forms or codes will transform the environs into a matrix of particular meanings which becomes part of psychic reality through acts of speech. As a person learns to subordinate his behaviour to a linguistic code, which is the expression of the role, different orders of relation are made available to him. The complex of meanings which a role-system transmits reverberates developmentally in an individual to inform his general conduct. On this argument it is the linguistic transformation of the role which is the major bearer of meanings: it is through specific linguistic codes that relevance is created, experience given a particular form, and social identity constrained.

Children who have access to different speech-systems (i.e. learn different roles by virtues of their status position in a given social structure) may adopt quite different social and intellectual procedures despite a common potential.

Reference

HYMES, D. (1961), 'Linguistic aspects of cross-cultural personality study', in B. Kaplan (ed.), *Studying Personality Cross-Culturally*, Row Peterson.

Part Six
Interpenetration of Meanings

These selections extend to all media of expression the implications of the previous section on the social coding of speech. Once the rules for Oxford academic dress have been exhaustively spelled out, we have the full scheme of academic statuses and events. Shiny black low-cut shoes in California were in logical contrast with soft-hued high boots. No mistake was possible about how that social world was constructed. The formality of speech, dress, comportment and table layout are all in harmony when the occasion prescribes: no detail can escape the structuring of the social order.

29 D. R. Venables and R. E. Clifford

Academic Dress

Excerpt from D. R. Venables and R. E. Clifford, *Academic Dress of the University of Oxford*, Private Publication, 1957, pp. 4–8.

Academic dress

The wearing of academic dress is compulsory at all formal ceremonies of the University and generally in the presence of high University officers, at lectures, at examinations and at most official meetings. *Subfusc* clothing is worn with full academic dress.

The dress now worn is much the same as in medieval times, but with certain modifications, the chief of which were made during the sixteenth century.

The Chancellor

The Chancellor of the University is elected by Convocation and holds the position for his lifetime. He is always a member of the University who has achieved notability in public life, and his appearances at ceremonies in Oxford are rare and formal.

At the Encenia the Chancellor occasionally presides over the meeting of Convocation and confers the honorary degrees on famous men and women.

The Chancellor wears an elaborate and distinctive robe made from heavy brocaded silk with gold lace trimming on the collar, facings, back and sleeves. The cap is made from black velvet and has a gold tassel.

The Vice-Chancellor

The Vice-Chancellor, who is always head of an Oxford college, is nominated each year by the Chancellor. It is possible at present for him to hold office for a period of two years.

He is the administrative head of the University and has many statutory powers, besides being the chairman of most of the important University boards and committees.

He wears the robe or gown of the degree to which he is entitled.

The Proctors

The Proctors are elected each year by two of the colleges in turn. They are in charge of discipline in the University and are also members of many boards and committees.

They wear a black full gown, with velvet sleeves and facings and edgings of a broad yellow and a narrow red stripe, together with a black hood lined with miniver fur. A square cap is worn.

Doctors

Doctors wear their full dress robes, white ties and bands at any function indicated on notices or in the *University Gazette* as being one on which 'Doctors will wear their robes'. Doctors of Divinity wear scarves with full dress robes.

Full dress is also worn at the Encaenia, the Encaenia garden party, the occasion of Royal visits and by those attending University sermons on special days, such as Christmas Day. It has also become customary for full dress to be worn at the Maison Française garden party.

At meetings of the Ancient House of Congregation (i.e. degree ceremonies) Doctors wear gowns, habits, hoods, bands and white ties, and a square cap. In Congregation or Convocation, they wear gowns with habits and hoods unless, being Masters of Arts also, they sit with the Masters and wear gowns only.

On any other occasions when full academic dress is specified Doctors wear robes, but not habits or hoods. At private parties, garden parties (other than the Encaenia or Maison Française), and when paying a formal visit to officials either publicly or privately, a black laced gown is worn.

Other graduates

All other graduates wear gowns, hoods and white ties, and a square cap on any occasion indicated by special notice as being one on which 'other graduates wear their hoods'. This applies to the Encaenia, visits of Royalty and any other special occasions. Gowns and hoods are required at the Encaenia garden party, but, by custom, ordinary ties are worn. Assessors and examiners wear gowns, hoods and white ties in the Examination Schools or other place when examining, as do Deans presenting candidates for matriculation or in the Ancient House of Congregation when presenting candidates for degrees.

Gowns only are worn at meetings of Congregation or Convocation, in in the presence of the Chancellor or Vice-Chancellor, either privately or publicly, and when dining in college.

When one of the high officers is invited to a private house, office, room or laboratory, his host does not wear academic dress, although both the Vice-Chancellor and other guests do.

Undergraduates

Undergraduates wear cap and gown in the presence of the Vice-Chancellor or other high officer of the University in their official capacity, also at matriculation ceremonies, examinations, lectures and University ceremonies. At degree ceremonies, examinations and matriculation ceremonies *subfusc* clothing must be worn.

Caps

Caps are worn with academic dress by men when out of doors and at all times by women. The Chancellor, Vice-Chancellor and the Proctors wear caps at all times except in church, in college or in a private place.

Members of other universities

Members of other universities do not wear academic dress within the precincts of the University of Oxford. The one exception is that members of the University of Cambridge wear their robes, as a matter of established custom, when preaching the University sermon at Oxford.

Wearing of bands

In addition to the special occasions when bands are worn as described above, the Vice-Chancellor and Proctors always wear them, as do Pro-Proctors when they are representing the Proctors and Pro-Vice-Chancellors representing the Vice-Chancellor. The Chancellor now wears bands instead of what used to be called a 'waterfall cravat'.

Subfusc clothing

In the Proctors' memorandum on the conduct and discipline of junior members of the University, *subfusc* is described as:

For men: a dark suit, dark socks, black boots or shoes, a white shirt, white collar and white bow tie.

For women: a white blouse, black tie, dark skirt, black stockings, black boots or shoes and, if desired, a dark coat.

30 T. Wolfe

Shiny Black Shoes

Excerpt from T. Wolfe, *The Electric Kool-Aid Acid Test*, Weidenfeld & Nicolson, 1968, pp. 5–6.

The cops now know the whole scene, even the costumes, the jesuschrist strung-out hair, Indian beads, Indian headbands, donkey beads, temple bells, amulets, mandalas, god's-eyes, fluorescent vests, unicorn horns, Errol Flynn dueling shirts – but they still don't know about the shoes. The heads have a thing about shoes. The worst are shiny black shoes with shoelaces in them. The hierarchy ascends from there, although practically all lowcut shoes are unhip, from there on up to the boots the heads like light, fanciful boots, English boots of the mod variety, if that is all they can get, but better something like hand-tooled Mexican boots with Caliente Dude Triple A toes on them. So see the FBI – black – shiny – laced up – FBI shoes – when the FBI finally grabbed Kesey –

There is another girl in the back of the truck, a dark little girl with thick black hair, called Black Maria. She looks Mexican, but she says to me in straight soft Californian:

'When is your birthday?'

'2 March.'

'Pisces,' she says. And then: 'I would never take you for a Pisces.'

'Why?'

'You seem too . . . *solid* for a Pisces.'

But I know she means stolid. I am beginning to feel stolid. Back in New York City, Black Maria, I tell you, I am even known as something of a dude. But somehow a blue silk blazer and a big tie with clowns on it and . . . a . . . pair of shiny lowcut black shoes don't set them all to doing the Varsity Rag in the head world in San Francisco. Lois picks off the marshmallows one by one; Cool Breeze ascends into the innards of his gnome's hat; Black Maria, a Scorpio herself, rummages through the Zodiac; Stewart Brand winds it through the streets; paillettes explode – and this is nothing special, just the usual, the usual in the head world of San Francisco, just a little routine messing up the minds of the citizenry en route, nothing more than psyche food for beautiful people, while giving some guy from New York a lift to the Warehouse to wait for the Chief, Ken Kesey, who is getting out of jail.

31 L. Wittgenstein

Wittgenstein's Tailor

Abridged from L. Wittgenstein, *Lectures and Conversations on Aesthetics, Psychology and Religious Belief*, edited by Cyril Barrett, Basil Blackwell, 1966, pp. 4–10.
  The footnotes were taken down by students in the summer of 1938. 'R' refers to Rush Rhees and 'T' refers to James Taylor – M.D.

11. [*Rhees:* What rule are we using or referring to when we say: 'This is the correct way'? If a music teacher says a piece *should* be played this way and plays it, what is he appealing to?]

12. Take the question: 'How should poetry be read? What is the correct way of reading it?' If you are talking about blank verse the right way of reading it might be stressing it correctly – you discuss how far you should stress the rhythm and how far you should hide it. A man says it ought to be read *this* way and reads it out to you. You say: 'Oh yes. Now it makes sense.' There are cases of poetry which should almost be scanned – where the metre is as clear as crystal – others where the metre is entirely in the background. I had an experience with the eighteenth-century poet Klopstock.[1] I found that the way to read him was to stress his metre abnormally. Klopstock put ⌣—⌣ etc. in front of his poems. When I read his poems in this new way, I said: 'Ah-ha, now I know why he did this.' What had happened? I had read this kind of stuff and had been moderately bored, but when I read it in this particular way, intensely, I smiled, said: 'This is *grand*', etc. But I might not have said anything. The important fact was that I read it again and again. When I read these poems I made gestures and facial expressions which were what would be called gestures of approval. But the important thing was that I read the poems entirely differently, more intensely, and said to others: 'Look! This is how they should be read.'[2] Aesthetic adjectives played hardly any role.

13. What does a person who knows a good suit say when trying on a suit at the tailor's? 'That's the right length,' 'That's too short', 'That's too narrow'. Words of approval play no rôle, although he will look pleased when the coat suits him. Instead of 'That's too short' I might say 'Look!' or instead of 'Right' I might say 'Leave it as it is.' A good cutter may not

  1. Friedrich Gottlieb Klopstock (1724–1803). Wittgenstein is referring to the Odes. Klopstock believed that poetic diction was distinct from popular language. He rejected rhyme as vulgar and introduced instead the metres of ancient literature. (Editor's note.)
  2. If we speak of the right way to read a piece of poetry, approval enters, but it plays a fairly small role in the situation – R.

use any words at all, but just make a chalk mark and later alter it. How do I show my approval of a suit? Chiefly by wearing it often, liking it when it is seen, etc.

14. (If I give you the light and shadow on a body in a picture I can thereby give you the shape of it. But if I give you the highlights in a picture you don't know what the shape is.)

15. In the case of the word 'correct' you have a variety of related cases. There is the first case in which you learn the rules. The cutter learns how long a coat is to be, how wide the sleeve must be, etc. He learns rules – he is drilled – as in music you are drilled in harmony and counterpoint. Suppose I went in for tailoring and I first learnt all the rules, I might have, on the whole, two sorts of attitude. (1) Lewy says: 'This is too short.' I say: 'No. It is right. It is according to the rules.' (2) I develop a feeling for the rules. I interpret the rules. I might say: 'No. It isn't right. It isn't according to the rules.'[3] Here I would be making an aesthetic judgement about the thing which is according to the rules in sense (1). On the other hand, if I hadn't learnt the rules, I wouldn't be able to make the aesthetic judgement. In learning the rules you get a more and more refined judgement. Learning the rules actually changes your judgement. (Although, if you haven't learnt harmony and haven't a good ear, you may nevertheless detect any disharmony in a sequence of chords.)

16. You could regard the rules laid down for the measurement of a coat as an expression of what certain people want.[4] People separated on the point of what a coat should measure: there were some who didn't care if it was broad or narrow, etc.; there were others who cared an enormous lot.[5] The rules of harmony, you can say, expressed the way people wanted chords to follow – their wishes crystallized in these rules (the word 'wishes' is much too vague).[6] All the greatest composers wrote in accordance with them. ([Reply to objection:] You can say that every composer changed the rules, but the variation was very slight; not all the rules were changed. The music was still good by a great many of the old rules. This though shouldn't come in here.) [...]

23. We talked of correctness. A good cutter won't use any words except words like 'Too long', 'All right'. When we talk of a Symphony of Beet-

3. Don't you see that if we made it broader, it isn't right and it isn't according to the rules – R.

4. These may be extremely explicit and taught, or not formulated at all – T.

5. But – it is just a fact that people have laid down such and such rules. We say 'people' but in fact it was a particular class . . . When we say 'people', these were *some* people – R.

6. And although we have talked of 'wishes' here, the fact is just that these rules were laid down – R.

hoven we don't talk of correctness. Entirely different things enter. One wouldn't talk of appreciating the *tremendous* things in Art. In certain styles in Architecture a door is correct, and the thing is you appreciate it. But in the case of a Gothic Cathedral what we do is not at all to find it correct – it plays an entirely different role with us.[7] The entire *game* is different. It is as different as to judge a human being and on the one hand to say 'He behaves well' and on the other hand 'He made a great impression on me.' [. . .]

31. You talk in entirely different terms of the Coronation robe of Edward II and of a dress suit.[8] What did *they* do and say about Coronation robes? Was the Coronation robe made by a tailor? Perhaps it was designed by Italian artists who had their own traditions; never seen by Edward II until he put it on. Questions like 'What standards were there?', etc. are all relevant to the question 'Could you criticize the robe as they criticized it?' You appreciate it in an entirely different way; your attitude to it is entirely different to that of a person living at the time it was designed. On the other hand 'This is a fine Coronation robe!' might have been said by a man at the time in exactly the same way as a man says it now.

7. Here there is no question of *degree* – R.
8. Edward the Confessor – T.

32 Anon

Etiquette: Dinner Party

Excerpt from Anon, *Modern Etiquette in Private and Public*, Frederick Warne, 1872, pp. 16–18.

Very soon after the last guest has arrived, the servant ought to announce dinner, and the host, after directing the gentlemen whom to take in, should offer his arm to the lady of the highest rank in the room, the gentleman of highest station taking the lady of the house.

Now this order of precedency in going in to dinner being likely, if violated, to give offence, it is well that the lady of the house should arrange with her husband how to marshal their guests before they arrive.

With respect to persons of title, these take precedence according to their titles; though, as eldest sons of peers have intermediate places in the scale (so to speak), we advise the lady to have by her Lodge's 'Orders for Precedency,' that she may make no mistakes. Foreign ambassadors are given the precedence of our nobility, out of courtesy, and with respect to their mission; archbishops rank with dukes; bishops with earls.

Ordinary foreign counts and barons have no precedence of title in England, but rank about with English baronets or great landed proprietors.

For *untitled* precedence:

An earl's grandson or granddaughter, and all *near relations* (untitled) of the aristocracy precede the esquires or *country gentlemen*.

Then come:

Wives of country gentlemen of no profession.
Clergymen's wives.
Naval officers and their wives.
Military men and their wives.
Barristers' wives.

There is no specified place for physicians or medical men and their wives, who, however, are ranked in the royal household as next to knights, and whose wives therefore would go out after those of barristers.

These rules appear doubtless to many unnecessary and absurd, but they are not really so; and perhaps there is no truer sign of good breeding than to know how to render 'honour to whom honour is due'. Assuredly they are of great use to prevent personal piques at supposed preferences and neglects.

The gentleman who takes you into the dining-room will sit at your right hand. Take off your gloves, and put them on your lap. Before you, on your plate, will be a table napkin, with a dinner-roll in it; take the bread out and put it at the side of your plate. Lay the opened table napkin in your lap, on your gloves, and then listen gracefully, and with attention, to your companion, who will do his best to amuse you till the soup is handed round.

The lady of the house should be at leisure to give her whole attention to her guests. If a clergyman be present, he is asked to say grace; if not, the gentleman of the house does so.

The present fashion of giving dinner parties *à la Russe*, is far preferable to the old mode of having the joints, etc. on the table; but it supposes that you have a sufficient number of waiters, as otherwise it would be impossible and ridiculous.

The table, then, is laid thus: in the centre is some exquisite ornament – an alabaster stand crowned with pineapples, beneath which hang clusters of grapes; or a frosted-silver tree, with deer, etc. beneath it, holding on its branches glass dishes filled with the most picturesque fruit. Round it the dessert dishes are placed; then small dishes of preserves, sweetmeats, etc. At the house of a nobleman, with whom we occasionally dine, the table – a round one – is encircled by small silver camels, bearing on their backs silver baskets, holding tiny fruits or sweetmeats.

On each plate a bill of fare is placed, so that the guests may see what will be handed round, and may be prepared to select, or wait for, whatever dishes they prefer.

Soup is then handed; wine is offered after it.

Now I must just say (as this book is written for those who do not profess to know much of society) that you should eat your soup from the *side* of your spoon, not take it from the point; that you should make no noise in eating it; that you should beware of tasting it while too hot, or of swallowing it fast enough to make you cough.

You must begin, or appear to begin, to eat as soon as it is put before you; not wait for other people.

Fish follows the soup. You must eat it with a fork, unless silver knives are provided. Break a little crust off your bread, to assist you in taking up your fish, but it is better to eat with the fork only, which you may do if it be turbot or salmon.

Put the sauce when it is handed to you on the side of your plate.

If you do not wish for soup or fish, decline it with a courteous 'No, thank you', to the servant.

After soup and fish come the side dishes, as they would be called, if they were on the table – the oyster or lobster patties, quenelles, etc.

Remember, that for these you use *the fork only;* as, indeed, you should for all dishes which do not absolutely require a knife. You must use a knife, of course, for cutlets of any kind, although they *are* side-dishes. It is proper to eat all soft dishes, as mince, etc., with the fork only.

Do not put your hands on the table, except to eat or carve (the latter is not required at a dinner *à la Russe*). Do not use your handkerchief if you can help it; if you *must* do so, let it be as inaudibly as possible.

Meat, chicken, or turkey are handed after the made-dishes. Then follow game, puddings, tarts, jellies, blancmange, etc.

For the partridge or pheasant, of course you use the knife and fork; all sweets are eaten with the fork, or spoon and fork, as you like; but the spoon is only required for cherry-tart, or anything of that nature, custard, etc.

Ladies scarcely ever eat cheese after dinner. If eaten, remember it should be with *a fork*, not a knife.

You should *never*, by any chance, put a knife near your mouth.

33 L. G. Allen

Etiquette: Table

Excerpt from L. G. Allen, *Table Service*, Little, Brown, 1915, pp. 24–7.

The center of the dining-table should be directly under the central light, unless this position would not permit the waitress to pass between the table and the sideboard. For dinner, lay the silence cloth upon the table. This cloth may be double-faced cotton flannel, knitted table padding, or an asbestos pad; the latter may be obtained in various sizes. The first two launder well; the last is easily handled and may be protected from soiling by the use of linen covers, which can be bought to fit the pads. The table-cloth appears to best advantage when ironed with few folds, which must be straight. A table-cloth should be unfolded on the table, not opened and thrown over it, as the latter method tends to crumple the cloth. The center fold of the cloth must form a true line through the center of the table, having the four corners at equal distances from the floor. The cloth never should hang less than nine inches on all sides below the edge of the table.

Place the centerpiece directly in the center of the table, taking care that the thread of the linen runs in the same direction as the thread of the cloth. Place in center of this a fern dish, growing plant, dish of fruit, or cut flowers. This is the conventional arrangement to be varied by individual taste. The decoration varies in elaborateness with the meal served, but whatever the arrangement, it should be either so low or so high that an unobstructed view may be had across the table.

Lay the covers, allowing twenty-four to thirty inches from plate to plate. A 'cover' consists of the plates, glasses, silver, and napkin to be used by each person. The covers on opposite sides of the table should be directly opposite each other, not out of line. Mark the position of the covers by laying the service or place plates, which should be not less than ten inches in diameter. In laying a bare table, the covers are marked by the plate doilies. A service plate is laid for each person, one inch from the edge of the table; this plate remains upon the table until it is necessary to replace it with a hot plate.

Next, lay the silver, which should always be placed in the order in which it is to be used, beginning at the outside and using toward the plate. Silver for the dessert course is never put on with the silver required for the other

Figure 1 Placing luncheon napkin

courses, except for the dinner which is served without a maid, when everything should be done to avoid the necessity of leaving the table. Neither is the table set with more than three forks. If more are required, they are placed with their respective courses. Either bring the salad or dessert silver in on the plate, or place it from a napkin or tray at the right, from the right, after the plate is placed. Some persons object to the first-named method, on account of the possible noise. The knife or knives are to be placed at the right of the plate, half an inch from the edge of the table, with the cutting edge toward the plate. Place spoons, with the bowls facing up, at the right of the knife; and forks, with the tines turned upward, at the left of the plate. The spoon for fruit or the small fork for oysters or hors-d'oeuvres is placed at the extreme right or on the plate containing this course. This statement does not include the serving of oysters or clams on the shell; then the fork is always found at the right.

Place the napkin, preferably flat and squarely folded, at the left of the forks. The hem and selvage of the napkin should be parallel with the forks and the edge of the table, this position bringing the embroidered letter, if there be one, in the right place. Napkins are sometimes given additional folds to save space.

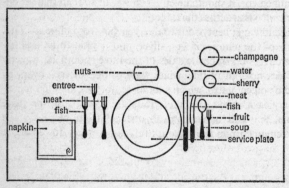

Figure 2 Formal dinner cover in detail

34 A. Fortescue and J. O'Connell

Etiquette: Altar

Abridged from A. Fortescue and J. O'Connell, *The Ceremonies of the Roman Rite Described*, Burns, Oates & Washbourne, 7th (revised and enlarged) edition, 1943, pp. 3–7.

The chief object in the sanctuary is the *altar* in the middle; this will be the High Altar of the church. All others are counted as side altars.

Altars

There are two kinds of altar; the fixed altar (*altare fixum*) and portable altar (*altare portatile*).

A *fixed altar* must be of stone with the table and base permanently united. A relic of at least one martyr is buried in it. The whole top (the 'mensa') of the altar is of stone and joined by stone to the ground; it is all consecrated as one thing. [. . .]

There should be some kind of canopy over the altar. This may hang from the roof of the church (a baldachin or tester) or may stand on columns (a ciborium or civory). It should cover not only the altar, but also the foot-pace, or at least the priest celebrating. The altar should not stand immediately against the wall of the church; at the consecration of an altar the rubrics require that the consecrating bishop go round it.

The altar is raised above the floor of the sanctuary by steps. Every altar should be raised at least one step; the High Altar will have three or more steps. There should be an uneven number. . . .

The proportion of beeswax in church candles is regulated by law. The Paschal candle, the two candles for Low Mass, six for High Mass, and the twelve necessary for Exposition and Benediction must have at least 65 per cent of real beeswax. All other candles used on an altar must have at least 25 per cent of beeswax. The firms which provide candles for Catholic churches stamp the percentage of beeswax on their candles.

Flowers on the altar are not necessary. They are not used in the great churches of Rome. But there is no law against them at certain times; and in England and Ireland custom is in favour of their use. They should, however, be used with the greatest restraint.

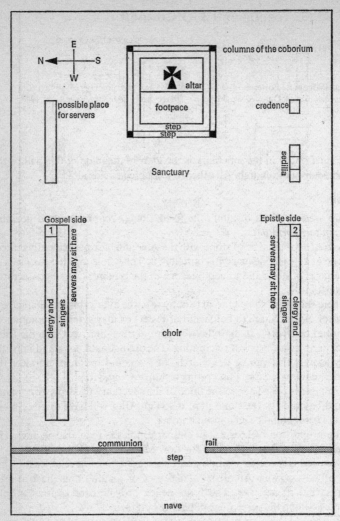

Figure 1 Plan of a parish church : choir and sanctuary

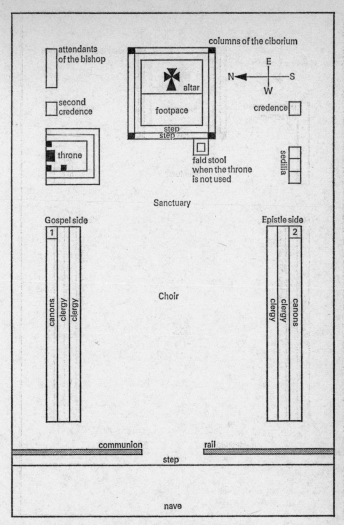

Figure 2 Plan of a cathedral church: choir and sanctuary

Part Seven
Provinces of Meaning

This section should be read against the background of Part Four. Alfred
Schutz considers how social realities are partitioned off from one another,
each with its own structuring of time and space so bounded that to cross
from one to another means a shock. He instances jokes, games, religion
and science as such bounded provinces of meaning. But since it is the same
people who are making the boundaries and crossing them with experiences
of shock, the idea of fully insulated provinces of meaning suggests two
reflections. On the one hand, if the insulation of a game is complete, the
triviality of the experience is assured, for it is by definition cut off from
all that has meaning for the players. On the other hand, insulation is very
difficult and unlikely. The two principal papers in Part Four, on the
classification of animals, show how the very form of the rules which assign
elements to categories carries the stamp of social concerns and imports
these concerns into such apparently neutral areas as animal taxonomy.
To achieve real insulation requires a deliberate breaking of the thread,
either by the monastic seclusion which enshrined the Glass Bead Game or
by a destructive and seemingly irrational refusal to accept rules from other
provinces.

These considerations throw doubt on the oft-vaunted insulation of music
from other experience. It is misleading to argue that music, by reason of its
abstract qualities, is a form of aesthetic enjoyment which is completely cut
off from social concerns.

Musical habits include scales, modes, theories of counterpoint and harmony, and
the study of the timbres, singly and in combination of a limited number of sound-
producing mechanisms. In mathematical terms these all concern discrete steps.
They resemble walking – in the case of pitches, on steppingstones twelve in
number.

As Cage is fully aware, the careful, limited walking on stepping-stones,
twelve in number, recalls the precise instructions for laying a dinner table
or an altar (see Part Six). The more the mathematical complexity, the more
the pressure of social judgements which assess the rules and the execution

of the piece in the same way as Wittgenstein's friend assesses his tailor's work. Just because mathematics and music are supremely capable of exploring formal properties, it cannot be argued that their power to move us lies in their capacity for being insulated. Formal correspondences connect different areas of experience.

35 A. Schutz

Multiple Realities

Excerpts from A. Schutz, *Collected Papers I, The Problem of Social Reality*,
Martinus Nijhoff, The Hague, 1967, pp. 207 and 229–233. First published in 1945.

In a famous chapter of his *Principles of Psychology* William James analyses
our sense of reality. Reality, so he states, means simply relation to our
emotional and active life. The origin of all reality is subjective, whatever
excites and stimulates our interest is real. To call a thing real means that
this thing stands in a certain relation to ourselves. 'The word "real" is, in
short, a fringe.' Our primitive impulse is to affirm immediately the reality of
all that is conceived, as long as it remains uncontradicted. But there are
several, probably an infinite number of various orders of realities, each
with its own special and separate style of existence. James calls them 'sub-
universes' and mentions as examples the world of sense or physical things
(as the paramount reality), the world of science, the world of ideal relations,
the world of 'idols of the tribe', the various supernatural worlds of mythology and religion, the various worlds of individual opinion, the worlds of
sheer madness and vagary. The popular mind conceives of all these subworlds more or less disconnectedly, and when dealing with one of them
forgets for the time being its relations to the rest. But every object we think
of is at last referred to one of these subworlds. 'Each world whilst it is
attended to is real after its own fashion; only the reality lapses with
the attention.' [. . .] James himself has pointed out that each of these sub-
universes has its special and separate style of existence; that with respect to
each of these sub-universes 'all propositions, whether attributive or existential, are believed through the very fact of being conceived, unless they
clash with other propositions believed at the same time, by affirming that
their terms are the same with the terms of these other propositions'; that
the whole distinction of real and unreal is grounded on two mental facts –
'first, that we are liable to think differently of the same; and second that,
when we have done so, we can choose which way of thinking to adhere to
and which to disregard.' James speaks therefore of a 'sense of reality'
which can be investigated in terms of a psychology of belief and disbelief.

In order to free this important insight from its psychologistic setting we
prefer to speak instead of many sub-universes of reality, of *finite provinces
of meaning* upon each of which we may bestow the accent of reality. We

speak of provinces of *meaning* and not of sub-universes because it is the meaning of our experiences and not the ontological structure of the objects which constitutes reality (see Husserl, 1931). Hence we call a certain set of our experiences a finite province of meaning if all of them show a specific cognitive style and are – *with respect to this style* – not only consistent in themselves but also compatible with one another. The italicized restriction is important because inconsistencies and incompatibilities of *some* experiences, all of them partaking of the same cognitive style, do not necessarily entail the withdrawal of the accent of reality from the respective province of meaning as a whole but merely the invalidation of the particular experience or experiences *within* that province. What, however, has to be understood under the terms 'specific cognitive style' and 'accent of reality'?

As an example let us consider again the world of everyday life as it was defined and analyzed in the preceding section. This world is certainly a 'sub-universe' or 'finite province of meaning' among many others, although one marked out as ultimate or paramount reality for the reasons mentioned in the last section. If we recapitulate the basic characteristics which constitute its specific cognitive style we find:

1. A specific tension of consciousness, namely wide-awakeness, originating in full attention to life.
2. A specific *epoché*, namely suspension of doubt.
3. A prevalent form of spontaneity, namely working (a meaningful spontaneity based upon a project and characterized by the intention of bringing about the projected state of affairs by bodily movements gearing into the outer world).
4. A specific form of experiencing one's self (the working self as the total self).
5. A specific form of sociality (the common intersubjective world of communication and social action).
6. A specific time-perspective (the standard time originating in an intersection between *durée* and cosmic time as the universal temporal structure of the intersubjective world).

These are at least some of the features of the cognitive style belonging to this particular province of meaning. As long as our experiences of this world – the valid as well as the invalidated ones – partake of this style we may consider this province of meaning as real, we may bestow upon it the accent of reality. And with respect to the paramount reality of everyday life we, within the natural attitude, are induced to do so because our practical experiences prove the unity and congruity of the world of working as valid and the hypothesis of its reality as irrefutable. Even more, this reality seems to us to be the natural one, and we are not ready to abandon our attitude toward it without having experienced a specific *shock* which compels us to break through the limits of this 'finite' province of meaning and to shift the accent of reality to another one.

To be sure, those experiences of shock befall me frequently amidst my daily life; they themselves pertain to its reality. They show me that the world of working in standard time is not the sole finite province of meaning but only one of many others accessible to my intentional life.

There are as many innumerable kinds of different shock experiences as there are different finite provinces of meaning upon which I may bestow the accent of reality. Some instances are: the shock of falling asleep as the leap into the world of dreams; the inner transformation we endure if the curtain in the theater rises as the transition into the world of the stageplay; the radical change in our attitude if, before a painting, we permit our visual field to be limited by what is within the frame as the passage into the pictorial world; our quandary, relaxing into laughter, if, in listening to a joke, we are for a short time ready to accept the fictitious world of the jest as a reality in relation to which the world of our daily life takes on the character of foolishness; the child's turning toward his toy as the transition into the playworld; and so on. But also the religious experiences in all their varieties – for instance, Kierkegaard's experience of the 'instant' as the leap into the religious sphere – are examples of such a shock, as well as the decision of the scientist to replace all passionate participation in the affairs of 'this world' by a disinterested contemplative attitude.

Now we are able to condense what we have found into the following theses:

1. All these worlds – the world of dreams, of imageries and phantasms, especially the world of art, the world of religious experience, the world of scientific contemplation, the play world of the child, and the world of the insane – are finite provinces of meaning. This means that:
(a) all of them have a peculiar cognitive style (although not that of the world of working within the natural attitude);
(b) all experiences within each of these worlds are, with respect to this cognitive style, consistent in themselves and compatible with one another (although not compatible with the meaning of everyday life);
(c) each of these finite provinces of meaning may receive a specific accent of reality (although not the reality accent of the world of working).

2. Consistency and compatibility of experiences with respect to their peculiar cognitive style subsists merely *within* the borders of the particular province of meaning to which those experiences belong. By no means will that which is compatible within the province of meaning P be also compatible within the province of meaning Q. On the contrary, seen from

P, supposed to be real, Q and all the experiences belonging to it would appear as merely fictitious, inconsistent and incompatible and vice versa.

3. For this very reason we are entitled to talk of *finite* provinces of meaning. This finiteness implies that there is no possibility of referring one of these provinces to the other by introducing a formula of transformation. The passing from one to the other can only be performed by a 'leap', as Kierkegaard calls it, which manifests itself in the subjective experience of a shock.[1]

4. What has just been called a 'leap' or a 'shock' is nothing else than a radical modification in the tension of our consciousness, founded in a different *attention à la vie*.

5. To the cognitive style peculiar to each of these different provinces of meaning belongs, thus, a specific tension of consciousness and, consequently, also a specific *epoché*, a prevalent form of spontaneity, a specific form of self experience, a specific form of sociality, and a specific time perspective.

6. The world of working in daily life is the archetype of our experience of reality. All the other provinces of meaning may be considered as its modifications.[2]

It would be an interesting task to try a systematic grouping of these finite provinces of meaning according to their constitutive principle, the diminishing tension of our consciousness founded in a turning away of our attention from everyday life. Such an analysis would prove that the more the mind turns away from life, the larger the slabs of the everyday world of working which are put in doubt; the *epoché* of the natural attitude which suspends doubt in its existence is replaced by other *epochés* which suspend belief in more and more layers of the reality of daily life, putting them in brackets. In other words, a typology of the different finite provinces of meaning could start from an analysis of those factors of the world of daily life from

1. For a discussion of the transition from the paramount reality to other finite provinces of meaning experienced through a shock, see *Symbol, Reality and Society*, pp. 343ff. (M.N.)

2. A word of caution seems to be needed here. The concept of finite provinces of meaning does not involve any static connotation as though we had to select one of these provinces as our home to live in, to start from or to return to. That is by no means the case. Within a single day, even within a single hour our consciousness may run through most different tensions and adopt most different attentional attitudes to life. There is, furthermore, the problem of 'enclaves', that is, of regions belonging to one province of meaning enclosed by another, a problem which, important as it is, cannot be handled within the frame of the present paper, which admittedly restricts itself to the outlining of a few principles of analysis. To give an example of this disregarded group of problems: any projecting within the world of working is itself, as we have seen, a fantasying, and involves in addition a kind of theoretical contemplation, although not necessarily that of the scientific attitude.

which the accent of reality has been withdrawn because they do not stand any longer within the focus of our attentional interest in life. What then remains outside the brackets could be defined as the constituent elements of the cognitive style of experiences belonging to the province of meaning thus delimited. It may, then, in its turn, obtain another accent of reality, or, in the language of the archetype of all reality, namely the world of our daily life – of quasi-reality.

Reference

HUSSERL, E. (1931), *General Introduction to Pure Phenomenology*.

36 E. E. Evans-Pritchard

Social Principles of Selection

Excerpts from E. E. Evans-Pritchard, *Witchcraft, Oracles and Magic among the Azande*, Clarendon Press, 1937, pp. 74–75, 80 and 114.

Since Azande recognize plurality of causes, and it is the social situation that indicates the relevant one, we can understand why the doctrine of witchcraft is not used to explain every failure and misfortune. It sometimes happens that the social situation demands a common-sense, and not a mystical, judgement of cause. Thus, if you tell a lie, or commit adultery, or steal, or deceive your prince, and are found out, you cannot elude punishment by saying that you were bewitched. Zande doctrine declares emphatically 'Witchcraft does not make a person tell lies'; 'Witchcraft does not make a person commit adultery'; 'Witchcraft does not put adultery into a man.' 'Witchcraft' is in yourself (you alone are responsible), that is, your penis becomes erect. It sees the hair of a man's wife and it rises and becomes erect because the only 'witchcraft' is, itself ('witchcraft' is here used metaphorically); 'Witchcraft does not make a person steal'; 'Witchcraft does not make a person disloyal.' Only on one occasion have I heard a Zande plead that he was bewitched when he had committed an offence and this was when he lied to me, and even on this occasion everybody present laughed at him and told him that witchcraft does not make people tell lies.

If a man murders another tribesman with knife or spear he is put to death. It is not necessary in such a case to seek a witch, for an objective towards which vengeance may be directed is already present. If, on the other hand, it is a member of another tribe who has speared a man his relatives, or his prince, will take steps to discover the witch responsible for the event.

It would be treason to say that a man put to death on the orders of his king for an offence against authority was killed by witchcraft. If a man were to consult the oracles to discover the witch responsible for the death of a relative who had been put to death at the orders of his king he would run the risk of being put to death himself. For here the social situation excludes the notion of witchcraft as on other occasions it pays no attention to natural agents and emphasizes only witchcraft. Also, if a man were killed in vengeance because the oracles said that he was a witch and had murdered another man with his witchcraft then his relatives could not say that he had been killed by witchcraft. Zande doctrine lays it down that he died at the hand of avengers because he was a homicide. If a man were to have expressed the view that his kinsman had been killed by witchcraft and to have acted upon his opinion by consulting the poison oracle, he might have been punished for ridiculing the king's poison oracle, for it was the poison oracle of the king that had given official confirmation of the man's guilt, and it was the king himself who had permitted vengeance to take its course.

In the instances given in the preceding paragraphs it is the natural cause and not the mystical cause that is selected as the socially significant one. In these situations witchcraft is irrelevant and, if not totally excluded, is not indicated as the principal factor in causation. As in our own society a scientific theory of causation, if not excluded, is deemed irrelevant in questions of moral and legal responsibility, so in Zande society the doctrine of witchcraft, if not excluded, is deemed irrelevant in the same situations. We accept scientific explanations of the causes of disease, and even of the causes of insanity, but we deny them in crime and sin because here they militate against law and morals which are axiomatic. The Zande accepts a mystical explanation of the causes of misfortune, sickness, and death, but he does not allow this explanation if it conflicts with social exigencies expressed in law and morals. [. . .]

From generation to generation Azande regulate their economic activities according to a transmitted body of knowledge, in their building and crafts no less than their agricultural and hunting pursuits. They have a sound working knowledge of nature in so far as it concerns their welfare. Beyond this point it has for them no scientific interest or sentimental appeal. It is true that their knowledge is empirical and incomplete and that it is not transmitted by any systematic teaching but is handed over from one generation to another slowly and casually during childhood and early manhood. Yet it suffices for their everyday tasks and seasonal pursuits. When in spite of it they fail, the reason for their failure is known in advance – it is due to witchcraft. [. . .]

Nevertheless, public opinion only attributes failure to witchcraft when all possibility of technical error has been eliminated. It is easy to see that this must be the case, for technical rules are in themselves a recognition of technical errors, and the rules could never be maintained unless errors were attributed to human responsibility. No Zande youth would ever learn to fashion a pot, weave a hat, make a spear, or carve a bowl if he attributed all his errors to witchcraft, for a man becomes a good craftsman by perceiving his own errors and those of others.

Looked at from this aspect it is easier to understand how Azande fail to observe and define the fact that not only may anybody be a witch, which they readily admit, but that most commoners are witches. Azande at once challenge your statement if you say that most people are witches. Notwithstanding, in my experience all except the noble class and commoners of influential position at court are at one time or another exposed by oracles as having bewitched their neighbours and therefore as witches. This must necessarily be the case, since all men suffer misfortunes and every man is some one's enemy. Every one is disliked by someone, and this somebody will some day fall sick or suffer loss and consult oracles about those who do not find favour in his eyes. But it is generally only those who make themselves disliked by many of their neighbours who are often accused of witchcraft and earn a reputation as witches.

Keeping our eyes fixed on the dynamic meaning of witchcraft, and recognizing therefore its universality, we shall better understand how it comes about that witches are not ostracized and persecuted; for what is a function of passing states and is common to most men cannot be treated with severity. The position of a witch is in no way analogous to that of a criminal in our own society, and he is certainly not an outcast living in the shadow of disgrace and shunned by his neighbours. I had certainly expected to find, not only that witchcraft was abhorrent to Azande, but that a witch, though not killed today owing to European rule, suffers social ostracism. I found that this was far from being the case. On the contrary, confirmed witches, known for miles around as such, live like ordinary citizens. Often they are respected fathers and husbands, welcome visitors to homesteads and guests at feasts, and sometimes influential members of the inner-council at a prince's court. Some of my acquaintances were notorious witches.

37 C. W. M. Hart and A. R. Pilling

Rules Ensure Correspondence between Provinces:
The Judicial Contest

Excerpt from C. W. M. Hart and A. R. Pilling, *The Tiwi of North Australia*,
Holt, Rinehart & Winston, 1960, pp. 80–83.

Thus the isolation of the Tiwi made the rule of the gerontocracy much
more absolute, and the enforcement of it much more effective than was
possible for any of the mainland tribes where violators of the rules could
skip across the border. Tiwi bachelors had to be satisfied, by and large,
with casual and temporary liaisons and even in these, because of the constant suspicion of the old husbands and the constant spying and scandal-
mongering of the old wives, they had to be prepared to be often caught and,
when caught, to be punished. Thus we come to another of the main
emphases in Tiwi culture – the enormous frequency of disputes, fights,
duels, and war parties arising directly or indirectly out of cases of seduction.
If we may call this area of life the legal area, then over 90 per cent of legal
affairs were matters in which women were in some way involved.

The Tiwi formula for handling seduction was very straightforward and
clear cut in its formal outline. Since senior men had young wives and young
men had not, seduction was necessarily viewed as an offense by a young
man against a senior man. Hence the charge was always laid by the senior
and the young man was always the defendant.[1] At night in camp the
accuser hurled his charges at the offender. We described earlier the alternatives available at this stage to both parties. Two of those alternatives were
for the old man to press the matter to a public 'trial,' either the next day, if
the camp was already a large one, or else on the next occasion when both
men were present in a big gathering.

The basic shape of all Tiwi trials was standardized in the form that we
have been calling the duel. Everybody present – men, women, children, and
dogs – formed a rough circle in an open space, sitting or standing according

---

1. Under pre-white conditions this had to be so. After the arrival of the Catholic
missionaries, some young men through Mission manipulation got a young wife at an
age that would have been impossible earlier. This resulted in an occasional case around
the Mission where a *young* husband charged a man older than himself with seducing
his wife. The resulting duel, with an older man as defendant, was regarded by the Tiwi
as both embarrassing and ludicrous, perhaps analogous to the average American's
attitude toward female professional wrestlers. (See Hart, 1954 for a case of this sort,
the duel of Bob *v.* Louis.)

to their degree of excitement at the moment. At one end stood the accuser, the old man, covered from head to foot in white paint, with his ceremonial spears in one hand and a bundle of the more useful hunting spears in the other. At the opposite end stood the defendant, with little or no paint on him, perhaps holding a hunting spear or two in his hand (a sign of insolence), perhaps holding only throwing sticks (less defiant, since the stick was an inferior weapon more appropriate to young men), or perhaps entirely weaponless (a sign of proper humility and the deference to his seniors that all bachelors ought to show in such situations). The accuser, with many gestures, particularly with much stamping of the feet and chewing of the beard, told the young man in detail precisely what he and all right-minded members of the community thought of him. This angry, loud harangue went into minute detail, not only about the actual offense, but the whole life career of the defendant, and paid particular attention to occasions in the past when the old man even remotely, or some of his relatives, even more remotely, had performed kindnesses toward either the young man or some of his relatives. It is difficult to summarize briefly one of these harangues, but the general formula, subject to much variation by each individual accuser, appeared to be the building up of as much contrast as possible between the criminal or antisocial character of the young man's actions and the fact that he was a member of a network of interpersonal relationships in which mutual aid and reciprocal obligations were essential. The Tiwi orators, of course, did not put the matter in such abstract terms. They listed the long catalogue of people who had done things for the young man since his birth, and for his ancestors and relatives, until the catalogue took in practically the whole tribe – past, present, and future. And what had he done to repay his obligations to all these people? 'Why, the miserable, ungrateful wretch spends his time hanging around my camp, etc., etc. And not only my camp, but last year it was widely believed that he was indulging in similar actions around the camp of my esteemed fellow-elder, So-and-So.' We do not think that we are overintellectualizing the content of these harangues if we say that they involved the old man's reminding the young man of his debt to society, and his attempting to convey the idea that social life needed mutual aid and trust between all its members.

After twenty minutes or so of this sociological abuse and blame-spinning, the old man threw aside his ceremonial spears and began to throw his hunting spears at the defendant. This active phase of the duel conformed to a stereotyped pattern which in some respects resembled baseball. The old man stood about ten feet farther away from the young man than the pitcher stands from the plate. The young man had to avoid being hit by the spears. To do this he was permitted to jump from side to side or into the air, or to duck, but he was expected always to land on approximately the same spot as he had been standing on when the first spear was thrown. Thus there was no marked strike zone, but an implied one. If the accused jumped well away from the strike zone, he was jeered by the crowd. If the old man was wild, he was jeered too, but more respectfully. Under such rules a modern baseball hitter, having no bat in his hand to worry about, would almost never be hit by a pitched ball, and the Tiwi young men were similarly never likely to be hit by an old man's spears. The main danger was the spear that pitched in the dirt. Although clearly outside the strike zone and hence an indication that the old man was really wild, such a spear was apt to carom off the ground at an unexpected angle and inflict a severe wound before the spectators (as collective umpires) had time to call it – in which case the duel was over and the accused was punished.[2]

Apart from those that unpredictably deflected off the ground, or even off a neighboring tree, the young man could dodge the old man's spears indefinitely if he wanted to. He was much younger and hence almost invariably in much better shape than the older man. But if he did this, the old man soon began to look a little ridiculous, and Tiwi society thoroughly disapproved of young men who made old men look ridiculous in public. Continued dodging and jumping and weaving of the body, no matter how gracefully they were done, were not prolonged by any young man who hoped in time to become a respected elder himself. The elders in the last analysis controlled bestowals, and holding one of them up to public ridicule was sure to antagonize all of them. So the young man, having for five or ten minutes demonstrated his physical ability to avoid being hit, then showed a proper moral attitude by allowing himself to be hit. This took even greater skill in bodily movement . Trying to lose a fight without making it too obvious to the crowd and without getting hurt too much oneself is a problem that confronts some professional athletes in our own culture, and few of them do it with as much skill as the younger Tiwi in the same situation. A fairly deep cut on the arm or thigh that bled a lot but healed quickly was the most desirable wound to help the old man inflict, and when the blood gushed from such a wound the crowd yelled approval and the duel was over. The young man had behaved admirably, the old man had vindicated his honor, the sanctity of marriage and the Tiwi constitution had been upheld, and everybody went home satisfied and full of moral rectitude. Seduction did not pay.

This was the Tiwi duel as it ideally should be conducted, and in perhaps as many as two-thirds of all such disputes it was so conducted. Divergences from this form clearly arose from the unpredictability of human beings and

2. Two cases of broken legs below the knee within six weeks of each other in 1928 give some indication of the force with which such badly aimed spears would bounce off the ground.

their fondness for trying to exercise choice instead of following a set pattern. Though the dice were heavily loaded against them, some Tiwi young men chose defiance instead of repentance. There were various avenues of defiance open to them. The mildest was to refuse to allow the old man's spears to hit the target. Slightly more brazen were the young men who turned up at the beginning of the duel with throwing sticks or hunting spears in their hands, even though they used these not to throw but to knock aside contemptuously the spears of the old man. More brazen still was the young man, rare but not unknown, who went so far as to throw missiles back at the older accuser. All such attempts to defy the traditional pattern of the duel met with the same response, and that very quickly. The duel began as usual with the two antagonists facing one another inside the circle of spectators. As soon as it became apparent that the young man was not conforming to the normal pattern of meekness and nonretaliation, there would be immediate activity on the sidelines. Two or three or four senior men would leave the spectators and range themselves alongside the accuser, spears in hand. Other senior men would quietly leave their seats and sit down in the audience alongside close relatives of the young defendant, particularly his full brothers or his father, if they were present, and gently lay restraining hands upon them. Within a few minutes there was no longer an old man facing a young man but as many as four or five old men facing one young man, and no sign of support for him. His close male relatives would keep their seats or (more often) allow themselves to be led away as if they did not want to witness what was coming next. Never, in any of these cases, did any supporter of the young man step into the ring and line up with him. He remained an isolate, faced by several older men, and of course he had no chance. It was easy to dodge the spears of one opponent, since they had to be thrown one at a time; it was impossible to dodge the spears of more than one, since they could be thrown more or less simultaneously.

Usually this baring of its teeth by society-at-large was enough. The group of elders did not need to throw many spears simultaneously. The accused capitulated by throwing aside his spears or throwing sticks, or if the defiance had been only of the mildest form – namely, an undue prolongation of the dodging – he allowed his accuser to score a direct hit and the duel ended in the normal way. In the rare cases of the accused refusing to give up, even when confronted by a menacing line of several elders, a concerted volley or two from them quickly knocked him out, and in pre-white days, usually killed him.[3] Crime thus paid even less for the accused who chose defiance

3. Since the coming of white administration, the Tiwi have found that when a man is killed in a native duel, there is a strong likelihood that white policemen will appear and will drag some of them off to Darwin where incomprehensible proceedings called murder trials then take place. To avoid such nonsense, since about 1925 they have

than it did for the accused who allowed himself to be wounded in a duel by a doddering ancient three times his age. The greater the amount of defiance, the more clear it became that the doddering ancient, acting ostensibly as an outraged husband, was the responsible agent of society dispensing public justice. If he needed help, all responsible elders went to his aid, and the kinsmen of the accused stood aside and let justice take its course.

---

tended to use throwing sticks rather than spears in their fighting. Throwing sticks, while dangerous, seldom kill people outright and as long as nobody is killed, the police in Darwin show no interest in native fights on the islands.

38 H. Hesse

Insulation makes the Finite Province Trivial: The Glass Bead Game

Excerpts from H. Hesse, *The Glass Bead Game*, Jonathan Cape, 1970, pp. 30–33 and 36–8. First published in 1943.

We shall now give a brief summary of the beginnings of the Glass Bead Game. It appears to have arisen simultaneously in Germany and in England. In both countries, moreover, it was originally a kind of exercise employed by those small groups of musicologists and musicians who worked and studied in the new seminaries of musical theory. If we compare the original state of the Game with its subsequent developments and its present form, it is much like comparing a musical score of the period before 1500, with its primitive notes and absence of bar lines, with an eighteenth-century score, let alone with one from the nineteenth with its confusing excess of symbols for dynamics, tempi, phrasing, and so on, which often made the printing of such scores a complex technical problem.

The Game was at first nothing more than a witty method for developing memory and ingenuity among students and musicians. And as we have said, it was played both in England and Germany before it was 'invented' here in the Musical Academy of Cologne, and was given the name it bears to this day, after so many generations, although it has long ceased to have anything to do with glass beads.

The inventor, Bastian Perrot of Calw, a rather eccentric but clever, sociable, and humane musicologist, used glass beads instead of letters, numerals, notes, or other graphic symbols. Perrot, who incidentally has also bequeathed to us a treatise on the *Apogee and Decline of Counterpoint*, found that the pupils at the Cologne Seminary had a rather elaborate game they used to play. One would call out, in the standardized abbreviations of their science, motifs or initial bars of classical compositions, whereupon the other had to respond with the continuation of the piece, or better still with a higher or lower voice, a contrasting theme, and so forth. It was an exercise in memory and improvisation quite similar to the sort of thing probably in vogue among ardent pupils of counterpoint in the days of Schütz, Pachelbel and Bach – although it would then not have been done in theoretical formulas, but in practice on the cembalo, lute or flute or with the voice.

Bastian Perrot in all probability was a member of the Journeyers to the East. He was partial to handicrafts and had himself built several pianos and clavichords in the ancient style. Legend has it that he was adept at playing the violin in the old way, forgotten since 1800, with a high-arched bow and hand-regulated tension of the bow hairs. Given these interests, it was perhaps only natural that he should have constructed a frame, modeled on a child's abacus, a frame with several dozen wires on which could be strung glass beads of various sizes, shapes, and colors. The wires corresponded to the lines of the musical staff, the beads to the time-values of the notes, and so on. In this way he could represent with beads musical quotations or invented themes, could alter, transpose, and develop them, change them and set them in counterpoint to one another. In technical terms this was a mere plaything, but the pupils liked it; it was imitated and became fashionable in England too. For a time the game of musical exercises was played in this charmingly primitive manner. And as is so often the case, an enduring and significant institution received its name from a passing and incidental circumstance. For what later evolved out of that students' sport and Perrot's bead-strung wires bears to this day the name by which it became popularly known, the Glass Bead Game.

A bare two or three decades later the Game seems to have lost some of its popularity among students of music, but instead was taken over by mathematicians. For a long while, indeed, a characteristic feature in the Game's history was that it was constantly preferred, used, and further elaborated by whatever branch of learning happened to be experiencing a period of high development or a renaissance. The mathematicians brought the Game to a high degree of flexibility and capacity for sublimation, so that it began to acquire something approaching a consciousness of itself and its possibilities. This process paralleled the general evolution of cultural consciousness, which had survived the great crisis and had, as Plinius Ziegenhalss puts it, 'with modest pride accepted the fate of belonging to a culture past its prime, as was the case with the culture of late antiquity: Hellenistic culture in the Alexandrian Age'.

So much for Ziegenhalss. We shall now attempt to sketch the further steps in the history of the Glass Bead Game. Having passed from the musical to the mathematical seminaries (a change which took place in France and England somewhat sooner than in Germany), the Game was so far developed that it was capable of expressing mathematical processes by special symbols and abbreviations. The players, mutually elaborating these processes, threw these abstract formulas at one another, displaying the sequences and possibilities of their science. This mathematical and astronomical game of formulas required great attentiveness, keenness, and concentration. Among mathematicians, even in those days, the reputation of being a good Glass Bead Game player meant a great deal; it was equivalent to being a very good mathematician.

At various times the Game was taken up and imitated by nearly all the scientific and scholarly disciplines, that is, adapted to the special fields. There is documented evidence for its application to the fields of classical philology and logic. The analytical study of musical values had led to the reduction of musical events to physical and mathematical formulas. Soon afterward philology borrowed this method and began to measure linguistic configurations as physics measures processes in nature. The visual arts soon followed suit, architecture having already led the way in establishing the links between visual art and mathematics. Thereafter more and more new relations, analogies, and correspondences were discovered among the abstract formulas obtained in this way. Each discipline which seized upon the Game created its own language of formulas, abbreviations, and possible combinations. Everywhere, the elite intellectual youth developed a passion for these Games, with their dialogues and progressions of formulas. The Game was not mere practice and mere recreation; it became a form of concentrated self-awareness for intellectuals. Mathematicians in particular played it with a virtuosity and formal strictness at once athletic and ascetic. It afforded them a pleasure which somewhat compensated for their renunciation of worldly pleasures and ambitions. For by then such renunciation had already become a regular thing for intellectuals. The Glass Bead Game contributed largely to the complete defeat of feuilletonism and to that newly awakened delight in strict mental exercises to which we owe the origin of a new, monastically austere intellectual discipline. [. . .]

To return now to the Glass Bead Game: what it lacked in those days was the capacity for universality, for rising above all the disciplines. The astronomers, the classicists, the scholastics, the music students all played their Games according to their ingenious rules, but the Game had a special language and set of rules for every discipline and subdiscipline. It required half a century before the first step was taken toward spanning these gulfs. The reason for this slowness was undoubtedly more moral than formal and technical. The means for building the spans could even then have been found, but along with the newly regenerated intellectual life went a puritanical shrinking from 'foolish digressions', from intermingling of disciplines and categories. There was also a profound and justified fear of relapse into the sin of superficiality and feuilletonism.

It was the achievement of one individual which brought the Glass Bead Game almost in one leap to an awareness of its potentialities, and thus to the verge of its capacity for universal elaboration. And once again this advance was connected with music. A Swiss musicologist with a passion for mathematics gave a new twist to the Game, and thereby opened the way for its supreme development. This great man's name in civil life can no longer be ascertained; by his time the cult of personality in intellectual fields had already been dispensed with. He lives on in history as Lusor (or also, Joculator) Basiliensis. Although his invention, like all inventions, was the product of his own personal merit and grace, it in no way sprang solely from personal needs and ambitions, but was impelled by a more powerful motive. There was a passionate craving among all the intellectuals of his age for a means to express their new concepts. They longed for philosophy, for synthesis. The erstwhile happiness of pure withdrawal each into his own discipline was now felt to be inadequate. Here and there a scholar broke through the barriers of his specialty and tried to advance into the terrain of universality. Some dreamed of a new alphabet, a new language of symbols through which they could formulate and exchange their new intellectual experiences.

Testimony to the strength of this impulse may be found in the essay 'Chinese Warning Cry', by a Parisian scholar of those years. The author, mocked by many in his day as a sort of Don Quixote (incidentally, he was a distinguished scholar in the field of Chinese philology), pointed out the dangers facing culture, in spite of its present honorable condition, if it neglected to develop an international language of symbols. Such a language, like the ancient Chinese script, should be able to express the most complex matters graphically, without excluding individual imagination and inventiveness, in such a way as to be understandable to all the scholars of the world. It was at this point that Joculator Basiliensis applied himself to the problem. He invented for the Glass Bead Game the principles of a new language, a language of symbols and formulas, in which mathematics and music played an equal part, so that it became possible to combine astronomical and musical formulas, to reduce mathematics and music to a common denominator, as it were. Although what he did was by no means conclusive, this unknown man from Basel certainly laid the foundations for all that came later in the history of our beloved Game.

The Glass Bead Game, formerly the specialized entertainment of mathematicians in one era, philologists or musicians in another era, now more and more cast its spell upon all true intellectuals. Many an old university, many a lodge, and especially the age-old League of Journeyers to the East, turned to it. Some of the Catholic Orders likewise scented a new intellectual atmosphere and yielded to its lure. At some Benedictine abbeys the monks devoted themselves to the Game so intensely that even in those early days the question was hotly debated – it was subsequently to crop up again now and then – whether this game ought to be tolerated, supported, or forbidden by Church and Curia.

After Joculator Basiliensis' grand accomplishment, the Game rapidly evolved into what it is today: the quintessence of intellectuality and art, the sublime cult, the *unio mystica* of all separate members of the *Universitas Literarum*. In our lives it has partially taken over the role of art, partially that of speculative philosophy. Indeed, in the days of Plinius Ziegenhalss, for instance, it was often called by a different name, one common in the literature of the Feuilletonistic Age. That name, which for many a prophetic spirit in those days embodied a visionary ideal, was: Magic Theater.

For all that the Glass Bead Game had grown infinitely in technique and range since its beginnings, for all the intellectual demands it made upon its players, and for all that it had become a sublime art and science, in the days of Joculator Basiliensis it still was lacking in an essential element. Up to that time every game had been a serial arrangement, an ordering, grouping, and confronting of concentrated concepts from many fields of thought and aesthetics, a rapid recollection of eternal values and forms, a brief, virtuoso flight through the realms of the mind. Only after some time did there enter into the Game, from the intellectual stock of the educational system and especially from the habits and customs of the Journeyers to the East, the idea of contemplation.

This new element arose out of an observed evil. Mnemonists, people with freakish memories and no other virtues, were capable of playing dazzling games, dismaying and confusing the other participants by their rapid muster of countless ideas. In the course of time such displays of virtuosity fell more and more under a strict ban, and contemplation became a highly important component of the Game. Ultimately, for the audiences at each Game it became the main thing. This was the necessary turning toward the religious spirit. What had formerly mattered was following the sequences of ideas and the whole intellectual mosaic of a Game with rapid attentiveness, practiced memory, and full understanding. But there now arose the demand for a deeper and more spiritual approach. After each symbol conjured up by the director of a Game, each player was required to perform silent, formal meditation on the content, origin, and meaning of this symbol, to call to mind intensively and organically its full purport.

39 Saint Francis

Techniques for Breaking the Claims of Socially Selected Meanings:
Brother Masseo's Path-Finding

Excerpt from Leo Sherley-Price (trs.) *The Little Flowers of Saint Francis*, Penguin,
1959, pp. 48–49.

One day Saint Francis was walking along the road with Brother Masseo,
and Brother Masseo had gone a short distance ahead. And reaching a place
where three roads met, from which one could travel to Siena, Florence, and
Arezzo, Brother Masseo asked: 'Father, which road should we take?'
'The road that God wills us to take,' replied Saint Francis. 'But how are
we to learn God's will?' asked Brother Masseo. 'By the sign that I will
show you,' replied Saint Francis. 'At this cross-roads where you are standing, I order you, by the merit of holy obedience, to spin round and round
as children do, and you are not to stop turning until I tell you.'

So Brother Masseo began to spin round and round, and he turned for so
long that he often fell to the ground out of giddiness. But as Saint Francis
did not tell him to stop, and he wished to obey him faithfully, he rose and
continued. At length, when he was spinning fast, Saint Francis cried: 'Stop
still, and don't move!' And he stood still, and Saint Francis asked him:
'In what direction are you facing?' 'Towards Siena,' Brother Masseo
replied. 'That is the road which God wants us to take,' said Saint Francis.

As they travelled along that road, Brother Masseo was very puzzled why
Saint Francis had made him spin round and round like a child in front of
layfolk passing by. But because of his veneration for the holy father he did
not presume to mention this to him.

As they neared Siena, the townsfolk heard of the Saint's coming, and
came out to meet him. And in their devotion to him, they picked up the
Saint and his companion and carried them to the bishop's residence, so that
they never set foot to the ground. Now at that very moment certain men of
Siena were fighting one another, and two of them had already been killed.
When Saint Francis arrived, he spoke to them with such devotion and
holiness that he reconciled them to one another in complete peace, unity,
and friendship. And when the Bishop of Siena learned of this holy action
that Saint Francis had performed, he invited him to his house and enter-
tained him with great honour that day and also that night. And on the

following morning Saint Francis, who in true humility sought nothing but the glory of God in all that he did, rose early with his companion and left without the bishop being aware of it.

Because of this Brother Masseo complained to himself as he walked along, saying: 'What has this good man been up to now? He has made me spin round like a child, and now he has not uttered a single word or offered his thanks to the bishop who treated him with so much honour.' And it seemed to Brother Masseo that Saint Francis had behaved unwisely. But later, being enlightened by God, he reconsidered the matter, and reproached himself in his heart, saying: 'Brother Masseo, you are too proud, for you criticize the ways of God, and deserve hell for your senseless presumption. Yesterday Brother Francis accomplished such holy things that had they been done by an angel of God, they could not have been more wonderful. So if he orders you to throw stones, you should obey him; for what he has done on this journey has been the result of God's working, as has been shown in the good results that followed. For had he not reconciled those men who were fighting among themselves, not only would many have been slain by the dagger – and this bloodshed had already begun – but many souls would have been dragged down to hell by the devil. So you are very stupid and proud when you criticize events which are clearly in accordance with the will of God.'

40 J. Cage

Indeterminacy

Excerpts from J. Cage, *Silence*, Calder & Boyars, 1968, pp. 155, 159 and 161.

    Of five aspects

  observe

20″ *two.*

      The highest purpose is to have no purpose
at all. This puts one in accord with nature
in her manner of operation. If someone comes
along and asks why?, there are answers.
30″ However there is a story I have found very helpful. What's so interesting about
technique anyway? *What if there are twelve tones in a
row?* What row? This seeing of cause and effect
is not emphasized but instead one makes an
identification with what is here and now. He
40″ then spoke of two qualities. Unimpededness and Inter-
penetration.

The relationship of things happening
at the same time is spontaneous
and irrepressible.
50″ It is you yourself
in the form you have
that instant taken.
To stop and figure it out
takes
time. [. . .]
11′00″ You won't find this in the books.
   'Why do you not do as I do? Letting
go of your thoughts
as though
they were
the cold ashes of a

10″ long
    dead fire ?' [. . .]
    The way to test a modern painting is this: If
    it is not destroyed by the action of
    shadows it is genuine oil painting.
10″ A cough or a baby crying will not
    ruin a good piece of modern music.
    This is —'s Truth. As contemporary music
    goes on changing in the way I am changing it
    what will be done is to more & more completely liberate sounds.
    Of course you do know structure is the division
20″ of whatever into parts. Last year when I talked
    here I made a short talk. *That was because I*
    was talking about something; but this year I
    am talking about nothing and of course
    will go on.

Part Eight
Formal Correspondences

To strive after pure expression, unsullied by any human purpose, is a taxing exercise, as the last three excerpts show. A lot of contrivance is necessary for saying nothing consistently for a long time. The provinces of meaning which carry least weight of social concern are loose strands, isolated bits of private meaning. By definition they would be unconnected with the mainstream interpretative effort which living in society demands. But it is not easy to escape the social structuring of experience. At one extreme the most remote mathematical games, at the other the heavy judgements of law or religion – in between lie the various hedged-off segments of behaviour, each with what Schutz calls its own cognitive style. But every distinctive province of meaning is press-ganged somehow to join the work of building shared assumptions. Either it becomes a source of analogy for use in the public system of knowledge – for example, the state of undress which starts in the context of home and intimacy is used to express public dishonour in the Bedouin coffee-house; or, at a more abstract level, breach of one rule is understood to entail breach of the whole set of rules. Meaning can be drawn across the boundaries in the opposite sense as well: the game that would be insignificant as a pastime gets emotional power by sucking into itself meanings from the wider society which its own structure portrays. The central problem of anthropology is to understand the coherence of culture. What Michael Halliday does for linguistics when he demonstrates how the syntax enunciates the theme, anthropology should be doing in the field of culture. The project is also central to the sociology of knowledge. For no approach to everyday knowledge can hope to escape triviality if it ignores the power of social concerns to impress their meanings through all levels of expression.

41 L. Wittgenstein

Pictorial Form

Excerpts from L. Wittgenstein, *Tractatus Logico-Philosophicus*, Routledge & Kegan Paul, second edition of new translation, 1971, pp. 15, 17 and 111. First published in 1921.

2.1 We picture facts to ourselves.

2.11 A picture presents a situation in logical space, the existence and non-existence of states of affairs.

2.12 A picture is a model of reality.

2.13 In a picture objects have the elements of the picture corresponding to them.

2.131 In a picture the elements of the picture are the representatives of objects.

2.14 What constitutes a picture is that its elements are related to one another in a determinate way.

2.141 A picture is a fact.

2.15 The fact that the elements of a picture are related to one another in a determinate way represents that things are related to one another in the same way.

Let us call this connection of its elements the structure of the picture, and let us call the possibility of this structure the pictorial form of the picture.

2.151 Pictorial form is the possibility that things are related to one another in the same way as the elements of the picture.

2.1511 *That* is how a picture is attached to reality; it reaches right out to it.

2.1512 It is laid against reality like a measure.

2.15121 Only the end-points of the graduating lines actually *touch* the object that is to be measured.

2.1513 So a picture, conceived in this way, also includes the pictorial relationship, which makes it into a picture.

2.1514 The pictorial relationship consists of the correlations of the picture's elements with things.

2.1515 These correlations are, as it were, the feelers of the picture's elements with which the picture touches reality.

2.16 If a fact is to be a picture, it must have something in common with what it depicts.

2.161 There must be something identical in a picture and what it depicts, to enable the one to be a picture of the other at all.

2.17 What a picture must have in common with reality, in order to be able to depict it – correctly or incorrectly – in the way it does, is its pictorial form.

2.171 A picture can depict any reality whose form it has.

A spatial picture can depict anything spatial, a coloured one anything coloured, etc.

2.172 A picture cannot, however, depict its pictorial form: it displays it.

2.173 A picture represents its subject from a position outside it. (Its standpoint is its representational form.) That is why a picture represents its subject correctly or incorrectly.

2.174 A picture cannot, however, place itself outside its representational form.

2.18 What any picture, of whatever form, must have in common with reality, in order to be able to depict it – correctly or incorrectly – in any way at all, is logical form, i.e. the form of reality.

2.181 A picture whose pictorial form is logical form is called a logical picture.

2.182 Every picture is *at the same time* a logical one. (On the other hand, not every picture is, for example, a spatial one.)

2.19 Logical pictures can depict the world. ...

5.5423 To perceive a complex means to perceive that its constituents are related to one another in such and such a way. This no doubt also explains why there are two possible ways of seeing the figure as a cube; and all similar phenomena. For we really see two different facts.

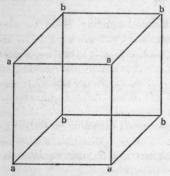

(If I look in the first place at the corners marked *a* and only glance at the *b*'s, then the *a*'s appear to be in front, and vice versa.)

42 S. M. Salim

Disorder Depicts Dishonour

Excerpt from S. M. Salim, *Marsh Dwellers of the Euphrates Delta* (L.S.E. Monograph on Social Anthropology, No. 23), Athlone Press, 1962, pp. 77–80.

The etiquette of the guest house shows clearly the esteem or even veneration in which it is held.

People who attend the guest house must come fully dressed, especially with the head rope (*'agāl*) and the outer cloak (*bishit*). They should not speak unless they are spoken to, especially if they are not of a high social status. Jokes and unnecessary laughter must be avoided, and in case of anger and disputes a tribesman must speak clearly and calmly. Anayid Ahl Mhammed, of Ahl ish-Shaikh clan, had constant trouble with his two sons, who used to quarrel frequently. One early morning they quarrelled and so angered their father that he hurried to ask the intervention of the *şirkal*. In his anger he went to the clan guest house without wearing his head rope. When he lodged his complaint he was unable to control himself enough to speak clearly. The *şirkal* listened to him very coldly, and when Anayid finished, he blamed him strongly for attending without a head rope and talking confusedly. Then the *şirkal* added insultingly, 'I thought that one of your old wives had run away with a lover.' Only a man who has been afflicted with great shame, such as the elopement of a wife, may attend a guest house without a proper head-dress, as he never wears it until he 'regains his honour'.

Etiquette is also a clear indication of social standing. Everyone who attends the guest house should sit in the place which corresponds to his social rank. People of high social status, such as *is-sāda*, Ahl Khayūn and *ajawid it-tayfa*, sit in the place of honour, which is usually distinguished by carpets and pillows. Social status is shown by the distance at which a tribesman sits from this place of honour, which is in the middle of the guest house by the hearth where coffee is brewed in winter, and near one of the two doorways in the summer.[1] The guest house owner can show his respect to an esteemed visitor or to a stranger, by personally leading him or showing him to his proper place, offering him a cigarette, or by ordering tea to be prepared and served to him as well as the usual coffee.

1. The tradition of Ahl Khayūn chiefs is to sit against the third pillar on the right-hand side in summer, and against the seventh in winter.

When entering the guest house and passing the first assembled tribesmen, the newcomer says '*As-salāmu 'alaykum*' ('Peace be with you'), to which all must answer, '*Wa 'alaykum is-salām*' ('And peace may be with you') or with one or more additional sentences according to the status of the newcomer.

The assembled people must show their respect to every newcomer according to his social status. A man must rise to his feet to those who are higher in rank than himself. For instance, all members of the commoner and the slave classes rise to those of the three higher ranks. One of the criteria of social standing of a *khayir* (good fellow) is *ila koma bil muḍīf* (lit. = 'to him there is a standing in the guest house'). According to the difference in rank between the persons already assembled and the newcomer, the act of rising itself varies from rising fully to the feet and standing respectfully until the newcomer is seated, to a mere gesture, sometimes no more than raising the hips a few inches from the ground.

When the new arrival is comfortably seated, every man in the guest house should salute him by saying '*Sabbaḥkum allah bil-khair*' ('May God make your morning good') and he should answer every one with the same sentence, standing or affecting to stand in answering those of the people of higher social status than himself. This complicated system of salutation, the failure to comply with which is taken as a serious lapse of good manners, becomes very confusing when people arrive in groups of threes and fours, and standings, sittings and salutations have to be performed quickly and accurately. One has to be quick-witted to act in full conformity with tribal convention.

Whenever food is served in guest houses on occasions such as a feast, marriage or funeral ceremonies, it is the tradition that the owner should invite every man present to eat. Since there are usually too many men to sit and eat at one time, food is laid on the floor and men called to eat in two or three groups, one after the other. Here the principle of ranking emerges again. As all participants are supposed to wash their hands before taking the meal, the owner or his younger brother or son, or perhaps a slave, goes round the assembly carrying a pitcher and basin. The owner invites everyone to wash his hands. He begins with the men of the highest social standing, a *sayyid* or *mūman*, and proceeds to men of lower status. If he happens to neglect someone or puts one man before another wrongly, he is corrected by those whom he tries to rank in a higher position. If another man carries the basin and pitcher, the owner announces the names and the washing of hands goes accordingly. When the first group is called to eat the owner must invite them personally and must see that the principle of social ranking is accurately applied. When the first group finish eating, the second group is called and more food may be brought if the remains are thought to be insufficient. Second servings lack the delicacies served for the first group. Again it is the tradition that the man of the highest social ranking should set aside the coffee and food for the coffee-man of the guest house, before starting to eat.

There is mobility between two sub-classes, the *ṣirkals*, *mukhtārs* and *ajawīd it-tayfa* and the ordinary commoners. This mobility is demonstrated in the guest house etiquette. Those commoners who approach the status of *ajawīd it-tayfa* are given better places and more ceremonial respect. A *ṣirkal* or one of *ajawīd it-tayfa* who, by his own misdeeds or those of his family, realizes that he has lost prestige, will take the initiative in seeking a lower place and no one will prevent him. Again, a commoner, for instance, would gain more respect and be seated in a better place after returning from a pilgrimage or a visit to one of the tombs of the Imams.

Formal social stratification may be complicated by age-status. An old slave may sit in a better place than a younger commoner, especially if he is known to be *khayir* (good fellow). Similarly, a younger *sayyid* or Khayūni may sit in a lower place than that of an old *ṣirkal* or *mukhtār*. It is important to mention that *is-sāda* are in most cases not allowed to take a lower place than their usual one, as respect to them is a religious duty. In the guest house of Ahl ish-Shaikh clan the sessions are presided over by Abdil Hadi Ahl Khayūn, a very old Khayūni chief, according to the principle of respecting the elder strictly followed by Ahl Khayūn. A younger Khayūni member sits well away from the elder member, though in doing so, he sits very much lower than his social standing in relation to the other guest demands. If an old Khayūni member leaves, a younger Khayūni member who has been sitting in a lower place may take his rightful place, indeed the others urge him to do so. But if a Khayūni went alone to a guest house, he would be seated in the best place regardless of his age.

The tribesmen know these rules and adhere to them strictly. Everyone knows the exact standing of everyone else and treats him accordingly. Particularly if he had been for some reason an irregular attender at guest house meetings, a man might out of politeness or humility take a lower place than was his by right, but the owner, or those whom he has made to sit unduly higher than himself, would urge him to move to his correct place. Quite often, when such a man insists on sitting in a lower place than his social status requires, those who fail to persuade him to sit in a higher place may correct their false position by changing their own places and sitting lower in relation to him.

Coffee is served in a little cup and each guest is offered three cups. Those who feel satisfied after the first or second cup can decline by shaking their empty cups to the coffee-man. People of high social status may be offered any number of cups till they decline by shaking them. The owner may honour a certain guest of rank, or a stranger, by asking his coffee-man to serve him with another round of coffee an hour or so after he has taken his first.

Those who commit mistakes, whether consciously or unconsciously, are corrected either directly by the *şirkal* or through a brother or a friend. If any tribesman deliberately infringes convention he may be checked and even dismissed from the guest house by the *şirkal*.

This rigid system of etiquette does not operate with the same accuracy in the smaller guest houses of the lineage headmen or notables, especially if the assembled people are few and all of the same lineage or neighbourhood and therefore on familiar terms. Even in the large clan guest houses when the people of rank have left, and only a few people remain, the atmosphere changes perceptibly to one of easy informality.

43 A. Segal

Breach of One Rule Breaches the System of Rules

Excerpts from A. Segal, 'Portnoy's Complaint and the sociology of literature', *The British Journal of Sociology*, vol. xxii, no. 3, September 1971, pp. 262–8.[1]

The striking thing about *Portnoy's Complaint* is that it provides a coherent world view of an individual man, the product of a particular generation and religious group, and the wider social conditions in which material achievements are regarded as a major sign of personal success and the source of social esteem. My purpose, however, is not to consider these social factors in themselves, but to see how they created a set of conditions by reference to which it becomes possible to make sense of the man's position.

Alexander Portnoy, thirty-three-year-old Jewish bachelor, lies (we assume) on his analyst's couch, yearning and pleading for deliverance from his tortured existence. He is a harried, oppressed yet self-conscious character whose major, if not sole pleasure lies in sexual gratification of the most varied kind with women who, in one way or another, prove to be unsuitable for the prospect of a permanent relationship. He is afflicted by the constant demands of his parents that he give them 'some pleasure in life' by marrying the right kind of girl, having children, and becoming a respected member of the community. These are precisely the things Portnoy cannot do, certainly not on their terms. Jewish women hold little attraction for him, and when it comes to the crunch, so to speak, they render him sexually impotent. This, of course, precludes the possibility of grandchildren for his parents. And his success in becoming Assistant Commissioner of Human Opportunity for the City of New York seems a different or unsatisfactory kind of achievement so far as his parents are concerned.

The sexual pleasure he receives from the series of non-Jewish women is short-term and dangerous, for he is constantly thinking about other women and the millions of female bodies he has not yet assailed, and he is haunted by the fear that his behaviour will lead to public exposure and scandal. Portnoy's dilemma is that he faces two alternatives almost equally unsatisfying and untenable: one, that he comply with his parents' wishes,

[1] I am indebted for their comments on the sociology of literature to Paul Filmer and Kuson Kumar, to Clive Kessler for an appreciation of the problems involved in understanding the novel and to Joan Dulchin for her suggestive comments.

thus getting them off his back but incurring his own permanent displeasure; two, that he pursue short-lived and specific satisfactions which involve the constant complaints of his parents and which, he fears, will lead to his public unmasking as some kind of sexual pervert. He has determinedly turned his back on the former possibility, is compelled to pursue the latter, yet yearns for a third alternative which is not forthcoming. Though he clearly understands his situation, Portnoy is reduced to continual feelings of personal doubt and anguish, anticipations of disaster, parental oppression and passing affairs which provide the sole gratification of eroticism. Why should this be so?

The explanation would appear, at first sight, to lend itself to a psychoanalytic interpretation, but not because the novel is set in the convention of a 'shrink's' case-study or because the patient expresses himself in the appropriate terminology. The image of Portnoy's mother standing over him with a large knife urging him to eat, an image which impressed itself upon him and continues to haunt him, suggests the infantile fear of castration; and the guilt, shame and anxiety feelings which dog him recall the residues of the Oedipus complex as yet not overcome. While this approach would shed a great deal of light on the problem, Portnoy's condition, I shall argue, can only be understood in terms of the multi-faceted experience and significance of being socialized in a peculiarly distinctive family setting. And this setting itself makes sense only in terms of the distinctions made and the ritualistic relationships developed between the world of the Jews and the world of the Goyim (non-Jews). To understand this argument, it is necessary to consider some of the typical features of life in the *shtetls* of nineteenth-century eastern Europe and the problems confronting Jewish immigrants in the United States, and to see these experiences as a background to the characteristic modes of upbringing which these experiences heavily influenced.[2]

If it can be put briefly, the insecurity of *shtetl* life rested upon a number of factors. The community was physically separated from the outside world and relationships with it were often proscribed. Access to prestigious and remunerative occupations and professions was impossible. Hence the Jews were reduced to general poverty and a subsistence living based on small-scale trading. Anti-semitism on occasion generated pogroms in which property and life were destroyed, and from which recourse to protection from attack could only be made to state officials, some of whom sanctioned the pogroms and used anti-semitism to their own political advantage. Hence the Jews turned inward in a kind of passive self-

2. I rely here in particular upon Zborowski and Herzog (1952) and Slater (1969). The theoretical orientation derives from Douglas (1966) and from discussions with Basil Bernstein.

protectiveness, impotent in the face of attacks from outside, developing a distrust of non-Jews, and learning to live with the constant fear of imminent catastrophe.

But the world-view of the Jews was not formed out of *shtetl* life. The scriptural injunction of the Old Testament to be holy was also an injunction to be separate. The daily ritual prescriptions and prohibitions enjoined on the so-called Chosen People served to demarcate them from all other communities in terms of monotheism initially, and endogamy, commensality and dietary laws. Of itself, this constellation of beliefs and practices would make relations with the outside world difficult, particularly during times of colonial occupation and dispersal. The *shtetl* and ghetto experience reinforced the religious basis of community life which ritualized its relationships with the outside. One form of this ritualization of relationships was to be seen in the dichotomy which described the Jews as morally superior yet powerless, and the Goyim as morally inferior but omnipotent.

Despite the changed material conditions of life in the New World, migration did not essentially alter these feelings. What it did, I want to suggest, was to fuse old attitudes with new surroundings in a highly peculiar fashion. For the first time for the majority of immigrants, the door to occupations of prestige, wealth and influence was open. But it was open not so much to the parents, who used the old skills and attitudes – business sense – to earn a living from lower-middle-class occupations, but to their children. The hopes of the community for a better life focused on the futures of the children, whose success would in turn illuminate and strengthen the community. In other words, the Jewish child became the centre of the aspirations of others: his achievements had to be carefully facilitated through the exclusion of harmful influences which by and large were attributed to outsiders; yet he was expected to make a *mensch* of himself, to get on in the world. He became the focal point of two contrary pressures: he was simultaneously exposed to the over-protectiveness and the ambitiousness of his parents, both pressures of which were supported by community values. The result, as Portnoy puts it, is that a Jewish man is regarded by his parents as a child.

'Mother, I'm thirty-three! I am the Assistant Commissioner of Human Opportunity for the City of New York. I graduated first in my law school class! Remember? I have graduated first from every class I've ever *been* in! At twenty-five I was already special counsel to a House Sub-committee – of the United States Congress, Mother! Of America! . . .' Oh, why go on? Why go on in my strangled high-pitched adolescent voice? Good Christ, a Jewish man with parents alive is a fifteen-year-old boy. . . .

Let us consider the patterns of this distinctive kind of socialization. As a child, Portnoy enjoys no privacy: his mother 'patrols the six rooms of our apartment the way a guerilla army moves across its own countryside – there's not a single closet or drawer of mine whose contents she hasn't a photographic sense of.' He is completely constricted by a sense of danger: his father's anxieties about work; his headaches and constipation; his mother's worries about his father; her prohibitions on eating out and apprehensions over ill-health. He fails to comprehend the strength of her reactions to his bad behaviour. Why should a child of five be asked to leave home, to be put outside in his coat, with the door closed and locked behind him? He doesn't even understand why his behaviour is bad. He is simply aware of being smothered in his mother's constant presence. His only pleasures are enjoyed when he can be left alone, to play baseball and to masturbate. And the latter, he fears, will induce cancer or send him blind. Masturbation and sexual fantasies become his sole sphere of autonomy. 'Doctor,' he says, 'do you understand what I was up against? My wang was all I really had that I could call my own.' As a grown man, he comes to find that the way out of the constricting familial environment is through the one channel of independence he has always possessed, which now takes the form of intercourse with non-Jewish women. The nature of familial constriction and the importance of sex with the *shikses* are two factors which require explanation. Both have obsessed and continue to obsess the man, and both run like *leit-motifs* through the book. They can be shown to be inextricably related in terms of the symbolic significance attributed to the distinction between the Jewish community and the Gentile community.

The Jewish world is defined and controlled by dietary laws which stipulate what can be eaten and what cannot be eaten and to some extent how food is to be eaten. Consumption of the wrong food threatens ill-health. Mrs Portnoy suspects her son of eating out.

'Just wait till your father hears what you do, in defiance of every health habit there could possibly be. Alex, answer me something. You're so smart, you know all the answers now, answer me this: how do you think Melvin Weiner gave himself colitis? Why has this child spent half his life in hospitals?'
'Because he eats *chazerai*.'

The humiliating sarcasm of the mother aside, the significance of this conversation lies in the double meaning of the term *chazerai*. It means literally 'piggishness', and is attached to abominations of food and mess, dirt or confusion in general. Contrasted to Jewish cleanliness and order, forbidden and therefore polluting food and disorder are *chazerai*: they partake of the realm of the Goyim. In other words, there is a direct symbolic association amongst non-Jewish customs, forbidden food, disorder, filth, pollution and ill-health. Portnoy wearies of the warnings of the consequences of contact with the realm of the Goyim.

Because I am sick and tired of *goyische* this and *goyische* that! If it's bad it's the *goyim*, if it's good it's the Jews! Can't you see, my dear parents, from whose loins I somehow leaped, that such thinking is a trifle barbaric? That all you are expressing is your *fear*? The very first distinction I learned from you, I'm sure, was not night and day, or hot and cold, but *goyische* and Jewish!

We can see further that while safety emanates from Jewishness, danger and fear emanate from non-Jewishness. But there is more. 'When duty, discipline and obedience give way,' Portnoy indicates,

what follows, there is no predicting. . . . Self-control, sobriety, sanctions – this is the key to a human life, saith all those endless dietary laws. Let the *goyim* sink *their* teeth into whatever lowly creature crawls and grunts across the face of the dirty earth, we will not contaminate our humanity thus. . . . They will eat *anything*, anything they can get their big *goy* hands on! And the terrifying corollary, *they will do anything as well.*

Contact with goyische practices, then, leads to unpredictability, the counterpart of disorder. In this unpredictability, furthermore, there resides power.

Yes, it's all written down in history, what they have done, our illustrious neighbours who own the world and know absolutely nothing of human boundaries and limits.

The blue-eyed, blonde and upright WASPS monopolize power; they are the means of the undoing and oppression of Portnoy's father, riddled by worry about his exhausting salesmanship with the goyische insurance company, and blockaded by constipation as a result. The Jews are socially impotent, despite their ethical superiority, and assume an appeasing attitude towards the powerful. Finally, the outside world represents unbridled pleasure-seeking of the kind forbidden to Jews. Their lapse into private pleasure induces waves of guilt. 'Come,' cries Portnoy,

someone, anyone, find me out and condemn me – I did the most terrible thing you can think of: I took what I am not supposed to have! Chose pleasure for myself over duty to my loved ones! Please, catch me, incarcerate me, before God forbid I get away with it completely – and go out and do again something I actually like!

The breaking of one rule involves an attack on the whole system of rules, rituals, personal identity and community. This can be seen clearly in the episode in which Portnoy, unable to confess any belief in religion, refuses to go to synagogue with his family. His refusal provokes from his father neither resignation, nor an attempt at persuasion, nor a single rebuke, but a series of abusive claims: that Portnoy is wearing unclean if not indecent clothes, that he start looking like a human being, that he is ignorant and his success at school is in some way perverse, that he has no respect nor love for his father, nor any respect for the Jewish people, their learning, their suffering and their history. By one specific attempt at independence, Portnoy, amidst the tears of all present, invokes upon himself a devastating and total attack.

Separation and distancing of children from the outside world produces a trained incompetence towards it, comprised of a physical, emotional and social incapacity. When the parents of a non-Jewish girlfriend, with whom he has been staying, say 'good morning' to him (a term never used in the Portnoy household, where communication assumes the form of argument and vilification), he is so surprised and incapacitated that he can only say 'thank you' in reply. He has been brought up to be polite.

I am marked like a road map from head to toe with my repressions. You can travel the length and breadth of my body over super-highways of shame and inhibition and fear. See, I am too good too, Mother, I too am moral to the bursting point – just like you! Did you ever see me try to smoke a cigarette? I look like Bette Davis. Today boys and girls not even old enough to be *barmitzvahed* are sucking on marijuana like it's peppermint candy, and I'm still all thumbs with a Lucky Strike.

Because the outside world is so incomprehensible, it calls forth an ineptness in dealing with it. The unknown becomes synonymous with the fearful. For all the help they gave him in becoming worldly, Portnoy claims he might have well been brought up by Hottentots and Zulus.

What in their world was not charged with danger, dripping with germs, fraught with peril? Oh, where was the gusto, where was the boldness and courage? Who filled these parents of mine with such a fearful sense of life?

This fearful sense of life, we can see, was the product and heritage of the historical separation of the Gentiles and the Jews, their ritual relationships of danger, fear and pollution, and the development of a world-view which held out the promise of safety from the outside in the observance of rules of religious significance. It was, and is, a total system of social organization and personal identity, and can be represented diagrammatically (Table 1).

Yet it is not always the case that the breaking of a single and specific rule embodies a total assault on the Jewish world. When the power relationship with the outside world is seen to be altered, the system is no longer endangered.

Why we can eat pig on Pell Street and not at home is because ... frankly I still haven't got the whole thing figured out, but at the time I believe it has largely to do with the fact that the elderly man who owns the place, and whom amongst ourselves we call '*Shmendrick*', isn't somebody whose opinion of us we have cause to worry about. Yes, the only people in the world whom it seems to me the

Table 1

Goyim		Jews
Qualities	Relations	Qualities
Power	Fear	Moral superiority
Filth	←———	Dietary laws
	Appeasement	
Disorder	←———	Health
	Pollution	
Pleasure	———→	Safety
	Danger	
Unpredictability	———→	Order

Jews are not afraid of are the Chinese. Because, one, the way they speak English makes my father sound like Lord Chesterfield; two, the insides of their heads are just so much fried rice anyway; and three, to them we are not Jews but *white* – and maybe even Anglo-Saxon. Imagine! No wonder the waiters can't intimidate us. To them we're just some big-nosed variety of WASP! Boy, do we eat! Suddenly, even the pig is no threat. . . .

What happens to Portnoy is that he falls away from the rules and rituals of Jewish life and experiences a progressive entry into the manifold realm of *goyische* practices. It all begins, he tells us, with the breaking of one dietary law – eating lobster – in the wrong context, away from home. . . .

Did I mention that when I was fifteen I took it out of my pants and whacked off on the 107 bus from New York? . . . Now, maybe the lobster is what did it. That taboo so easily and simply broken, confidence may have been given to the whole slimy, suicidal Dionysian side of my nature; the lesson may have been learned that to break the law, all you have to do is – just go ahead and break it!

Now, at the age of thirty-three, his only pleasure is in intercourse with forbidden women. He speaks of three: Mary Jane Reed, whom he calls The Monkey; Kay Campbell, The Pumpkin; and Sarah Abbott Maulsby, The Pilgrim. They are not just Gentile women: they are more like a representative sample of the class and regional structure of Christian American Womanhood. Mary Jane Reed, from the coalmines of West Virginia, is pure proletarian and rural; Kay Campbell has a mid-West, respectable middle-class background (her father is a real estate agent and town councillor); and Sarah Abbott Maulsby is an upper-class New England descendant of the earliest Protestant settlers. Portnoy's sexuality is, in fact, an expression of his search for power, a power that he feels he can acquire personally through erotic contact with the WASPS.

What I'm saying, Doctor, is that I don't seem to stick my dick up these girls, as much as I stick it up their backgrounds – as though through fucking I will discover America. *Conquer* America – maybe that's more like it. Columbus, Captain Smith, Governor Winthrop, General Washington – now Portnoy. As though my manifest destiny is to seduce a girl from each of the forty-eight states. As for Alaskan and Hawaiian women, I really have no feelings either way, no scores to settle, no coupons to cash in, no dreams to put to rest – who are they to me, a bunch of Eskimos and Orientals?

It is here that the key to understanding Portnoy's condition and the Jewish world-view which his character so vividly portrays is to be found. His search for power is not power-seeking for its own sake. His sexuality has been his sole sphere of autonomy in family life as a child. It now becomes the means of the assertion of his independence. It is his only way out. Yet he is enmeshed by the definitional constraints of his background, but in an inverted form. Just as it was in order for his family to eat pork in the Chinese restaurant, because the Chinese are excluded from the WASP establishment and therefore are bereft of power in relation to the Jews, so it is that Portnoy is uninterested in sex with the non-powerful – the Hawaiians and Alaskans. His independence resides in the act of intercourse with the powerful. This is why his attempts with Israeli women are complete failures. It is not through some process of identification between his castrating mother and Jewish women in general that they induce impotence in him. It is because they do not fit in with the definitional scheme of things. Portnoy is impotent with them because he sees them as members of the socially powerless Jewish community. He can derive nothing from a relationship with them, and he is as contemptuous of them as he is of all those outside the WASP world. His sexual potency, and thus his assertion of independence, can only be supported and fulfilled through contact with the powerful as they are defined in the traditional Jewish world-view. And Portnoy is trapped because he can only express his desire for independence from the Jewish world against that world and in terms of the Jewish scheme of things. His salvation only makes sense in relation to the Jewish symbolic separation of the Gentiles and the Jews. This is the ultimate irony of the book. He becomes Assistant Commissioner of Human Opportunity because he never had any human opportunity. He is engaged in exposing unjust practices and unlawful discriminations in New York because he suffered from the same things as he sees them in his family. The job itself, ameliorative of social ills, is nothing more than an extension of childhood rebellion; not an attempt to change the world through any radical break with it, but to work within its confines. He *is* the Jewish joke in the book, but is robbed of the punch-line which is told by someone else: his analyst and representative of the same world.

Portnoy's complaint is this: in order to overcome his condition he must shed the Jewish identity with which he has been imbued. But this would involve the undermining of the channel of his independence – sex with the *goyim* on a compulsive scale – which is ironically both his present emancipation from the Jewish world and his imprisonment in its scheme of things. The circle is complete. And why? Because the values, prohibitions and practices which govern the socialization of the child in the Jewish family are at the same time the definers of the ritual separation of the Jews and the Gentiles. Thus, encroachment into the Gentile world entails violations of those values, prohibitions and practices which have been the mechanisms of the development of social identity. These values, prohibitions and practices have a total and multivalent quality: reference to one involves the same intellectual, emotional and moral responses as does reference to all others. Thus when one is invoked, all are invoked; when one is threatened, all are threatened. The only meaningful relationship with the world, and the source and structure of identity, is to be found in this divorce of the two realms and the interlaced and multivalent aspects within each. The ritual relationships between the two are changed only when its basis – the power relationship – is perceived as changed. It is under this condition that the Jewish world-view is in danger of collapse. But so long as the uneven power relationship is seen to remain, it continues as the foundation of both separation and the distinctive problem of identity with which Portnoy, in the refusal to accept his assigned position, is confronted. This is the latent structure of meaning which emerges from Roth's novel.

References

BRAMSTED, E. K. (1964), *Aristocracy and the Middle Classes in Germany*, Phoenix.
COSER, L. A. (1963), *Sociology Through Literature*, Prentice-Hall.
DOUGLAS, M. (1966), *Purity and Danger*, Routledge & Kegan Paul; Penguin, 1970.
GOLDMAN, L. (1964), *Pour une sociologie du Roman*, Gallimard.
LUKACS, G. (1969), *The Historical Novel*, Penguin.
MERRILL, F. E. (1967), 'Stendhal and the self: a study in the sociology of literature' in J. G. Manis and B. N. Meltzer (eds.), *Symbolic Interaction: A Reader in Social Psychology*, Allyn & Bacon.
SLATER, M. K. (1969), 'My son the doctor: aspects of mobility among American Jews', *Amer. Soc. Rev.*, vol. 34, no. 3.
ZBOROWSKI, M., and HERZOG, E. (1952), *Life is People: The Culture of the Shtetl*, International Universities Press.

44 R. Vailland

The Racketeer in Life and in Play

Excerpts from R. Vailland, *The Law*, Jonathan Cape, 1958, pp. 35–44 and 50–56.
First published in 1957.

Tonio, don Cesare's confidential man, was admitted as sixth member of a
game which was starting up, on the initiative of Matteo Brigante, in one of
the cafés of the Old Town. The Law can be played by five, six, seven or
more; but six is a good number.

In Porto Manacore, Matteo Brigante controlled everything – including
The Law. He was a former bosun's mate in the Royal Italian Navy. He had
begun to control the town immediately upon his return to his native town
in 1945, after the defeat. He was nearing his fifties, but he had retained the
bosun's manner; you were always expecting to see him put a whistle
brusquely to his mouth. It was a thin mouth, beneath a narrow, black, stiff
moustache, and he always kept the lips pressed together, even when he
laughed. Controlling everything, but doing nothing, he had never been
convicted by the tribunals, except once, well before the war, which was for
having *accoltellato*, knifed, a boy who had deprived one of his sisters of her
virginity. It was a crime which did him honour, one of those crimes of
honour for which the southern courts show every indulgence. He controlled the men who fished from boats, the men who fished with the *tra-
bucco* and the men who fished with dynamite. He controlled the sellers of
lemons, the buyers of lemons and the thieves of lemons. He controlled those
who allowed themselves to be robbed in the olive-presses and those who
robbed them. He controlled the smugglers who went out to meet yachts
laden with American cigarettes and the customs men who prowled along
the coast in their motor launches, suddenly throwing on searchlights that
probed every cove, or not throwing them on if Brigante had made a deal so
that they would turn a blind eye. He controlled those who made love and
those who didn't, the cuckolds and those who made them cuckolds. He
gave information to thieves and information to the police, which allowed
him to control both the thieves and the police. People paid him to control
and people paid him not to control; and thus he levied his tax on every
operation, commercial or non-commercial, conducted within the bounds
of Porto Manacore or the neighbouring areas. Matteo Brigante had such a

lot of controlling to do that he had enticed Pizzaccio, the assistant baker, away from the *pizzeria* and had taken him into his service as first assistant controller.

This evening, before going on to control the ball put on by the town corporation for the summer visitors, Brigante, the racketeer, had invited his lieutenant to play at The Law. Pizzaccio was the nickname of the former baker's assistant; it could be translated as 'dud Pizza'; similarly, in the heroic years of the city of Florence, Lorenzaccio had been the pejorative of Lorenzo.

The other players in the game were the American, a one-time emigrant to Guatemala who had returned to end his days in his home land, where he had bought a small olive plantation; the Australian, another one-time emigrant, who delivered fruit and fish in his light van; and lastly don Ruggero, don Ottavio's son, a student at Naples Law School, who preferred, during the vacations, to run after the wives of his father's peasants and get drunk in the cafés rather than flirt with the daughters of Manacore's leading citizens – a bunch of half-wits, in his opinion.

With his two hundred lire concealed from the vigilance of his wife Maria, Tonio was not on equal footing with his companions. But he could keep his end up for quite a time. The stake for each game was in fact fixed at a litre of Andria, a red wine 14° proof and costing a hundred and twenty lire. With six people playing, there were four losers. A hundred and twenty divided by four made thirty. Two hundred divided by thirty made six, with twenty left over. With two hundred lire, Tonio could chance his luck six times – or even seven times, for the landlord would certainly give him credit for ten lire. Besides, it was neither the amount of money risked nor the quantity of wine drunk which provided the point of the game of The Law, but the law itself, bitter when you had to bow to it, delectable when you imposed it.

The Law is played throughout southern Italy. It comprises two phases. The object of the first phase is to designate a winner, who is called *padrone*, chief; this is accomplished as rapidly as possible, sometimes with the cards, sometimes with the dice; the chief could equally well be chosen by drawing straws. This evening they chose tarot cards as the instrument of fate.

Pizzaccio won the first round of tarot and was thus designated chief.

The landlord produced a jug of wine which he placed beside Pizzaccio; a few men who were drinking at the bar came up and made a circle round the table. No one spoke.

It is after the designation of the chief that the second phase of the game of The Law begins. It comprises two episodes. First of all the chief chooses a *sotto-padrone*, a deputy.

Pizzaccio let his eyes rest successively on each of the other five players; then his attention returned to this one, to that one, feigning perplexity. He kept them waiting. He knew The Law well.

'Get on with it,' said the landlord. 'Your pizza's cooked.'

'It's not quite done yet,' said Pizzaccio.

At that moment he had his eyes on Tonio.

'Tonio,' he began, 'has a pretty sister-in-law . . .'

Everyone's attention focused on Tonio who sat motionless, his eyes lowered, his hands spread flat on the table.

The winner, the chief, who dictates the law, has the right to speak and not to speak, to interrogate and to reply in place of the interrogated, to praise and to blame, to insult, to insinuate, to revile, to slander and to cast a slur on people's honour; the losers, who have to bow to the law, are bound to submit without sound or movement. Such is the fundamental rule of the game of The Law.

'There is something to be said,' Pizzaccio pursued, 'for choosing yourself a deputy with a pretty sister-in-law. If I made Tonio deputy, perhaps he would lend me la Marietta. . . .'

Attention remained fastened on Tonio. They knew he was hanging around Marietta, who did not want him. In Manacore, especially on the marsh, that false wilderness where relatives were always on the alert, the men became madly obsessed with the women of the family – sisters, sisters-in-law, daughters. Pizzaccio's thrusts always found the mark; it was a real pleasure to listen to him playing at The Law. Tonio remained silent and motionless in his freshly starched white jacket. Bravo for him too!

'Come to think of it,' Pizzaccio said slowly, 'if I want to get la Marietta, Brigante's the one I ought to turn to. . . .'

It was not unknown that Matteo Brigante, too, was hanging around Marietta, that he often paid visits to the house with the colonnades and that the girl replied with a provocative laugh to his double-edged remarks. Whenever Tonio saw him walking calmly across the bridge which spanned the outlet of the lake and heading for don Cesare's villa, his features froze and he made no reply to the visitor's greeting, even though he was scared of him. Brigante loved virgins. The fiancés, the suitors, the brothers and the fathers hesitated to attack the racketeer. But the need to avenge their honour can make people do silly things. So Brigante always carried his grafting knife with him, a formidable weapon, as sharp as a razor; a legal weapon too, the most common of working tools in a land of fruit growers, dangerous and on the right side of the law, like Brigante himself; he was the most artful of duellists with a grafting knife. Never would Tonio dare to defy him openly. None of this was unknown. Which was why everyone's attention remained fastened on Tonio.

'You'll pass Marietta on to me?' asked Pizzaccio of Matteo Brigante.

'After I have opened the way.'

'The going will be easier,' said Pizzaccio. 'I appoint you deputy.'

There was a murmur of approval. The game was developing well, straight and clean, without any blurring of the outlines.

Tonio had not batted an eyelid. Bravo for him too!

With the designation of the deputy the first episode of the second phase of the game of The Law ended.

The losers paid. The American, the Australian, don Ruggero and Tonio each gave thirty lire to the landlord.

Pizzaccio, chief of the game, poured himself a glass of wine and put his lips to it. Thus began, according to rule, the second episode of the second phase of the game of The Law.

'A wine fit for a king!' exclaimed Pizzaccio. 'Taste it, deputy.'

It was piquant to hear Pizzaccio take the tone of chief to Matteo Brigante, his chief in real life. These reversals of the hierarchy, an echo of the saturnalia of ancient Rome, gave an added edge to the interest of The Law.

Brigante poured himself a glass of wine and tasted it.

'It would be a sin,' he said, 'to give such a wine to pigs.'

'Do as you like,' said Pizzaccio. 'You're the deputy.'

Brigante drained his glass.

'I could do with another,' he said.

'It is your right,' replied Pizzaccio.

Brigante poured himself a second glass. The jug held seven. There were only four left.

It sometimes happens that the chief and the deputy drink the whole jug, without offering a single glass to the losers. It is their right. This has point only last thing at night, and only then if fate and malignity have combined to prevent one or more players from being appointed, even once, chief or deputy; their exasperation is increased by the sight of those who dictate the law silently emptying the jug before their eyes. The sting of this gesture is not always negligible. But Pizzaccio and Brigante were too skilled to employ it early in the game, when everyone still had control of his nerves.

Brigante slowly emptied his second glass of wine.

'I'm dying of thirst,' said don Ruggero.

'Shall we stand him a glass?' asked Brigante.

'Do as you like,' said Pizzaccio.

Brigante filled don Ruggero's glass at once. There had been no point in keeping on tenterhooks a boy who spent the greater part of the year in Naples and who had become indifferent to the maliciousness of Porto Manacore; his heart was too lofty, by birth, to be humiliated by the shafts of the other players. Don Ruggero was a mediocre person to play against. They willingly admitted him, however, so as not to vex him, because he willingly lent his Vespa and his canoe and was always ready to stand drinks, and also because, once he warmed to the game, he was capable of malice, the most precious of virtues for The Law.

There were only three glasses left in the jug.

'You'll stand me a glass?' the American asked Brigante.

'You'll stand me a glass?' is the time-honoured formula and the request must be made to the deputy and not to the chief. Don Ruggero had therefore broken the rule by calling out: 'I'm dying of thirst.' For the reasons which have just been explained, no one had called attention to his crime.

'Shall we stand him a glass?' Brigante asked his chief, in accordance with The Law.

'Do as you like,' said Pizzaccio.

'I don't think we ought to stand him a glass,' said Matteo Brigante. 'He's too much of a niggard. We shouldn't encourage people to be niggards.'

'Is he really a niggard?' asked Pizzaccio.

'He's even more niggardly than his olives,' said Brigante.

The avarice of the American was as notorious as the poor state of his olive grove. The latter was undoubtedly the cause of the former. The American had returned in glory from Guatemala; he spoke of the miraculous orchards of the United Fruit Company, for whom he had worked as an area manager. He had forgotten the sly ways of the South; the land agent had made him pay a high price for olive trees which no longer yielded fruit; the transaction had left him permanently bitter. Brigante and Pizzaccio turned the blade in the wound for a long time. The eyes of the players and the spectators did not leave the American's face, which turned still greener. In the night he would have an attack of malaria. But he stood up to it well, not saying a word, not making a movement. An agreeable victim, but Tonio was preferable; the wounds which sprang from setbacks in love were the most diverting to see inflicted.

'You'll stand me a glass?' the Australian asked in turn.

He asked in an assured voice, being in business with Brigante, who had nothing to gain by persecuting him. In his van he transported, underneath the crates of fruit, the cartons of American cigarettes collected along the coastline; he always sent an exact tally to the racketeer, who was thus enabled to check the smugglers' declarations. In the case of the Australian, as in the case of don Ruggero, everyday considerations competed against the demands of The Law; reality modified the laws of good theatre; the game does not exist which is governed solely by its own rules; even in games of pure chance, like roulette, the player who can lose without feeling the pinch has a better chance of winning.

Pizzaccio and Brigante made a few nasty jokes, for the sake of form, and the Australian received his wine.

Then Pizzaccio poured himself a glass and drank it slowly, in silence. It was his privilege as chief. He turned to Tonio.

'You're not asking for any?'

'No,' replied Tonio.

'It is your right.'

Brigante emptied the last glass at a single gulp. Thus ended the first game of the evening.

The tarot cards designated the American as chief of the second game. He chose don Ruggero as deputy, considering him the one player who would have the nerve to humiliate Matteo Brigante if the occasion presented itself. But don Ruggero was growing bored. He was thinking of the hunt for foreign women in the streets of Naples when the boats arrived from Capri, of the English, the Swedes, the Americans (huntresses who hypocritically disguised themselves as game), of the French even, who had joined the horde for some years past – Frenchmen must have lost their proverbial virility; Mussolini, thought don Ruggero, had been right to speak of the decadence of that nation. He conducted the game distractedly, personally drinking three glasses one after another; the sooner he got drunk, the sooner this tedious provincial evening would be at an end. When Tonio asked him: 'You'll stand me a glass?', he said no, without giving any explanation; humiliating Tonio was not his idea of fun; he might equally well have said yes; it was almost by chance that he said no; or perhaps it was because Tonio's air of constraint had reminded him of a foreign woman who, the day after, had pretended to remember nothing.

They began the third game at once. The cards designated Brigante as chief, and he chose Pizzaccio as deputy.

Brigante attacked Tonio even before he had drunk his glass of honour.

'Aren't you going to ask my deputy for anything?'

'No,' replied Tonio.

He kept his hands flat on the table, his plump, white, personal attendant's hands, and his eyes fixed on his hands.

'Why,' insisted Brigante, 'don't you ask Pizzaccio to stand you a glass? You've already lost three games and you haven't had a single glass. As I see it, you'd be within your rights if you quenched your thirst.'

'It's my right not to ask for any.'

There was a murmur of approval. Tonio had not yielded to the provocation.

'Tonio doesn't crack in a hurry,' Brigante said to Pizzaccio. 'And yet I was told he was don Cesare's personal attendant, his deputy. A deputy ought to make himself respected. . . .'

'In don Cesare's house,' said Pizzaccio, 'it's the women who are the real deputies. . . .'

'You'd better explain that to me,' said Brigante.

'Thirty years ago,' Pizzaccio began, 'old Julia had a lovely pair of tits. When don Cesare had played with them to his heart's content, he married her off to some poor devil who died of shame.'

'I see,' said Brigante. 'This poor devil passed himself off as don Cesare's personal attendant, but it was la Julia who laid down the law.'

'At that time,' Pizzaccio continued, 'you were in the navy. You can't know what went on. But things turned out exactly as you guessed . . . Before he died, the poor devil gave Julia three daughters. The eldest is named Maria.'

'Tonio's Maria!' exclaimed Brigante.

'Wait till I explain . . . When Maria was sixteen, don Cesare took a fancy to her. Her tits were even fuller than her mother's had been. Don Cesare led her on so nicely, she got big in the belly. There was nothing for it but to find some cuckold to marry her; Tonio came along. . . .'

Talk your heads off, thought Tonio. *When my turn comes to be chief or deputy, you'll hear plenty more. You play the gentleman, Matteo Brigante, now that you have an account with the Bank of Naples, but people haven't forgotten that every sailor in Ancona tumbled your wife, while you were sailing in the king's ships; it was with the money she put away in her stocking that you bought the flat you're living in today, in the old palace. And you, Pizzaccio, messed up pizza, who go with the male German tourists for five hundred lire . . .*

Thus thought Tonio, preparing to make his tormentors swallow their own poison, sharpening the words he would hurl at them. All attention focused on him. But he remained silent and motionless, frozen, in his freshly starched white jacket. It was Matteo Brigante and Pizzaccio who were beginning to crack.

'If I understand you,' said Brigante, 'Tonio passes himself off as don Cesare's personal attendant, but it's Maria who has the whip hand . . .'

'She's had the whip hand for a very long time,' said Pizzaccio.

He gave a little laugh, a chuckle. He bent towards Tonio to get a better look at him.

'But,' he continued, 'it was soon Elvira's, Maria's sister's, turn to be eighteen . . .'

'Don Cesare passed the whip over to her,' said Brigante.

'It's Marietta's turn next,' said Pizzaccio.

'Don Cesare's a real bull.'

'Good bulls,' said Pizzaccio, 'never grow old. You should see how Marietta wriggles when he looks at her.'

Brigante, in turn, bent towards Tonio.

'As houses go,' he said, 'you might say your house is quite a house.'

'The door open and the shutters closed,' added Pizzaccio without a pause.

Talk your heads off, thought Tonio. In his mind he was sharpening terrible words for when his turn came to dictate the law. But at the same time he was calculating that he had already spent three times thirty lire; there were only four games left in which he could take his chance at being designated chief. With six people playing, you could sometimes lose fifteen or twenty times in a row. The Law is not a game which follows the course of justice, since the player who does not start off with a little capital cannot try his luck to the full.

Thus thought Tonio, without shifting his eyes from the plump, white hands resting flat on the table. His hands did not tremble, but the hollow of his chest began to tighten with anguish at the idea that he had only four chances left of becoming chief this evening.

Several spectators had withdrawn from the table and were debating the turn the game had taken, in lowered voices. Some considered Brigante was putting too much aggression into his game and Pizzaccio too much servility towards his chief; The Law demanded a greater detachment towards the victim and more variety in the choice of victims; the wounds should be inflicted as though in sport. Others, however, praised the two men warmly; the attack should be concentrated on a single objective and the mortification of the victim should be complete. Such were the two opposing schools of thought.

Matteo Brigante and Pizzaccio, realizing that their style was the cause of discussion, rapidly put an end to the series of exchanges. They each poured themselves a glass.

'To the health of don Cesare's women,' said Pizzaccio.

'You'll stand me a glass?' asked the Australian.

The game was under way again. [. . .]

The Law was definitely taking a pleasant turn. Seven games already, and the cards still hadn't made Tonio chief. And no one had chosen him as deputy. For The Law to be agreeable there had to be a victim, clearly designated, whom fate and the players could hound till he was exhausted; only thus did this poor man's game become as exciting as a hunt or a bullfight – still more exciting, the victim being a man.

For the eighth game the proprietor gave Tonio credit: he had already lost his two hundred lire and ten more besides. The cards were slow to reveal themselves and for a moment it seemed probable that don Cesare's servant would win. This would have been a matter for regret. Not that it need inevitably be regretted that fate should suddenly change its humour and begin to favour the victim. The turning of the tables can sometimes have piquant consequences. It all depends on the quality of the victim. When Matteo Brigante or Pizzaccio, after a long spell of losing, suddenly found themselves in a position to dictate The Law, the memory, still rankling, of the humiliations they had received gave fire to their natural spite and multiplied its resources; as when a bull of character which you think is finished suddenly charges, going for the man's body; there is no finer sight. But Tonio, by the eighth game, was already too mortified to raise much of a charge; by nature he was sly; but he had lost the cool-headedness which the best sly touches demand; concern over money, the idea of being in debt, also helped to weigh him down; had he won at this late hour, he would not have been able to carry victory to the point of annihilating the enemy, as should a good general and a good player at The Law. Luckily the cards finally pronounced for don Ruggero, who was proclaimed chief. He was beginning to take an interest in the game and appointed Matteo Brigante deputy, considering him the most vicious of his companions.

Tonio stood up.

'I owe you forty lire . . .' he said to the proprietor.

He pushed back his chair and strode towards the door.

'He's running out on us,' cried Pizzaccio. 'He's got no guts.'

'Good night all,' said Tonio.

'Tonio!' shouted don Ruggero.

Tonio was already half out of the door.

'What do you want?' he asked don Ruggero.

'You haven't the right to leave,' said don Ruggero.

'You'd better listen to him,' said the proprietor to Tonio. 'He'll be a lawyer before long. He knows what he's talking about.'

'You haven't the right to leave,' continued don Ruggero, 'because you haven't fulfilled your part of the contract.'

There was a murmur of approval. Don Ruggero was getting the game off to an elegant start.

'Listen to me,' pursued don Ruggero. 'You're don Cesare's confidential man. Suppose you engaged a boy for him. You and the boy make a verbal contract with one another. You see what I'm driving at?'

Tonio listened with knitted brows, a set look on his face.

'Under the terms of this verbal agreement,' pursued don Ruggero, 'you haven't the right to dismiss the boy without notice. But neither has the boy the right to leave his job without notice. Do you agree?'

'Yes,' said Tonio, with hesitation.

'By starting the game, you made a verbal agreement with us. You haven't the right to leave without notice.'

'I don't feel up to it,' said Tonio. 'Good night all.'

But he hesitated to take the final stride.

Don Ruggero made a sweeping gesture with his arm.

'I call you all as witness. Don Cesare's confidential man is setting an example for breaking an agreement without notice.'

'Good night all,' repeated Tonio. But he still hesitated.

'I withdraw my credit,' said the proprietor. 'I don't give credit to a man who doesn't respect his agreements.'

'Here's a new situation,' proclaimed don Ruggero.

He shot out of his chair, went up to Tonio and put his hand on his shoulder.

'When one isn't allowed credit, one has to pay before leaving. Give him the forty lire you owe him.'

'I haven't got any money,' said Tonio.

'A clear case of sponging. This is a job for the courts.'

There was a renewed murmur of approval and some applause. A law student, when he was prepared to take the trouble, could add some neat trimmings to the game of The Law.

'It's true,' cried the Australian. 'I saw it happen one day in Foggia. The chap hadn't paid for his meal. The proprietor called the police and they arrested him.'

'I don't want to be awkward,' said the proprietor. 'If he promises to stay till the end of the game, I'll give him back his credit.'

They applauded the proprietor. They surrounded Tonio. They pushed him towards the table.

'You've got me,' he kept saying. 'I know you've got me.'

But he returned to his seat.

'You'll stand me a glass?' the Australian at once asked Matteo Brigante, the deputy.

'That depends,' replied Brigante. 'First let's see what your answers are like.'

'Go ahead and ask . . .'

'I'd like to know why it is that Tonio can't take a joke.'

'Marietta's got under his skin.'

'A good answer. But tell me: why should Marietta get under his skin?'

'I was looking at her the other day, when I went to pick up supplies from don Cesare's fishermen. She'd got nothing on under her frock. The sweat was making the material stick to her skin. You could see the lot – breasts like lemons, a behind like a pair of pomegranates.'

'What does Tonio want from Marietta? That's what I'd like to know.'

'Her virginity,' replied the Australian. 'But Tonio isn't the only one who's after Marietta's virginity.'

'Who'll get it, do you think?'

'Don Cesare,' replied the Australian.

'No,' said Matteo Brigante.

'I tell you it will be don Cesare,' repeated the Australian.

'No,' Brigante repeated violently.

The Australian was insistent. Don Cesare was one of the real old noblemen. No one had ever heard of his not having the virginity of a girl from his household. His father, too, had been a real bull of an overlord. His grandfather the same. Certainly don Cesare was seventy-two now; but his mistress, Elvira, didn't complain. A family in which the men had always remained bulls up to a ripe old age. At eighty his grandfather had still been enjoying the girls of the marsh.

The Australian spoke with a kind of jubilation. Quite a number of drinkers had gradually grouped themselves around the table. The café was full. The jubilation spread to everyone. They repeated: 'An old bull! An old goat!' It was as though don Cesare's virility brought honour to the whole gathering.

'You gave the wrong answer,' said Matteo Brigante. 'You shan't have any wine.'

'You'll stand me a glass?' asked the American in his turn.

'First tell me who will get Marietta's virginity . . .'

'I know the answer to that,' said the American. 'My olives are on the edge of the marsh. I don't miss a thing. I know what don Cesare's women plan to do with Marietta's virginity.'

'Tell us.'

'Marietta is for the agronomist.'

'You're lying,' said Matteo Brigante.

He had drunk a good deal of wine since the start of the game, having been almost continually chief or deputy. His play now lacked finesse. This was not necessarily regrettable; there came a time, during a really animated game, when brutality brought a satisfying vigour to The Law. Most of the onlookers, too, had been drinking heavily; the laughter and the exclamations were growing louder.

The American related how Marietta's mother and her two sisters, Maria and Elvira, had lured the agronomist. Marietta was going to work for him. He wouldn't be able to keep his hands off the lemons and the pomegranates.

'Has Marietta got hooves, then?' asked don Ruggero.

There was an enormous laugh. The erection of the model pen had convinced the whole town that the agronomist shared the tastes of the men of the marsh. He was lodging his mistresses in a palace.

The onlookers imitated the bleating of the goat; each had his own way of bleating. Some scraped the ground with their feet, like the male goat when he is about to charge. Others lowered their heads and sketched imaginary horns in the air with their hands. No one now paid any attention to Tonio. Marietta was a splendid little she-goat. One character leaning across a corner of the table was waggling his rump and calling Marietta's name at every start. At this there was no end to the laughing and bleating.

When they had calmed down a little:

'You gave the wrong answer,' said Brigante to the American. 'You shan't have any wine.'

They booed Matteo Brigante.

'You'll stand me a glass?' asked Pizzaccio.

He smiled, looking very sure of himself.

'Tell us what your findings are?' asked Brigante.

'It's not don Cesare who will rape Marietta. Nor will it be the agronomist. It will be you, Matteo Brigante.'

They booed Pizzaccio. He was too servile with his chief-in-real-life. It was no longer a game.

'You have given a good answer,' Matteo Brigante said firmly.

They booed again.

Brigante filled a glass and offered it to Pizzaccio.

'If you like,' he said, 'you can ask me for a second glass of wine, for a third, for the whole jug if you like . . .'

The booing redoubled. The café became a riot.

Brigante hammered his fist on the table.

'Listen to me,' he shouted.

It took some time to restore silence.

'Listen to me,' he went on, 'I'm going to tell you how I, Matteo Brigante, go about raping a virgin.'

There was a great silence.

Brigante bent towards Tonio.

'Listen carefully,' he said. 'I'm going to give you a lesson. But you won't be able to make use of it. You've got no guts.'

Attention fastened for a moment on Tonio, the victim selected by The Law. But it returned at once to Matteo Brigante who was now on his feet.

'Let's suppose,' he began, 'that Marietta was standing there, by the table. . . .'

He gave a clear, detailed and precise account of what each of them dreamed of accomplishing.

Tonio had turned as white as his freshly starched white jacket. Some of the characters were watching him out of the corner of their eyes, ready to collar him. But he made no move, all eyes for Brigante's mime.

Brigante was particularly insistent about the brutality with which he would rupture the hymen. Since he was thin, hard-boned and wiry, this was all the more impressive.

Tonio stared at him with the vacant expression of people watching television.

'And that's it,' concluded Brigante.

The silence was prolonged a moment more, and then the applause exploded. Several onlookers took their turn at miming the gestures of raping. Others began to bleat again; the bleats became ear-splitting. Still others clashed their heads together, miming the struggle of two male goats for the possession of a female.

45 M. A. K. Halliday

The Syntax Enunciates the Theme

Excerpt from M. A. K. Halliday, 'Linguistic Function and Literary Style: an inquiry into the language of William Golding's "The Inheritors"'. This paper appeared in the proceedings of the Second Style in Language Conference in Bellagio, 1969, and is published in Seymour Chatman (ed.), *Literary Style: A Symposium*, New York, Oxford University Press, 1971, reprinted by permission. Reprinted in M. A. K. Halliday, *Explorations in the Functions of Language*, Edward Arnold, 1973.

Here we might be inclined to talk of semantic choice and syntactic choice: what the author chooses to say, and how he chooses to say it. But this is a misleading distinction; not only because it is unrealistic in application (most distinctions in language leave indeterminate instances, although here there would be suspiciously many) but more because the combined effect is cumulative: the one does not weaken or cut across the other but reinforces it. We have to do here with an interaction, not of meaning and form, but of two levels of meaning, both of which find expression in form, and through the same syntactic features. The immediate thesis and the underlying theme come together in the syntax; the choice of subject matter is motivated by the deeper meaning, and the transitivity patterns realize both. This is the explanation of their powerful impact.

The foregrounding of certain patterns in syntax as the expression of an underlying theme is what we understand by 'syntactic imagery', and we assume that its effect will be striking. But in *The Inheritors* these same syntactic patterns also figure prominently in their 'literal' sense, as the expression of subject matter; and their prominence here is doubly relevant, since the literal use not only is motivated in itself but also provides a context for the metaphorical – we accept the syntactic vision of things more readily because we can see that it coincides with, and is an extension of, the reality. *The Inheritors* provides a remarkable illustration of how grammar can convey levels of meaning in literature; and this relates closely to the notion of linguistic functions which I discussed at the beginning. The foregrounded patterns, in this instance, are ideational ones, whose meaning resides in the representation of experience; as such they express not only the content of the narrative but also the abstract structure of the reality through which that content is interpreted. Sometimes the interpretation matches our own, and at other times, as in the drawing of the bow in passage A below, it conflicts with it; these are the 'opposed conditions of use' referred to earlier. Yet each tells a part of the story. Language, by the multiplicity of its functions, possesses a fugue-like quality in which a number of themes unfold simultaneously; each one of these themes is apprehended in various settings. Hence one recurrent motive in the text is likely to have more than one value in the whole.

The Inheritors is prefaced by a quotation from H. G. Wells' *Outline of History:*

... We know very little of the appearance of the Neanderthal man, but this ... seems to suggest an extreme hairiness, an ugliness, or a repulsive strangeness in his appearance over and above his low forehead, his beetle brows, his ape neck, and his inferior stature. ... Says Sir Harry Johnston, in a survey of the rise of modern man in his *Views and Reviews*: 'The dim racial remembrance of such gorilla-like monsters, with cunning brains, shambling gait, hairy bodies, strong teeth, and possibly cannibalistic tendencies, may be the germ of the ogre in folk-lore. ...'

The book is, in my opinion, a highly successful piece of imaginative prose writing; in the words of Kinkead-Weekes and Gregor, in their penetrating critical study (1967), it is a 'reaching out through the imagination into the unknown'. The persons of the story are a small band of Neanderthal people, initially eight strong, who refer to themselves as 'the people'; their world is then invaded by a group of more advanced stock, a fragment of a tribe, whom they call at first 'others' and later 'the new people'. This casual impact – casual, that is, from the tribe's point of view – proves to be the end of the people's world, and of the people themselves. At first, and for more than nine tenths of the book (pages 1–216), we share the life of the people and their view of the world, and also their view of the tribe: for a long passage (pages 137–180) the principal character, Lok, is hidden in a tree watching the tribe in their work, their ritual and their play, and the account of their doings is confined within the limits of Lok's understanding, requiring at times a considerable effort of 'interpretation'. At the very end (pages 216–33) the standpoint shifts to that of the tribe, the inheritors, and the world becomes recognizable as our own, or something very like it. I propose to examine an aspect of the linguistic resources as they are used first to characterize the people's world and then to effect the shift of world-view.

For this purpose I shall look closely at three passages taken from different parts of the book; these are reproduced below. Passage A is representative of the first, and much longer, section, the narrative of the people; it is taken from the long account of Lok's vigil in the tree. Passage C is taken from the short final section, concerned with the tribe; while passage B spans the transition, the shift of standpoint occurring at the paragraph division within this passage. Linguistically, A and C differ in rather significant ways, while B is in certain respects transitional between them.

The clauses of passage A [56][1] are mainly clauses of action [21], location

1. The figures in square brackets show numbers of occurrences.

(including possession) [14] or mental process [16]; the remainder [5] are attributive (for a discussion of clause types see Halliday, 1970). Usually [46], the process is expressed by a finite verb in simple past tense. Almost all [19] of the action clauses describe simple movements (*turn, rise, hold, reach, throw, forward* etc.); and of these the majority [15] are intransitive; the exceptions are *the man was holding the stick, as though someone had clapped a hand over her mouth, he threw himself forward* and *the echo of Liku's voice in his head sent him trembling at this perilous way of bushes towards the island.* The typical pattern is exemplified by the first two clauses, *the bushes twitched again* and *Lok steadied by the tree,* and there is no clear line, here, between action and location: both types have some reference in space, and both have one participant only. The clauses of movement usually [16] also specify location, e.g. *the man turned sideways in the bushes, he rushed to the edge of the water;* and on the other hand, in addition to what is clearly movement, as in *a stick rose upright,* and what is clearly location, as in *there were hooks in the bone,* there is an intermediate type exemplified by [*the bushes*] *waded out,* where the verb is of the movement type but the subject is immobile.

The picture is one in which people act, but they do not act on things; they move, but they move only themselves, not other objects. Even such normally transitive verbs as *grab* occur intransitively: *he grabbed at the branches* is just another clause of movement (cf. *he smelled along the shaft of the twig*). Moreover a high proportion [exactly half] of the subjects are not people; they are either parts of the body [8] or inanimate objects [20], and of the human subjects half again [14] are found in clauses which are not clauses of action. Even among the four transitive action clauses, cited above, one has an inanimate subject and one is reflexive. There is a stress set up, a kind of syntactic counterpoint, between verbs of movement in their most active and dynamic form, that of finite verb in independent clause (see Halliday, 1964), in the simple past tense characteristic of the direct narrative of events in a time sequence, on the one hand, and on the other hand the preference for non-human subjects and the almost total absence of transitive clauses. It is particularly the lack of transitive clauses of action with human subjects (there are only two clauses in which a person acts on an external object) that creates an atmosphere of ineffectual activity. The scene is one of constant movement, but movement which is as much inanimate as human and in which only the mover is affected – nothing else changes. The syntactic tension expresses this combination of activity and helplessness.

No doubt this is a fair summary of the life of Neanderthal man. But Passage A is not a description of the people. The section from which it is taken is one in which Lok is observing and, to a certain extent, interacting with the tribe; they have captured one of the people, and it is for the most part their doings that are being described. And the tribe are not helpless. The transitivity patterns are not imposed by the subject matter; they are the reflexion of the underlying theme, or rather of one of the underlying themes – the inherent limitations of understanding, whether cultural or biological, of Lok and his people, and their consequent inability to survive when confronted with beings at a higher stage of development. In terms of the processes and events as we would interpret them, and encode them in our grammar, there is no immediate justification for the predominance of intransitives; this is the result of their being expressed through the medium of the semantic structure of Lok's universe. In our interpretation, a goal-directed process (or, as I shall suggest below, an externally caused process) took place: someone held up a bow and drew it. In Lok's interpretation, the process was undirected (or, again, self-caused): *a stick rose upright* and *began to grow shorter at both ends*. (I would differ slightly here from Kinkead-Weekes and Gregor, who suggest, I think, that the form of Lok's vision is perception and no more. There may be very little processing, but there surely is some; Lok has a theory – as he must have, because he has language.)

Thus it is the syntax as such, rather than the syntactic reflection of the subject matter, to which we are responding. This would not emerge if we had no account of the activities of the tribe, since elsewhere – in the description of the people's own doings, or of natural phenomena – the intransitiveness of the syntax would have been no more than a feature of the events themselves, and of the people's ineffectual manipulation of their environment. For this reason the vigil of Lok is a central element in the novel. We find, in its syntax, both levels of meaning side by side: Lok is now actor, now interpreter, and it is his potential in both these roles that is realized by the overall patterns of prominence that we have observed, the intransitives, the non-human subjects and the like. This is the dominant mode of expression. At the same time, in passage A, among the clauses that have human subjects, there are just two in which the subject is acting on something external to himself, and in both these the subject is a member of the tribe; it is not Lok. There is no instance in which Lok's own actions extend beyond himself; but there is a brief hint that such extension is conceivable. The syntactic foregrounding, of which this passage provides a typical example, thus has a complex significance: the predominance of intransitives reflects, first, the limitations of the people's own actions; second, the people's world view, which in general cannot transcend these limitations – but within which there may arise, thirdly, a dim apprehension of the superior powers of the 'others', represented by the rare intrusion of a transitive clause such as *the man was holding the stick out to him*. Here the syntax leads us into a third level of meaning, Golding's concern with the nature of humanity; the intellectual and spiritual developments that contribute to the present human condition, and the conflicts that arise within it, are realized in the form of conflicts between the stages of that development – and, syntactically, between the types of transitivity.

Passage A is both text and sample. It is not only these particular sentences and their meanings that determine our response, but the fact that they are part of a general syntactic and semantic scheme. That this passage is representative in its transitivity patterns can be seen from comparison with other extracts.[2] It also exemplifies certain other relevant features of the language of this part of the book. We have seen that there is a strong preference for processes having only one participant: in general there is only one nominal element in the structure of the clause, which is therefore the subject. But while there are very few complements,[3] there is an abundance of adjuncts [44]; and most of these [40] have some spatial reference. Specifically, they are (a) static [25], of which most [21] are place adjuncts consisting of preposition plus noun, the noun being either an inanimate object of the immediate natural environment (e.g. *bush*) or a part of the body, the remainder [4] being localizers (*at their farthest, at the end* etc.); and (b) dynamic [15], of which the majority [10] are of direction or non-terminal motion (*sideways,* [*rose*] *upright, at the branches, towards the island* etc.) and the remainder [5] perception, or at least circumstantial to some process that is not a physical one (e.g. [*looked at Lok*] *along his shoulder,* [*shouted*] *at the green drifts*). Thus with the dynamic type, either the movement is purely perceptual or, if physical, it never reaches a goal: the nearest thing to terminal motion is *he rushed to the edge of the water* (which is followed by *and came back*!).

The restriction to a single participant also applies to mental process clauses [16]. This category includes perception, cognition and reaction, as well as the rather distinct sub-category of verbalization; and such clauses in English typically contain a 'phenomenon', that which is seen, understood, liked etc. Here however the phenomenon is often [8] either not expressed at all (e.g. [*Lok*] *gazed*) or expressed indirectly through a preposition, as in *he smelled along the shaft of the twig;* and sometimes [3] the subject is not a human being but a sense organ (*his nose examined this stuff and did not like it*). There is the same reluctance to envisage the 'whole man' (as distinct from a part of his body) participating in a process in which other entities are involved.

2. The other extracts examined for comparison were three passages of similar length: p. 61, from 'He remembered the old woman...'; pp. 102–3, from 'Then there was nothing more...'; p. 166, from 'At that moment the old man rushed forward...'.

3. By 'complement' is understood all nominal elements other than the subject: direct object, indirect object, cognate object and adjectival and nominal complement. 'Adjuncts' are non-nominal elements (adverbs and prepositional phrases).

There is very little modification of nouns [10, out of about 100]; and all modifiers are non-defining (e.g. *green drifts, glittering water*) except where [2] the modifier is the only semantically significant element in the nominal, the head noun being a mere carrier demanded by the rules of English grammar (*white bone things, sticky brown stuff*). In terms of the immediate situation, things have defining attributes only if these attributes are their sole properties; at the more abstract level, in Lok's understanding the complex taxonomic ordering of natural phenomena that is implied by the use of defining modifiers is lacking, or is only rudimentary.

We can now formulate a description of a typical clause of what we may call Language A, the language in which the major part of the book is written and of which passage A is a sample, in terms of its process, participants and circumstances:

1. There is one participant only, which is therefore subject; this is:

(a) actor in a non-directed action (action clauses are intransitive), or participant in a mental process (the one who perceives, etc.), or simply the bearer of some attribute or some spatial property;

(b) a person (*Lok, the man, he* etc.), or a part of the body, or an inanimate object of the immediate and tangible natural environment (*bush, water, twig* etc.);

(c) unmodified, other than by a determiner which is either an anaphoric demonstrative (*this, that*) or, with parts of the body, a personal possessive (*his* etc.).

2. The process is:

(a) action (which is always movement in space), or location-possession (including e.g. *the man had white bone things above his eyes* = 'above the man's eyes there were . . .'), or mental process (thinking and talking as well as seeing and feeling – a 'cunning brain'! – but often with a part of the body as subject);

(b) active, non-modalized, finite, in simple past tense (one of a linear sequence of mutually independent processes).

3. There are often other elements which are adjuncts, i.e. treated as circumstances attendant on the process, not as participants in it; these are

(a) static expressions of place (in the form of prepositional phrases), or, if dynamic, expressions of direction (adverbs only) or of non-terminal motion, or of directionality of perception (e.g. *peered at the stick*);

(b) often obligatory, occurring in clauses which are purely locational (e.g. *there were hooks in the bone*).

A grammar of Language A would tell us not merely what clauses occurred in the text but also what clauses could occur in that language (see Thorne, 1965). For example, as far as I know the clause *a branch curved downwards over the water* does not occur in the book; neither does *his hands felt along the base of the rock*. But both of them could have done. On the other hand, *he had very quickly broken off the lowest branches* breaks four rules: it has a human actor with a transitive verb, a tense other than simple past, a defining modifier, and a non-spatial adjunct. This is not to say that it could not occur. Each of these features is improbable, and their combination is very improbable; but they are not impossible. They are improbable in that they occur with significantly lower frequency than in other varieties of English (such as, for example, the final section of *The Inheritors*).

Before leaving this passage, let us briefly reconsider the transitivity features in the light of a somewhat different analysis of transitivity in English. I have suggested elsewhere (1967–8 cf. Fillmore, 1968), that the most generalized pattern of transitivity in modern English, extending beyond action clauses to clauses of all types, those of mental process and those expressing attributive and other relations, is one that is based not on the notions of actor and goal but on those of cause and effect. In any clause, there is one central and obligatory participant – let us call it the 'affected' participant – which is inherently involved in the process. This corresponds to the actor in an intransitive clause of action, to the goal in a transitive clause of action, and to the one who perceives, etc., in a clause of mental process; *Lok* has this function in all the following examples: *Lok turned away, Fa drew Lok away, Lok looked up at Fa, Lok was frightened, curiosity overcame Lok*. There may then be a second, optional participant, which is present only if the process is being regarded as brought about by some agency other than the participant affected by it: let us call this the 'agent'. This is the actor in a transitive clause of action and the initiator in the various types of causative; the function of *Tuami* in *Tuami waggled the paddle in the water* and *Tuami let the ivory drop from his hands*. As far as action clauses are concerned, an intransitive clause is one in which the roles of 'affected' and 'agent' are combined in the one participant; a transitive clause is one in which they are separated, the process being treated as one having an external cause.

In these terms, the entire transitivity structure of Language A can be summed up by saying that there is no cause and effect. More specifically: in this language, processes are seldom represented as resulting from an external cause; in those instances where they are, the 'agent' is seldom a human being; and where it is a human being, it is seldom one of the people. Whatever the type of process, there tends to be only one participant; any other entities are involved only indirectly, as circumstantial elements (syntactically, through the mediation of a preposition). It is as if doing was as passive as seeing, and things no more affected by actions than by perceptions: their role is as in clauses of mental process, where the object of perception is not in any sense 'acted on' – it is in fact the perceiver that is the 'affected' participant, not the thing perceived – and likewise tends to be expressed circumstantially (e.g. *Lok peered at the stick*). There is no effective relation between persons and objects: people do not bring about events in which anything other than they themselves, or parts of their bodies, are implicated.

There are, moreover, a great many, an excessive number, of these circumstantial elements; they are the objects in the natural environment, which as it were take the place of participants, and act as curbs and limitations on the process. People do not act on the things around them; they act within the limitations imposed by the things. The frustration of the struggle with the environment, of a life 'poised . . . between the future and the past', is embodied in the syntax: many of the intransitive clauses have potentially transitive verbs in them, but instead of a direct object there is a prepositional phrase. The feeling of frustration is perhaps further reinforced by the constant reference to complex mental activities of cognition and verbalization. Although there are very few abstract nouns, there are very many clauses of speaking, knowing and understanding (e.g. *Lok understood that the man was holding the stick out to him*); and a recurrent theme, an obsession almost, is the difficulty of communicating memories and images (*I cannot see this picture*) – of transmitting experience through language, the vital step towards that social learning which would be a precondition of their further advance.

Such are some of the characteristics of Language A, the language which tells the story of the people. There is no such thing as a Language B. Passage B is simply the point of transition between the two parts of the book. There is a Language C: this is the language of the last sixteen pages of the novel, and it is exemplified by the extract shown as passage C below. But passage B is of interest because it is linguistically also to some extent transitional. There is no doubt that the first paragraph is basically in Language A and the second in Language C; moreover the switch is extremely sudden, being established in the first three words of B2, when Lok, with whom we have become closely identified, suddenly becomes *the red creature*. Nevertheless B1 does provide some hints of the change to come.

There are a few instances [4] of a human 'agent' (actor in a transitive clause); not many, but one of them is Lok, in *Lok . . . picked up Tanakil*. Here is Lok acting on his environment, and the object 'affected' is a human being, and one of the tribe! There are some non-spatial adjuncts, such as *with an agonized squealing, like the legs of a giant*. There are abstract nominals: *demoniac activity, its weight of branches*. And there are perhaps more modifiers and complex verb forms than usual. None of these features is occurring for the first time; we have had forward-looking flashes throughout, e.g. (page 191) *He had a picture of Liku looking up with soft and adoring eyes at Tanakil, guessed how Ha had gone with a kind of eager fearfulness to meet his sudden death;* and compare (pages 212–3) '*Why did you not snatch the new one?*' and '*We will take Tanakil. Then they will give back the new one.*', both spoken by the more intelligent Fa (when transitive action clauses do occur in Language A, they are often in the dialogue). But there is a greater concentration of them in B1, a linguistic complexity that is also in harmony with the increased complexity of the events, which has been being built up ever since the tribe first impinged on the people with the mysterious disappearance of Ha (page 65). The syntax expresses the climax of the gradual overwhelming of Lok's understanding by new things and events; and this coincides with the climax in the events themselves as, with the remainder of the people all killed or captured, Lok's last companion, Fa, is carried over the edge of the waterfall. Lok is alone; there are no more people, and the last trace of his humanity, his membership of a society, has gone. In that moment he belongs to the past.

Lok does not speak again, because there is no one to speak to. But for a while we follow him, as the tribe might have followed him, although they did not – or rather we follow *it*; there can be no *him* where there is no *you* and *me*. The language is now Language C, and the story is that of *homo sapiens*; but for a few paragraphs, beginning at B2, as we remain with Lok, the syntax harks back to the world of the people, just as in B1 it was beginning to look forward. The transition has taken place; *it was a strange creature, smallish, and bowed* that we had come to know so well. But it is still the final, darkening traces of this creature's world that we are seeing, fleetingly as if in an escaping dream.

A brief sketch of B2: There are very few transitive clauses of action [4]; in only one of these is Lok the agent – and here the 'affected' entity is a part of his own body: *it put up a hand*. The others have *the water* and *the river* as agent. Yet nearly half [22] the total number of clauses [47] have Lok as subject; here, apart from a few [4] mental process clauses, the verb is again one of simple movement or posture, and intransitive (*turn, move, crouch* etc.; but including for the first time some with a connotation of attitude like *sidle* and *trot*; compare it with *broke into a queer, loping run*). The remaining subjects are inanimate objects [19] and parts of the body [6]. But there are differences in these subjects. The horizons have widened; in addition to *water* and *river* we now have *sun* and *green sky* – a reminder that the new people walk upright: cf. (page 143) *they did not look at the earth but straight ahead*; and there are now also human evidences and artefacts: *path, rollers, ropes*. And the parts of the body no longer see or feel; they are subjects only of intransitive verbs of movement (e.g. *its long arms swinging*), and mainly in non-finite clauses, expressing the dependent nature of the processes in which they participate. A majority [32] of the finite verbs are still in simple past tense; but there is more variation in the remainder, as well as more non-finite verbs [8], reflecting a slightly increased proportion of dependent clauses that is also a characteristic of Language C. And while in many clauses [21] we still find spatial adjuncts, these tend to be more varied and more complex (e.g. *down the rocks beyond the terrace from the melting ice in the mountains*).

This is the world of the tribe; but it is still inhabited, for a brief moment of time, by Lok. Once again the theme is enunciated by the syntax. Nature is no longer totally impenetrable; yet Lok remains powerless, master of nothing but his own body. In passages A and B taken together, there are more than fifty clauses in which the subject is Lok; but only one of these has Lok as an agent acting on something external to himself, one that has already been mentioned: *Lok picked up Tanakil*. There is a double irony here. Of all the positive actions on his environment that Lok might have taken, the one he does take is the utterly improbable one of capturing a girl of the tribe – improbable in the event, at the level of subject matter (let us call this 'level one'), and improbable also in the deeper context ('level two') since Lok's newly awakened power manifests itself as power over the one element in the environment that is 'superior' to himself. It is at a still deeper 'level three' that the meaning becomes clear. The action gets him nowhere; but it is a syntactic hint that his people have played their part in the long trek towards the human condition.

By the time we reach passage C, the transition is complete. Here, for the first time, the majority of the clauses [48, out of 67] have a human subject; of these, more than half [25] are clauses of action, and most of these [19] are transitive. Leaving aside two in which the thing 'affected' is a part of the body, there is still a significant increase in the number of instances [17], contrasting with 5 in the whole of A and B together] in which a human agent is acting on an external object. The world of the inheritors is organized as ours is; or at least in a way that we can recognize. Among these are two clauses in which the subject is *they*, referring to the people ('the devils': e.g. *they have given me back a changeling*); in the tribe's scheme of things, the people are by no means powerless. There is a parallel here with the earlier part. In passage A the actions of the tribe are encoded in terms of the world view of the people, so that the predominance of intransitive clauses is interpreted at what we called 'level two', although there is a partial reflection of 'level one' in the fact that they are marginally less predominant when the subject matter concerns the tribe. Similarly, in passage C references to the people are encoded in terms of the world view of the tribe, and transitive structures predominate; yet the only member of the people who is present – the only one to survive – is the captured baby, whose infant behaviour is described in largely intransitive terms (pages 230–31). And the references to the people, in the dialogue, include such formulations as '*They cannot follow us, I tell you. They cannot pass over water*', which is a 'level one' reassurance that, in a 'level two' world of cause and effect whose causes are often unseen and unknown, there are at least limits to the devils' power.

We can now see the full complementarity between the two 'languages', but it is not easy to state. In Language A there is a level two theme, that of powerlessness. The momentary hints of potency that we are given at level one represent an antithetic variation which, however, has a significance at level three: the power is ascribed to the tribe but signifies Lok's own incipient awareness, the people's nascent understanding of the human potential. This has become a level two theme in Language C; and in like fashion the level two theme of Language A becomes in Language C a level one variation, but again with a level three significance. The people may be powerless, but the tribe's demand for explanations of things, born of their own more advanced state, leads them, while still fearfully insisting on the people's weakness in action, to ascribe to them supernatural powers.

While there are still inanimate subjects in the clauses [11], as there always are in English, there is no single instance in passage C of an inanimate agent. In A and B we had *the echo of Liku's voice in his head sent him trembling* [. . .], *the branches took her, the water had scooped a bowl out of the rock;* in C we have only *the sail glowed, the sun was sitting in it, the hills grow less*. Likewise all clauses with parts of the body as subject [8] are now intransitive, and none of them is a clause of mental process. Parts of the body no longer feel or perceive; they have attributes ascribed to them (e.g. *his teeth were wolf's teeth*) or they move (*the lips parted, the mouth was opening and shutting*). The limbs may move and posture, but only the whole man perceives and reacts to his environment. Now, he also shapes his environment: his actions have become more varied – no longer simply movements; we find here *save, obey* and *kiss* – and they produce results. Something, or someone, is affected by them.

Just as man's relation to his environment has altered, so his perception of it has changed; the environment has become enlarged. The objects in it are no longer the *twig, stick, bush, branch* of Language A, nor even the larger but still tangible *river, water, scars in the earth*. In passage B2 we already had *air* and *sun* and *sky* and *wind*; in C we have *the mountain . . . full of golden light, the sun was blazing, the sand was swirling* (the last metaphorically); and also human artefacts: *the sail, the mast*. Nature is not tamed: the features of the natural environment may no longer be agents in the transitivity patterns, but nor are they direct objects. What has happened is that the horizons have broadened. Where the people were bounded by tree and river and rock, the tribe are bounded by sky and sea and mountain. Although they are not yet conquered, the features that surround them no longer circumscribe all action and all contemplation. Whereas Lok *rushed to the edge of the water and came back*, the new people *steer in towards the shore*, and *look across the water at the green hills*.

The establishment of a syntactic norm (for this is what it is) is thus a way of expressing one of the levels of meaning of the work: the fact that a particular pattern constitutes a norm *is* the meaning. The linguistic function of the pattern is therefore of some importance. The features that we have seen to be foregrounded in *The Inheritors* derive from the ideational component in the language system; hence they represent, at the level at which they constitute a norm, a world-view, a structuring of experience that is significant because there is no *a priori* reason why the experience should have been structured in this way rather than in another. More particularly, the foregrounded features were selections in transitivity. Transitivity is the set of options whereby the speaker encodes his experience of the processes of the external world, and of the internal world of his own consciousness, together with the participants in these processes and their attendant circumstances; and it embodies a very basic distinction of processes into two types, those that are regarded as due to an external cause, an agency other than the person or object involved, and those that are not. There are, in addition, many further categories and sub-types. Transitivity is really the cornerstone of the semantic organization of experience; and it is at one level what *The Inheritors* is about. The theme of the entire novel, in a sense, is transitivity; man's interpretation of his experience of the world, his understanding of its processes and of his own participation in them. This is the motivation for Golding's syntactic originality; it is because of this that the syntax is effective as a 'mode of meaning' (Firth, 1957). The particular transitivity patterns that stand out in the text contribute to the artistic whole through the functional significance, in the language system, of the semantic options which they express.

This is what we understand by relevance: the notion that a linguistic feature 'belongs' in some way as part of the whole. The pursuit of prominence is not without significance for the understanding and evaluation of a literary work; but nor is it sufficient to be a rewarding activity in itself (see Fowler, 1966). It has been said of phonological foregrounding that 'there must be appropriateness to the nexus of sound and meaning'; and this is no less true of the syntactic and semantic levels, where however the relationship is not one of sound and meaning but one of meaning and meaning. Here 'relevance' implies a congruence with our interpretation of what the work is about, and hence the criteria of belonging are semantic ones. We might be tempted to express the relevance of syntactic patterns, such as we find in *The Inheritors*, as a 'unity of form and meaning', parallel to the 'sound and meaning' formulation above; but this would I think be a false parallel. The syntactic categories are *per se* the realizations of semantic options, and the relevance is the relevance of one set of meanings to another – a relationship among the levels of meaning of the work itself.

In *The Inheritors*, the syntax is part of the story. As readers, we are reacting to the whole of the writer's creative use of 'meaning potential'; and the nature of language is such that he can convey, in a line of print, a complex of simultaneous themes, reflecting the variety of functions that language is required to serve. And because the elements of the language, the words and phrases and syntactic structures, tend to have multiple values, any one theme may have more than one interpretation: in expressing some content, for example, the writer may invite us at the same time to interpret it in quite a different functional context – as a cry of despair, perhaps. It is the same property of language that enables us to react to hints, to take offence and do all the other things that display the rhetoric of everyday verbal interaction. A theme that is strongly foregrounded is especially likely to be interpreted at more than one level. In *The Inheritors* it is the linguistic representation of experience, through the syntactic resources of transitivity, that is especially brought into relief, although there may be other themes not mentioned here that stand out in the same way. Every work achieves a unique balance among the types and components of meaning, and embodies the writer's individual exploration of the functional diversity of language.

Extracts from *The Inheritors*:
A (pages 106–7)

The bushes twitched again. Lok steadied by the tree and gazed. A head and a chest faced him, half-hidden. There were white bone things behind the leaves and hair. The man had white bone things above his eyes and under the mouth so that his face was longer than a face should be. The man turned sideways in the bushes and looked at Lok along his shoulder. A stick rose upright and there was a lump of bone in the middle. Lok peered at the stick and the lump of bone and the small eyes in the bone things over the face. Suddenly Lok understood that the man was holding the stick out to him but neither he nor Lok could reach across the river. He would have laughed if it were not for the echo of the screaming in his head. The stick began to grow shorter at both ends. Then it shot out to full length again.

The dead tree by Lok's ear acquired a voice.

'Clop!'

His ears twitched and he turned to the tree. By his face there had grown a twig: a twig that smelt of other, and of goose, and of the bitter berries that Lok's stomach told him he must not eat. This twig had a white bone at the end. There were hooks in the bone and sticky brown stuff hung in the crooks. His nose examined this stuff and did not like it. He smelled along the shaft of the twig. The leaves on the twig were red feathers and reminded him of goose. He was lost in a generalized astonishment and excitement. He shouted at the green drifts across the glittering water and heard Liku crying out in answer but could not catch the words. They were cut off suddenly as though someone had clapped a hand over her mouth. He rushed to the edge of the water and came back. On either side of the open bank the bushes grew thickly in the flood; they waded out until at their farthest some of the leaves were opening under water; and these bushes leaned over.

The echo of Liku's voice in his head sent him trembling at this perilous way of bushes towards the island. He dashed at them where normally they would have been rooted on dry land and his feet splashed. He threw himself forward and grabbed at the branches with hands and feet. He shouted:

'I am coming!'

B (pages 215–7)

1. Lok staggered to his feet, picked up Tanakil and ran after Fa along the terrace. There came a screaming from the figures by the hollow log and a loud bang from the jam. The tree began to move forward and the logs were lumbering about like the legs of a giant. The crumplefaced woman was struggling with Tuami on the rock by the hollow log; she burst free and came running towards Lok. There was movement everywhere, screaming, demoniac activity; the old man was coming across the tumbling logs. He threw something at Fa. Hunters were holding the hollow log against the terrace and the head of the tree with all its weight of branches and wet leaves was drawing along them. The fat woman was lying in the log, the crumpled woman was in it with Tanakil, the old man was tumbling into the back. The boughs crashed and drew along the rock with an agonized squealing. Fa was sitting by the water holding her head. The branches took her. She was moving with them out into the water and the hollow log was free of the rock and drawing away. The tree swung into the current with Fa sitting limply among the branches. Lok began to gibber again. He ran up and down on the terrace. The tree would not be cajoled or persuaded. It moved to the edge of the fall, it swung until it was lying along the lip. The water reared up over the trunk, pushing, the roots were over. The tree hung for a while with the head facing upstream. Slowly the root end sank and the head rose. Then it slid forward soundlessly and dropped over the fall.

2. The red creature stood on the edge of the terrace and did nothing. The hollow log was a dark spot on the water towards the place where the sun had gone down. The air in the gap was clear and blue and calm. There was no noise at all now except for the fall, for there was no wind and the green sky was clear. The red creature turned to the right and trotted slowly towards the far end of the terrace. Water was cascading down the rocks beyond the terrace from the melting ice in the mountains. The river was high and flat and drowned the edge of the terrace. There were long scars in the earth and rock where the branches of a tree had been dragged past by the water. The red creature came trotting back to a dark hollow in the side of the cliff where there was evidence of occupation. It looked at the other figure, dark now, that grinned down at it from the back of the hollow. Then it turned away and ran through the little passage that joined the terrace to the slope. It halted, peering down at the scars, the abandoned rollers and broken ropes. It turned again, sidled round a shoulder of rock and stood on an almost imperceptible path that ran along the sheer rocks. It began to sidle along the path, crouched, its long arms swinging, touching, almost as firm a support as the legs. It was peering down into the thunderous waters but there was nothing to be seen but the columns of glimmering haze where the water had scooped a bowl out of the rock. It moved faster, broke into a queer loping run that made the head bob up and down and the forearms alternate like the legs of a horse. It stopped at the end of the path and looked down at the long streamers of weed that were moving backwards and forwards under the water. It put up a hand and scratched under its chinless mouth.

C (pages 228–9)

The sail glowed red-brown. Tuami glanced back at the gap through the mountain and saw that it was full of golden light and the sun was sitting in it. As if they were obeying some signal the people began to stir, to sit up and look across the water at the green hills. Twal bent over Tanakil and kissed her and murmured to her. Tanakil's lips parted. Her voice was harsh and came from far away in the night.

'Liku!'

Tuami heard Marlan whisper to him from by the mast.

'That is the devil's name. Only she may speak it.'

Now Vivani was really waking. They heard her huge, luxurious yawn and the bear skin was thrown off. She sat up, shook back her loose hair and looked first at Marlan then at Tuami. At once he was filled again with lust and hate. If she had been what she was, if Marlan, if her man, if she had saved her baby in the storm on the salt water . . .

'My breasts are paining me.'

If she had not wanted the child as a plaything, if I had not saved the other as a joke . . .

He began to talk high and fast.

'There are plains beyond those hills, Marlan, for they grow less; and there will be herds for hunting. Let us steer in towards the shore. Have we water . . . but of course we have water! Did the women bring the food? Did you bring the food, Twal?'

Twal lifted her face towards him and it was twisted with grief and hate.

'What have I to do with food, master? You and he gave my child to the devils and they have given me back a changeling who does not see or speak.'

The sand was swirling in Tuami's brain. He thought in panic: they have given me back a changed Tuami; what shall I do? Only Marlan is the same . . . smaller, weaker but the same. He peered forrard to find the changeless one as something he could hold on to. The sun was blazing on the red sail and Marlan was red. His arms and legs were contracted, his hair stood out and his beard, his teeth were wolf's teeth and his eyes like blind stones. The mouth was opening and shutting.

'They cannot follow us, I tell you. They cannot pass over water.'

References

FILLMORE, C. J. (1968), 'The case for case', in E. Bach and R. T. Harris (eds.), *Universals in Linguistic Theory*, Holt, Rinehart & Winston.

FIRTH, J. R. (1957), 'Modes of meaning', *Essays and Studies (The English Association)*.

FOWLER, R. (1966), 'Linguistic theory and the study of literature', in R. Fowler (ed.), *Essays on Style and Language: Linguistic and Critical Approaches to Literary Style*, Routledge & Kegan Paul.

GOLDING, W. (1955), *The Inheritors*, Faber & Faber.

HALLIDAY, M. A. K. (1964), 'Descriptive linguistics in literary studies', in A. Duthie (ed.), *English Studies Today: Third Series*, Edinburgh University Press.

HALLIDAY, M. A. K. (1967–8), 'Notes on transitivity and theme in English', *J. Ling*, vol. 3, nos. 1 & 2, vol. 4, no. 2.

HALLIDAY, M. A. K. (1970), 'Language structure and language function', in J. Lyons (ed.), *New Horizons in Linguistics*, Penguin.

HYMES, D. H. (1960), 'Phonological aspects of style: some English sonnets', in T. A. Sebeok (ed.), *Style in Language*, MIT and Wiley.

KINKEAD-WEEKES, M., and GREGOR, I. (1967), *William Golding: a Critical Study* Faber & Faber.

Further Reading

Part One
Tacit Conventions

J. Beattie, 'Aspects of Nyoro symbolism', *Africa*, vol. 38, 1968, pp. 413–42.

M. Douglas, *Purity and Danger: an Analysis of Concepts of Pollution and Taboo*, Routledge & Kegan Paul, 1966; Penguin, 1970.

E. E. Evans-Pritchard, 'Lévy-Bruhl's theory of primitive mentality', *Bulletin of Faculty of Arts*, 1934, vol. 2, no. 1, Egyptian University, Cairo.

E. E. Evans-Pritchard, *Nuer Religion*, Clarendon Press, 1956.

L. Faron, 'Symbolic values and the integration of society among the Mapuche of Chile', *Amer. Anthrop.*, vol. 64, 1962, pp. 1151–64.

A. I. Hallowell, *Culture and Experience*, University of Pennsylvania Press, 1955.

A. M. Hocart, *The Life-Giving Myth*, Methuen, 1970.

H. Hubert and M. Mauss, *Sacrifice: its Nature and Function*, Cohen & West, 1964.

G. Kepes (ed.), *Sign, Image and Symbol*, Studio Vista, 1966.

A. Loisy, *Essai historique sur le sacrifice*, Paris, 1921.

J. Middleton, *Lugbara Religion*, Oxford University Press, 1960.

R. Needham, 'Right and left in Nyoro symbolic classification', *Africa*, vol. 37, 1967, pp. 425–52.

W. H. Rassers, *Panji, the Culture Hero*, Martinus Nijhoff, 1959.

G. Reichel-Dolmatoff, *Amazonian Cosmos: the Sexual and Religious Symbolism of the Tukano Indians*, Chicago University Press, 1971.

A. Richards, *Chisungu: a Girl's Initiation Ceremony among the Bemba of North Rhodesia*, Faber, 1956.

R. F. Spencer (ed.), *Forms of Symbolic Action*, Proceedings of the 1969 spring meeting of the American Ethnological Society, 1970.

V. W. Turner, *The Drums of Affliction: a Study of Religious Processes Among the Ndembu of Zambia*, Clarendon Press, 1968.

Part Two
The Logical Basis of Constructed Reality

B. Beck, 'Colour and heat in S. Indian ritual', *Man* (NS), vol. 4, 1969, pp. 553–72.

T. O. Beidelman, '*Utani*: some Kaguru notions of death, sexuality and affinity', *S.West. J. Anthrop.*, vol. 22, 1966, pp. 354–80.

T. O. Beidelman, 'Some hypotheses regarding Nilo-Hamitic symbolism and social structure: Baraguya folklore', *Anthrop. Quart.*, vol. 41, 1968, pp. 78–89.

R. Bulmer, 'Karam colour categories', *Kivung*, vol. 1, 1968, pp. 120–33.

H. C. Conklin, 'Hanunoo colour categories', *S. West. J. Anthrop.*, vol. 11, 1955, pp. 339–44.

R. Firth, 'Twins, birds and vegetables: problems of identification in primitive religious thought', *Man* (NS), vol. 1, 1966, pp. 1–17.

D. Hicks, 'A structural analysis of Aweikoma symbolism', *Ethnos*, 1966, pp. 96–111.

E. R. Leach, 'The structure of symbolism', in J. S. la Fontaine (ed.), *The interpretation of ritual*, Tavistock, 1972.

C. Lévi-Strauss, *The savage mind*. Weidenfeld & Nicolson, 1966.

C. Lévi-Strauss, *Totemism*. Penguin Books, 1969.

G. Lienhardt, 'Modes of thought', In E. E. Evans-Pritchard *et al.* (eds.), *The Institutions of Primitive Society*, Blackwell, 1954.

J. Middleton, 'Some categories of dual classification among the Lugbara of Uganda', *History of Religions*, vol. 7, 1968, pp. 187–208.

G. B. Milner, 'Siamese twins, birds and the double helix', *Man* (NS), vol. 4, 1969, pp. 5–23.

R. Needham, 'Alliance and classification among the Lamet', *Sociologus*, vol. 10, 1960, pp. 97–118.

D. R. Price-Williams, 'Abstract and concrete modes of classification in a primitive society', *Brit. J. educ. Psych.*, vol. 32, 1962, pp. 50–61.

P. Rigby, 'Dual symbolic classification among the Gogo of central Tanzania', *Africa*, vol. 36, 1966, pp. 1–17.

W. E. H. Stanner, 'Religion, totemism, and symbolism', in R. M. and C. H. Berndt (eds.), *Aboriginal Man in Australia*, Angus & Robertson, 1965.

N. Yalman, 'On some binary categories in Sinhalese religious thought', *Trans. N. Y. Acad. Sci.*, Ser. 11, vol. 24, 1962, pp. 408–20.

Part Three
Orientations in Time and Space

N. Allen, 'The vertical dimension in Thulang classification', *J. Anthrop. Soc. Oxford*, vol. 3, 1972, pp. 81–94.

J. A. Barnes, 'Time flies like an arrow', *Man* (NS), vol. 6, 1971, pp. 537–52.

T. O. Beidelman, 'Kaguru time reckoning: an aspect of the cosmology of an East African people', *S. West. J. Anthrop*, vol. 19, 1963, pp. 9–20.

P. Bourdieu, 'The attitude of the Algerian peasant toward time', in J. Pitt-Rivers (ed.), *Mediterranean Countrymen*, Mouton, 1963.

C. E. Cunningham, 'Order in the Atoni house', *Bijdr. Taal.-Land-Volkenk*, vol. 120, 1964, pp. 34–68.

D. B. Eyde, 'On Tikopia social space', (with a comment by R. Firth), *Bijdr. Taal.-Land-Volkenk*, vol. 123, 1969, pp. 40–70.

M. Freedman, 'Geomancy', *Proc. R. Anthrop. Inst.*, 1968, pp. 5–15.

A. van Gennep, *The Rites of Passage*, Routledge & Kegan Paul, 1960.

C. Geertz, *Person, Time and Place in Bali*, Cultural Rep., Ser. 14, S.E. Asia Studies, Yale University, 1966.

E. Haugen, 'The semantics of Icelandic orientation', *Word*, vol. 13, 1957, pp. 447–60. H. Hubert and M. Mauss., 'Étude sommaire de la représentation du temps dans la religion et la magie', in *Mélanges d'histoire des religions*, Alcan, 1929.

A. Jackson, 'Sound and ritual', *Man* (NS), vol. 3, 1968, pp. 293–99.

E. R. Leach, *Political Systems of Highland Burma*, 1954

E. R. Leach, 'Two essays concerning the symbolic representation of time', in *Rethinking anthropology*, London: Athlone Press.

J. Littlejohn, 'The Temne house', *Sierra Leone Stud.*, vol. 14, 1960, pp. 63–79.

J. Littlejohn, 'Temne space', *Anthrop. Quart.* 36, 1963, pp. 1–17.

R. Needham, 'Percussion and transition', *Man* (NS), vol. 2, 1967, pp. 606–14.

M. Panoff, 'The notion of time among the Maenge people of New Britain', *Ethnology*, vol. 8, 1969, pp. 153–66.

J. D. Sapir, '*Kujaama:* symbolic separation among the Diola Fogny', *Amer. Anthrop.*, vol. 72, 1970, pp. 1330–48.

L. V. Thomas, 'L'espace social chez les Diola', *Notes afr.*, vol. 111, 1966, pp. 89–97.

Part Four
Physical Nature Assigned to Classes

W. H. Alkre, 'Porpoises and taro', *Ethnology*, vol. 7, 1968, pp. 280–9.

E. N. Anderson, 'Sacred fish', *Man* (NS), vol. 4, 1969, pp. 443–49.

T. O. Beidelman, 'Right and left hand among the Kaguru', *Africa*, vol. 31, 1961, pp. 250–7.

T. O. Beidelman, 'The blood covenant and the concept of blood in Ukaguru', *Africa* 33, vol. 1963, pp. 321–42.

T. O. Beidelman, 'Pig (*guluwe*): an essay on Ngulu sexual symbolism', *S.West. J. Anthrop.*, vol. 20, 1964, pp. 359–92.

T. O. Beidelman, 'The ox and Nuer sacrifice: some Freudian hypotheses about Nuer symbolism', *Man* (NS), vol. 1, 1966, pp. 453–67.

T. O. Beidelman, 'Some Nuer notions of nakedness, nudity and sexuality', *Africa*, vol. 38, 1968, pp. 113–32.

P. Bourdieu, 'The sentiment of honour in Kabyle society', in J. G. Peristiany (ed.), *Honour and Shame*, Weidenfeld & Nicolson, 1965.

R. Bulmer, 'Worms that croak and other mysteries of Karam natural history', *Mankind*, vol. 6, 1968, pp. 621–39.

R. Bulmer, 'Which came first, the chicken or the egg head?', In J. Pouillon and P. Maranda (eds.), *Echanges et communications*, Mouton, 1970.

R. Bulmer and M. J. Tyler, 'Karam classification of frogs', *J. Polynes. Soc.*, vol. 77, 1968, pp. 333–85.

J. Buxton, 'Animal identity and human peril: some Mandari images', *Man* (NS), vol. 3, 1968, pp. 35–49.

M. Douglas, 'Animals in Lele religious symbolism', *Africa* 27, 1957, pp. 46–58.

M. Douglas, *The Lele of the Kasai*, Oxford University Press. 1963.

J. J. Fox, 'Sister's child as plant: metaphors in an idiom of consanguinity', in R. Needham (ed.), *Rethinking kinship and marriage*, Tavistock (Ass. Social Anthrop. Mongr. 11), 1971.

D. J. Freeman, 'Iban augury', *Bijdr. Taal.-Land-Volkenk*, vol. 117, 1961, pp. 141–67.

C. Geertz, 'Deep play: notes on the Balinese cockfight', *Daedalus*, vol. 101, 1972, pp. 1–37.

C. R. Hallpike, 'Social hair', *Man* (NS), vol. 4, 1969, pp. 256–64.

J. Littlejohn, 'The choreography of the left hand and the right', *New Society*, vol. 228, 1967, pp. 198–9.

M. Mauss, 'Les techniques du corps', *J. de la Psychologie*, vol. 32, 1935, pp. 271–93.

R. Needham, 'The left hand of the Mugwe: an analytical note on the structure of Meru symbolism', *Africa*, vol. 30, 1960, pp. 20–33.

F. Panoff, 'Food and faeces: a Melanesian rite', *Man* (NS), vol. 5, 1970, pp. 237–52.

J. Pitt-Rivers, 'Spiritual power in Central America: the *naguals* of Chiapas', in M. Douglas (ed.), *Witchcraft Confessions and Accusations*, Tavistock (Ass. Social Anthrop. Mongr. 9). 1970.

E. ten Raa, 'The moon as a symbol of life and fertility in Sandawe thought', *Africa*, vol. 39, 1969, pp. 24–53.

P. Rigby, 'The symbolic role of cattle in Gogo ritual', in T. O. Beidelman (ed.), *The Translation of Culture*, Tavistock. 1971.

M. Ruel, 'Were animals and the introverted witch', in M. Douglas (ed.), *Witchcraft Confessions and Accusations*, Tavistock (Ass. Social Anthrop. Mongr, 9), 1970.

M. Ruel, 'Lions, leopards and rulers', *New Society*, vol. 380, 1970, pp. 54–6.

A. Strathern and M. Strathern, 'Marsupials and magic: a study of spell symbolism among the Mbowamb', in E. Leach (ed.), *Dialectic in Practical Religion*, Cambridge University Press (Camb. Pap. Social Anthrop. 5). 1968.

E. Z. Vogt, 'Human souls and animal spirits in Zinacantan', in J. Pouillon and P. Maranda, (eds.), *Echanges et communications*, Mouton, 1970.

Part Five
The Limits of Knowledge

P. Berger, *The Social Reality of Religion*, Faber & Faber, 1969.

P. Berger and T. Luckmann, *The Social Construction of Reality*, Allen Lane, 1969.

B. Berlin and P. Kay, *Basic Colour Terms*, University of California Press, 1969.

E. A. Burt, *The Metaphysical Foundations of Modern Physical Sciences*, Routledge & Kegan Paul, 1949.

R. M. W. Dixon, 'Virgin birth' (letter), *Man* (NS), vol. 3, 1968, pp. 653–4.

M. Douglas, 'Dogon culture: profane and arcane', *Africa*, vol. 38, 1968, pp. 16–25.

M. Douglas, 'The social control of cognition: some factors in joke perception', *Man* (NS), vol. 3, 1968, pp. 361–76.

A. Forge, 'Learning to see in New Guinea', in P. Mayer (ed.), *Socialisation: The Approach from Social Anthropology*, Tavistock (Ass. Social Anthrop. Mongr. 8), 1970.

R. Horton, 'African traditional thought and western science', *Africa*, vol. 37, 1967, pp. 50–71 and 155–87.

F. Kafka, 'The investigations of a dog', In *Metamorphosis and Other Stories*, Penguin, 1961.

T. Luckmann, *The Invisible Religion*, Macmillan, 1968.

S. J. Tambiah, 'The magical power of words', *Man* (NS), vol. 3, 1968, pp. 175–208.

L. S. Vygotsky, *Thought and Language*. MIT Press, 1962.

B. R. Wilson, (ed.) *Rationality*, Blackwell, 1970.

Part Six
Interpenetration of Meanings

R. C. Birdwhistell, *Introduction to Kinesics*, Allen Lane, 1971.

G. Calme-Griaule, *Ethnologie et langage: la parole chez les Dogon*, Gallimard, 1966.

E. E. Evans-Pritchard, 'Nuer spear symbolism', *Anthrop. Quart.*, vol. 26, 1953, pp. 1–19.

J. C. Faris, *Nuba Personal Art*, Duckworth, 1972.

R. Firth, 'Postures and gestures of respect', In *Echanges et communications*, (ed.) J. Pouillon & P. Maranda, Mouton, 1970.

R. Firth, 'Verbal and bodily rituals of greeting and parting', in J. S. la Fontaine (ed.), *The Interpretation of Ritual*. London: Tavistock, 1972.

A. Forge, 'Art and environment in the Sepik', *Proc. R. anthrop. Inst.*, 1965, pp. 23–31.

S. Freud, *The Interpretation of Dreams*, Hogarth Press, 1956.

A. F. Gell, 'Penis sheathing and ritual status in a west Sepik village', *Man*, (NS), vol. 6, 1971, pp. 165–81.

C. Humphrey, 'What is primitive art?', *New Society*, vol. 388, 1970, pp. 393–5.

C. Humphrey, 'Some ideas of Saussure applied to Buryat magical drawings', in E. Ardener (ed.), *Social Anthropology and Language*, Tavistock, (Ass. Social Anthrop. Mongr. 10). 1971.

A. Kyermaten, 'The royal stools of Ashanti', *Africa*, vol. 39, 1969, pp. 1–10.

E. R. Leach, 'The legitimacy of Solomon', in *Genesis as Myth and Other Essays*, Cape, 1969.

N. Munn, 'Walbiri graphic signs', *Amer. Anthrop.*, vol. 64, 1962, pp. 972–84.

N. Munn, 'Totemic designs and group continuity in Walbiri cosmology', in M. Reay (ed.), *Aborigines Now*, Angus and Robertson, 1964.

C. Odugbesan, 'Femininity in Yoruba religious art', in M.Douglas and P. Kaberry (eds.), *Man in Africa;* Tavistock, 1969.

K. E. Read, 'Morality and the concept of the person among the Gahuku-Gama', *Oceania*, vol. 25, 1955, pp. 233–82.

A. Strathern and M. Strathern, *Self Decoration in Mount Hagen*, Duckworth, 1971.

J. Westcott, 'The sculpture and myths of Eshu-Elegba, the Yoruba trickster: definition and interpretation in Yoruba iconography', *Africa*, vol. 32, 1962, pp. 336–54.

R. G. Willis, 'The head and the loins: Lévi-Strauss and beyond', *Man*, (NS), vol. 2, 1967, pp. 519–34.

Part Seven
Provinces of Meaning

T. O. Beidelman, 'Swazi royal ritual', *Africa*, vol. 36, 1966, pp. 373–405.

W. Blythe, *The Impact of Chinese Secret Societies in Malaya*, Oxford University Press, 1969.

R. K. Dentan, 'Labels and rituals in Semai classification', *Ethnology*, vol. 9, 1970, pp. 16–25.

E. E. Evans-Pritchard, 'Nuer modes of address', *Uganda J.*, vol. 12, 1948, pp. 166–71.

J. W. Fernandez, 'Symbolic consensus in a Fang reformative cult', *Amer. Anthrop.*, vol. 67, 1965, pp. 902–29.

J. W. Fernandez, 'Unbelievably subtle words: representation and integration in the sermons of an African reformative cult', *History of Religions*, vol. 6, 1966, pp. 43–69.

R. Horton, 'The Kalabari *Ekine* society: a borderline of religion and art', *Africa*, vol. 33, 1963, pp. 94–114.

J. Huizinga, *Homo Ludens: a Study of the Play Element in Culture*, Routledge & Kegan Paul, 1949.

M. Jaspan, 'Symbols at work: aspects of kinetic and mnemonic representation in Redjang ritual', *Bijdr. Taal-Land-Volkenk*, vol. 123, 1967, pp. 476–516.

L. Lamphere, 'Symbolic elements in Navajo ritual', *S. West. J. Anthrop.* 25, 1969, pp. 279–305.

D. Laycock, 'Three native card games of New Guinea and their European ancestors', *Oceania*, vol. 37, 1966, pp. 48–53.

N. MacKenzie (ed.), *Secret Societies*, Aldus, 1967.

P. Opie and I. Opie, *The Lore and Language of Schoolchildren*, Clarendon Press, 1959.

H. A. Powell, 'Cricket in Kiriwina', *Listener*, vol. 48 (No. 1227), 1952, pp. 384–5.

E. ten. Raa, 'Procedure and symbolism in Sandawe riddles', *Man* (NS), vol. 1, 1966, pp. 391–97.

F. Rehfisch, 'Competitive gift exchange among the Mambila', *Cah. Etud. Afr.*, vol. 3, 1962, pp. 91–103.

V. W. Turner, *Chihamba, the White Spirit*. Manchester University Press, (Rhodes–Livingstone Pap. 33), 1962.

H. Webster, *Primitive Secret Societies*, Macmillan, 1932.

Part Eight
Formal Correspondences

E. Auerbach, *Literary Language and its Public*, Routledge & Kegan Paul, 1965.

R. M. W. Dixon, 'Noun classes', *Lingua*, vol. 21, 1968, pp. 104–25.

M. Douglas, *Natural symbols: Explorations in Cosmology*, Barrie & Rockliffe, 1970.

M. Douglas, 'Do dogs laugh? A cross-cultural approach to body symbolism', *J. Psychosom. Res.*, vol. 15, 1971, pp. 387–90.

L. Dumont, *Homo Hierarchicus: The Caste System and its Implications*, Weidenfeld & Nicolson, 1970.

S. Langer, *Philosophy in a New Key*, Harvard University Press, 1942.

A. C. Mayer, *Caste and Kinship in Central India: A Village and its Region*, Routledge & Kegan Paul, 1960.

C. Lévi-Strauss and R. Jakobson, 'Charles Baudelaire's "Les Chats"', in M. Lane. (ed.), *Structuralism: a Reader*, London: Cape, 1970.

M. Riffaterre, *Essais de stylistique structurale: présentation et traditions par Daniel Delas*, Flammarion, 1971.

V. W. Turner, *The Forest of Symbols: Aspects of Ndembu Ritual*. Cornell University Press, 1967.

V. W. Turner, *The Ritual Process: Structure and Anti-Structure*, Routledge & Kegan Paul, 1969.

Acknowledgements

For permission to reproduce the Readings in this volume, acknowledgement is made to the following sources:

1 Routledge & Kegan Paul and Humanities Press
2 Martinus Nijhof
3 Prentice-Hall
4 The Clarendon Press
5 Routledge & Kegan Paul and Humanities Press
6 Routledge & Kegan Paul and The Free Press
7 The Clarendon Press
8 Royal Anthropological Institute of Great Britain and Ireland
9 Martinus Nijhof
10 The Clarendon Press
11 Martinus Nijhof
12 The Clarendon Press
13 The Bobbs-Merrill Co Inc.
14 Prentice-Hall
15 Calder & Boyars
16 Pergamon Press
17 International African Institute
18 Librairie Plon
19 Mr P. Gidal
20 Incorporated Council of Law reporting for England and Wales
21 Routledge & Kegan Paul and the Free Press
22 Routledge & Kegan Paul
24 *Ethnology* and Dr S. J. Tambiah
25 Royal Anthropological Institute of Great Britain and Ireland
26 Martinus Nijhoff
27 Routledge & Kegan Paul and Humanities Press
28 Routledge & Kegan Paul
29 D. R. Venables
30 Weidenfeld & Nicholson Ltd and A. D. Peters
31 Basil Blackwell Publishers
32 Frederick Warne & Co Ltd.
34 Burns, Oates & Washbourne
35 Martinus Nijhoff
36 The Clarendon Press
37 Holt, Rinehart & Winston
38 Jonathan Cape and Holt, Rinehart & Winston
39 Penguin Books
40 Calder & Boyars

41 Routledge & Kegan Paul and Humanities Press
42 The Athlone Press
43 Routledge & Kegan Paul and A. Segal
44 Jonathan Cape and Alfred A. Knopf
45 Oxford University Press

Author Index

Subject Index

Thailand – *continued*
  sacrifice in, 140, 142–3, 144, 164
  sexual relations in, 127, 128, 129, 130,
    135–7, 143, 146–8, 163
  spatial divisions, 127, 145, 156–7,
    157–8, *see also* House divisions
  spirit cults in, 136, 142, 144, 159
  villages, 127–8, 132, 133
  witchcraft in, 132
Therapy, hospitals and perception of
    time in, 83–6
Time, 10
  consciousness of, 74
  experience of, 74, 228, 230
  in films, 111
  in hospitals, 82, *see also* Timetables
  Husserl on, 73–4
  Kabyle, 104
  in music, 90–91
  Ngoni structuring of, 71
  Nuer structuring of, 75–81, *see also*
    Nuer, time notions of
  phenomenology of, 73
  planning of in hospitals, 82–3, 84–5,
    86, *see also* Timetables
  primitive forms of, 73
  situations and, 87–9
Timetables, in hospitals, 83–6
Tiwi

duelling, 235–9
  rules of, 236–8
gerontocracy among, 235, 238
missions among, 235
sexual relations among, 235
Totemism, 12, 160
  Australian aboriginal, 12, 32
  Nuer, 69
Transexuality, 115
Transvestites, 87
Trobriand magic, 162

Vietnam, 132
  peace talks, table design at, 92–4

Witchcraft
  Azande, 24–5, 234
    as explanation of misfortune, 24–5,
      232, 233
    social situation of, 232–3
  Thai, 132
Wittgenstein, L.
  on language, 17, 29, 201
  on logic, 29–30, 31

Zande, *see* Azande
Zulus, 262
Zuñi, 36, 124
  animal classification, 34